A

HISTORY OF EGYPT

From the Earliest Times to the XVIth Dynasty

BY

W. M. FLINDERS PETRIE, D.C.L.
EDWARDS PROFESSOR OF EGYPTOLOGY IN UNIVERSITY COLLEGE, LONDON

WITH NUMEROUS ILLUSTRATIONS

ISBN: 978-1-63923-666-4

All Rights reserved. No part of this book maybe reproduced without written permission from the publishers, except by a reviewer who may quote brief passages in a review to be printed in a newspaper or magazine.

Printed: February 2023

Published and Distributed By:
Lushena Books
607 Country Club Drive, Unit E
Bensenville, IL 60106
www.lushenabks.com

ISBN: 978-1-63923-666-4

This History will comprise Six Volumes:

Vol. I. Dynasties I.-XVI. By W. M. F. PETRIE
Vol. II. ,, XVII.-XX. By W. M. F. PETRIE
Vol. III. ,, XXI.-XXX. By W. M. F. PETRIE
Vol. IV. Ptolemaic Egypt
Vol. V. Roman Egypt. By J. G. MILNE
Vol. VI. Arabic Egypt. By STANLEY LANE POOLE

PREFACE

THE aim in producing the present history has been to place in the hands of students a book of reference which shall suffice for all ordinary purposes; while stating the information in such a form that any person who is likely to read such a work may grasp a general view of the course of one of the oldest civilisations of the world. A history that merely states the facts on the writer's authority may do well enough for the general reader; but for the student such writing is almost useless, and references are essential. In these pages every fact and every object has at least one authority stated for it, except where it rests on the author's personal observation. But it has not been needful to give more than one reference, usually the most accessible or useful, on each fact. Those who want to read up all the literature on any detail, will naturally refer to Wiedemann's *Geschichte*, which is an index to the subject so invaluable that no one can do much without it. And though every writer since that work has appeared must naturally be indebted to its pages, if dealing with Egyptian history or monuments, yet the present work is based on an actual examination of every accessible book that is here quoted.

This history, however, does not aim at being a bibliography of the subject; nor has it seemed desirable to bring in theories or views which appear to have passed away, and not to need present attention. While endeavouring to notice everything that a student should bear in mind on each period, yet more space has been given in proportion to new facts or new theories, *pro* and *con*, than to those which will be already familiar to persons who have read works on the subject. Similarly, in the illustrations, it has been sought to give such as are not commonly known, wherever it was suitable to do so. In this way this work is not only complete in itself, but may serve as a supplement, brought down to date, to the other histories that have appeared. It will be found to provide illustrations, later information, and more chronological discussion than exists in the present histories of Brugsch, Wiedemann, or Meyer.

In the matter of chronology—the backbone of history—it is sought here to glean everything that can be noticed as to the internal history of each period. And on the still more difficult question of general chronology, an attempt has been made to give some main outline of it to assist the memory. Where dates are confessedly so uncertain, it may seem presumptuous to keep a running head-date to the pages; but yet it is better to thus assist the reader's ideas of the relative periods of different rulers, than to refuse any such help on the ground that it can only be approximate. In the last chapter the actual bases of our present chronology are fully stated; and it must always be remembered by the reader that the range of uncertainty may be about

PREFACE

a century in the earlier parts of this volume, diminishing perhaps to about a generation by the close of the volume. No greater accuracy than this is in the least professed in the numbers here assigned. But as their relation to one another over short periods is probably correct within a few years, it is needful to state them to the nearest year.

In the very vexed question of transliteration, a course has been followed which will probably not satisfy either of the extreme parties. The names are neither reduced to unpronounceable skeletons, nor are they dressed out in ornate vocalisation. The skeleton and comma system may be very well for purely philological purposes, but is a gratuitous obstacle to the reader who has not taken a preliminary course of such work; while the following of Greek and Coptic vocalisation renders it difficult to trace the word in hieroglyphics. Hence a system has been adopted very near to that which is most familiar to the English reader in other books.

Throughout this work I have received continual help from my constant friend, Mr. F. Ll. Griffith, whose special knowledge of the language has provided many new translations of texts here quoted, and whose familiarity with the literature has often been of great service to me.

This volume is but the first of a series which is intended to embrace the whole history of Egypt down to modern times. It is expected that three volumes will treat of the period of the Pharaohs, one volume of the Ptolemies, one volume of the Roman age, and one volume of Arabic Egypt. So far as practicable, the same system will be maintained throughout, though by different writers; and the aim of all will be to provide a general history, with such fulness and precision as shall suffice for the use of students. The material is necessarily restricted here to the dynastic history; and there is no intention of including a history of art, civilisation, or literature, which would each require a volume as large as this.

CONTENTS

CHAP.		PAGE
	PREFACE	v
	LIST OF ILLUSTRATIONS	x
	LIST OF ABBREVIATIONS	xiv
I.	PREHISTORIC EGYPT	1
II.	THE FIRST THREE DYNASTIES	16
III.	FOURTH DYNASTY	30
IV.	FIFTH DYNASTY	68
V.	SIXTH DYNASTY	86
VI.	SEVENTH TO TENTH DYNASTIES	108
VII.	ELEVENTH DYNASTY	123
VIII.	TWELFTH DYNASTY	145
IX.	THIRTEENTH AND FOURTEENTH DYNASTIES	200
X.	THE HYKSOS	233
XI.	NOTES ON CHRONOLOGY	248
	INDEX	255

LIST OF ILLUSTRATIONS

FIG.		PAGE
1.	Diagram of great fault forming Nile valley, looking north	2
2.	Diagram of great fault, eroded into a gorge, fed by water-tunnelled caverns in the cliffs	3
3.	Diagram of gorge filled with débris, forming present Nile bed	3
4.	Diagram of a collapsed cavern, showing features actually observed above Nile level, and inferred below Nile level. Scale 1 inch to 800 feet	4
5.	Cliffs channelled by rainfall, looking through the mouth of a channel, Valley of Tombs of Kings, Thebes	4
6.	Palæolithic flint, water-worn, Esneh. (B. Mus.)	5
7.	Flint implements, Kahun. XIIth dynasty	8
8.	Aquiline type, upper part of diorite statue of Khafra, IVth dynasty	10
9.	Snouty type (G. Mus.)	11
10.	Large-eyed type, upper part of statue of Mertitefs, IVth dynasty	11
11.	Men of the land of Pūn	12
12.	Sculptures on statue of Min, Koptos	13
13.	Philistines (Medinet Habu)	15
14.	List of kings on the Table of Abydos. Sety I., XIXth dynasty	17
15.	Portion of the Turin papyrus, showing three kings of the XIIIth, and the beginning of the XIVth dynasty	18
16.	Late scarabs of Mena	24
17.	The step pyramid of Sakkara	25
18.	Granite statue, Memphis	26
19.	Wooden panels of Hesy (G. Mus.)	27
20.	Head of Hesy	28
21.	Vase lid of Sneferu (G. Mus.)	31
22.	Section of pyramid of Medum. Scale 1 inch to 200 feet	32
23.	Pyramid angle, 14 on 11; mastaba angle, 4 on 1	33
24.	Pyramid temple of Medum, drawn from measurements	34

LIST OF ILLUSTRATIONS

FIG.		PAGE
25.	Rahotep and Nefert, painted limestone (G. Mus.)	37
26.	Plaque of Khufu (F.P. Coll.)	38
27.	The Nine Pyramids of Gizeh from the south	39
28.	Rock tablet of Khufu, Wady Maghara	43
29.	Names of Khafra from a statue	47
30.	West side of granite temple, showing passage and causeway leading askew up to temple of second pyramid	49
31.	Plan of granite temple. Scale $\frac{1}{400}$	50
32.	The Sphinx, side view	52
33.	Khafra. Diorite statue (G. Mus.)	54
34.	Steatite cylinder of Menkaura. $\frac{1}{2}$ scale (F.P. Coll.)	55
35.	Section of the pyramid of Menkaura	57
36.	Statuette of Menkaura (G. Mus.)	62
37.	Scarab of Menkaura, and restoration by Hatshepsut	62
38.	Scarab of Shepseskaf (F.P. Coll.)	64
39.	Cylinder of Userkaf (B. Mus.)	70
40.	Cylinder of Sahura. $\frac{1}{2}$ scale (F.P. Coll.)	71
41.	Cylinder of Neferarkara. $\frac{1}{2}$ scale	73
42.	Scarab of Kakaa (B. Mus.)	74
43.	Scarab of Shepseskara (G. Coll.)	74
44.	Scarab of An (F.P. Coll.)	75
45.	Statuette of Ra·en·user (G. Mus.)	77
46.	Slab with figure of Menkauhor, found re-used in Serapeum (P. Mus.)	78
47.	Scarab of Assa (F.P. Coll.)	79
48.	Flint ink slab of Assa (F.P. Coll.)	80
49.	Stele at Elephantine. Scale $\frac{1}{40}$	82
50.	Section and plan of passages of the pyramid of Unas. Scale $\frac{1}{500}$	83
51.	Alabaster jar lid of Teta. Scale $\frac{1}{4}$	87
52.	Scarab of Pepy I. (M. Coll.)	89
53.	Rubble walls and chips forming the mass of the pyramid of Pepy I. At the right is the top of the chamber masonry	91
54.	Cylinder of Pepy I. (Tylor Coll.)	96
55.	Alabaster vase of Merenra (Flor. Mus.)	97
56.	Scarab of Merenra (F.P. Coll.)	101
57.	Rosette of Pepy II. (G. Coll.)	101
58.	Slab of Pepy II., Koptos	103
59.	Types of scarabs of Pepy and following dynasties	103
60.	Scarab of Nebkhara (H. Coll.) ?	106
61.	Alabaster of Horneferhen. $\frac{1}{2}$ scale (F.P. Coll.)	106
62.	Scarab of Neby (G. Coll.)	113
63.	Earliest symmetrical scarabs (B. Mus.; F.P. Coll.)	113
64.	Scarab of Raenka (P. Mus.)	113
65.	Scarab of Khety (P. Mus.)	114
66.	Copper-work, brazier of Khety (P. Mus.)	114
67.	Wooden palette of Kameryra (P. Mus.)	115

FIG.		PAGE
68.	Scarab of Maāabra (G. Mus.)	116
69.	Scarab of Skhanra (F.P. Coll.)	116
70.	Scarab of Khauserra (G. Coll.)	117
71.	Scarab of Aahotepra (F.P. Coll.)	117
72.	Scarab of Aa (G. Mus.)	117
73.	Base of statue of Khyan, Bubastis (G. Mus.)	118
74.	Cylinders and scarabs of Khyan	119
75.	Scarab of Uazed (G. Coll.)	121
76.	Scarab of Yapeqher (M. Coll.)	122
77.	Prince Antef (part of stele, G. Mus.)	126
78.	Coffin of Antef I. (P. Mus.)	127
79.	Coffin of Antef II. (P. Mus.)	128
80.	Pyramidion of Antef III. (B. Mus.)	129
81.	Coffin of Antef III. (B. Mus.)	130
82.	Scarab of Mentuhotep II. (P. Mus.)	131
83.	Stele of Antef IV., Elephantine	133
84.	Scarab of Antef V. (F.P. Coll.)	134
85.	Slab with head of Antef V., Koptos	135
86.	Scarab of Mentuhotep III. (B. Mus.)	138
87.	Figures at Shut er Regal	139
88.	Scarab of Sankhkara (F.P. Coll.)	141
89.	Scarab of Amenemhat I. (E. Coll.)	148
90.	Head of Amenemhat I., red granite, Tanis	150
91.	Slab of Amenemhat I., Koptos	152
92.	Scarab of Usertesen I. (F.P. Coll.)	156
93.	Bust of Usertesen I., black granite, Tanis	158
94.	Road up to tomb of Ameny, Beni Hasan	159
95.	Usertesen I., Abydos	161
96.	Usertesen I., Koptos	162
97.	Scarab of Amenemhat II. (G. Coll.)	164
98.	Sarbut el Khadem	166
99.	Cylinder of Usertesen II. (B. Mus.)	168
100.	Pyramid of Illahun from the south	169
101.	Section and plan of passages in pyramid of Illahun. Scale $\frac{1}{1000}$	170
102.	Chief and women of Aamu	173
103.	Queen Nefert, Tanis	175
104.	Scarab of Usertesen III. (P. Mus.)	176
105.	Inlaid pectoral made under Usertesen III., Dahshur	177
106.	View of Semneh	180
107.	Scarab of Amenemhat III.	184
108.	Head of Amenemhat III., from his statue at St. Petersburg	185
109.	Plan of passages in Hawara pyramid. Scale $\frac{1}{1000}$	186
110.	Alabaster altar of Ptah neferu, Hawara pyramid	188
111.	Two tablets of Amenemhat III., Wady Maghara	189
112.	Map of the ancient Lake Moeris in the Fayum basin. The shaded part is that reclaimed from the lake by Amenemhat III.	190
113.	Scarab of Amenemhat IV. (P. Mus.)	196

LIST OF ILLUSTRATIONS xiii

FIG.   PAGE
114. Scarab of Sebekneferu (G. Coll.) 197
115. Cylinder of Sebekneferu (B. Mus.) 197
116. Cowroids of Sehotepabra (F.P. Coll.) 208
117. Scarabs of Rasebekhotep (F.P. and H. Colls.) . . 208
118. Cylinder of Sebekhotep I. (B. Mus.) 209
119. Grey granite statue of Mermeshau, Tanis . . . 210
120. Scarab of Sebekhotep II. (G. Mus.) 210
121. Stele of Sebekhotep II. Royal daughters adoring Min 211
122. Scarab of Neferhotep (F.P. Coll.) 212
123. } Black basalt statuette of Neferhotep (Bologna Mus.) . { 213
124. }   { 214
125. Scarab of Sebekhotep III. (F.P. Coll.) 215
126. Red granite statue of Sebekhotep III., Tanis . . 216
127. Grey granite colossus of Sebekhotep III., Island of Arqo 216
128. Scarab of Khakara (F.P. Coll.) 218
129. Scarab of Sebekhotep IV. (G. Coll.) 218
130. Scarab of Sebekhotep V. (G. Mus.) 219
131. Scarab of Aaab (F.P. Coll.) 219
132. Scarab of Merneferra (G. Mus.) 220
133. Scarab of Merhotepra (P. Mus.) 220
134. Scarab of Nebmaātra (P. Mus.) 220
135. Scarab of Nehesi (Brent Coll.) 221
136. Basalt statuette of Sebekemsaf, Thebes (F.P. Coll.) . 223
137. Scarab of Upuatemsaf (H. Coll.) 225
138. Cartouches of Khen·zer (P. Mus.) 226
139. Scarab of Neferabra (T. Mus.) 229
140. Black granite fish offerers, Tanis 237
141. Black granite sphinx, Tanis 238
142. } Granite head, Bubastis . . . . . . { 239
143. }   { 240
144. Cartouche of Apepa I., Gebelen (G. Mus.) . . . 241
145. Scarabs of Apepa I. 242
146. Black granite altar of Apepa II., Cairo (G. Mus.) . 243
147. Obelisk of Ra·āa·seh, Tanis 244
148. Scarab of Dudumes (F.P. Coll.) 245
149. Cylinders of Sebeqkara (F.P. Coll.) 245
150. Rock marking, Silsileh 246
151. Scarab of Rahotep (F.P. Coll.) 246

LIST OF ABBREVIATIONS

The following abbreviations are used to denote the works and the collections most frequently quoted. The distinction between pages and plates is sufficiently shown by the character of numerals employed.

A.	L'Anthropologie (Journal).
A.E.	L'Archéologie Egyptienne, Maspero.
A.R.	Archæological Report, Egypt Exploration Fund.
A.Z.	Zeitschrift Aeg. Sprache.
B.A.G.	Berlin Anthrop. Gesellsch.
B.G.	Brugsch, Geographie.
B.H.	,, History (English edition).
B. Mus.	British Museum.
B.R.	Brugsch, Recueil.
B.T.	,, Thesaurus.
C.E.	Chabas, Melanges Egn.
C.M.	Champollion, Monuments.
C.N.	,, Notices.
C.O.E.	Congrès Oriental, St. Etienne, 1878.
E. Coll.	Edwards Collection.
E.G.	Ebers, Gozen zum Sinai.
F.H.	Fraser, Graffiti of Hat-nub.
F. Mus.	Florence Museum.
F.P. Coll.	Flinders Petrie Collection.
G. Bh.	Griffith, Beni Hasan.
G. Coll.	Grant Collection.
G.H.	Golenischeff, Hammamat.
G.K.	Griffith, Kahun Papyri.
G. Mus.	Ghizeh Museum.
G.S.	Griffith, Siut.
H. Coll.	Hilton Price Collection.
J.A.I.	Jour. Anthrop. Inst.
L.A.	Lepsius, Auswahl.
L.D.	,, Denkmäler.
L.K.	,, Königsbuch.
L.L.	,, Letters (English edition).
Lb. D.	Lieblein, Dictionary of Names.
M.A.	Mariette, Abydos Catalogue.
M.A. ii.	,, Abydos ii.
M.A.F.	Mission Archl. Franc.
M. Coll.	Murch Collection.
M.D.	Monuments Divers.
M.G.	Meyer, Geschichte.
M.I.	De Morgan, Monuments et Inscriptions.
M.K.	Mariette, Karnak.
M.M.	,, Mastabas.
Ms. A.	Maspero, L'Archéol. Egn.
Ms. C.	,, Contes Pop.

LIST OF ABBREVIATIONS

Ms. G.	Maspero, Guide Bulak.
My. E.	Murray, Egypt.
N.A.	Naville, Ahnas.
N.B.	,, Bubastis.
N. Bh.	Newberry, Beni Hasan.
P.H.	Petrie, Hawara.
P.I.	,, Illahun.
P.K.	,, Kahun.
P.M.	,,. Medum.
P. Mus.	Paris (Louvre) Museum.
P.N.	Petrie, Nebesheh.
P.P.	,, Pyramids.
P.R.	Pierret, Recueil Inscrip. Louvre.
P.S.	Petrie, Season 1887.
P. Sc.	,, Historical Scarabs.
P.T. i. and ii.	,, Tanis, i. and ii.
Pr. M.	Prisse, Monuments.
R.A.	De Rougé, Album.
R.C.	Revue Critique.
R.E.	De Rougé, Études Egn.
R.P.	Records of the Past.
R.S.D.	De Rougé, Six Dynasties.
Rec.	Recueil de Travaux Egyptn. (Journal).
S.B.A.	Soc. Bibl. Arch. Proc.
S.B.A.T.	,, ,, Trans.
S. Cat. F.	Schiaparelli, Catalogue Florence.
S.S.A.	Schack-Schackenborg, Unterwiss. des K. Amenemhat.
S.T.	Schiaparelli, Tomba Herchuf
W.G.	Wiedemann, Geschichte.
W.G.S.	,, ,, Supplement.

The above works, and others, can be consulted in the Edwards Library, University College, London.

The transliteration used here is as follows :—

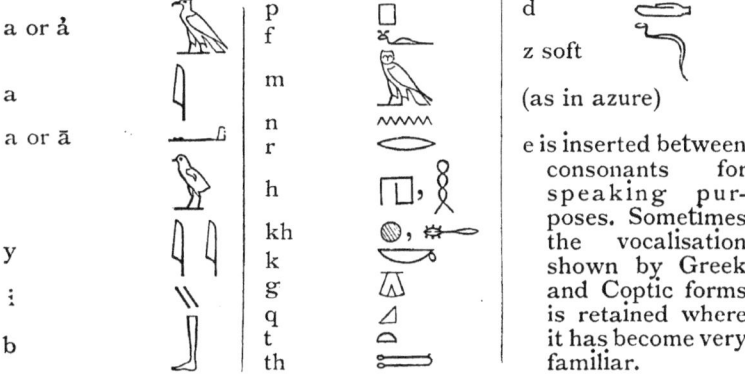

a or å

a

a or ā

y

i

b

p
f
m
n
r
h
kh
k
g
q
t
th

d

z soft
(as in azure)

e is inserted between consonants for speaking purposes. Sometimes the vocalisation shown by Greek and Coptic forms is retained where it has become very familiar.

ADDENDA

Page 34, line 14 from bottom, *add* "A statue of Henka, keeper of his two pyramids, was found at Medum (Berl. Mus.; B.C. 51)."

,, 89, *after* "Rock graffiti, Hat-nub," *add*—
"Dendera, block (Dümichen, Dendera, iv. a).
,, mentioned at (*L. c.* i.).
,, offerings by Pepy represented (*L. c.* ii.)."

,, 96, line 3 from foot, *after* "Collections," *add* "see Cailliaud, Voyage à L'Oasis, Pl. xxxvii. 17-18."
after ; *add* "also a slate pendant reading 'King Pepy, beloved of Tahuti' (at Bologna)."

,, 148, *after* "Hammamat," *add*—
"Dendera, Blocks (Dümichen, Dendera, iii. f, iv. b)."

,, 190, line 3 from top, *add*—
"dated in his 43rd year (Vyse, Pyramids, iii. 94)."

,, 195, line 2 from top, statue is from Memphis (B.R. 2).

A HISTORY OF EGYPT

CHAPTER I

Prehistoric Egypt

WITHIN the period of human records Egypt has changed but little, if at all, in its conditions of the surface and the climate. The statements of writers show this for the last two thousand years, and the subjects and state of the monuments show the same for other periods, back to the fourth dynasty. But, as in Europe, the remains of man before letters reach into very different conditions of land and of climate. Prehistoric man having been so far but little noticed in Egypt, there is a great field for additional research; and we cannot yet say to what geological period his advent must be assigned. This leads us to sketch briefly what has been observed as to the surface history of the Nile Valley, subsequent to the geological deposits of the rocks which form the basis of the land.

The floor of Egypt is the Eocene limestone, which is found at many points around the Mediterranean; but the uniformity of the gaunt grey masses of the Tertiary or Jurassic limestones, which are doubtless familiar to most travellers in the moister climates of Gibraltar, Marseilles, Malta, Athens, and in Palestine, is replaced by a warm brown in Egypt, where lichens cannot hide the surface, and where weathering is so slight. This limestone extends inward about five hundred miles from the coast. South of that is the Nubian sandstone, interrupted by the granite hills of Aswan.

At the close of the Eocene period this limestone deposit was elevated, and formed a wide, low tableland, over which ran the drainage of north-east Africa; hemmed in, as it is, by the mountains of the eastern desert, from obtaining any discharge into the Red Sea. Of this period there are remains in the thick beds of coarse gravel and boulders, river-rolled, which crown the present hills between the Fayum and the Nile, and which must have been deposited before the present valleys were worn in the tableland.

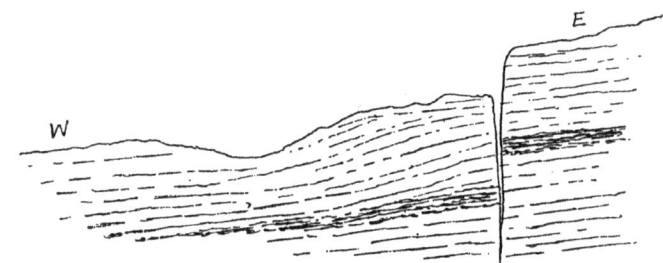

FIG. 1.—Diagram of great fault forming Nile valley, looking north.

The next stage was a difference of level during the Miocene period, caused by further elevation of the eastern desert. This must have risen in all about a thousand feet above sea level, and mostly opposite the peninsula of Sinai. Then occurred the usual result of such a change: a grand fracture took place (Fig. 1), at least two hundred miles long, from the old coast line up to Asyut. Not only may this be seen by the geologist in comparing the strata on opposite sides of the Nile, which show a difference of 250 ft., but it is obvious to every traveller that still the eastern desert is far higher than the western, that while on the east the ground rises into high mountains, on the west it falls

PREHISTORIC EGYPT 3

into deep hollows of the Oases and the Fayum, even as much as two hundred feet below the Nile. The river, which was already in this region, as the high gravels show, fell into the cleft of this great fault (Fig. 2); and it seems probable that the surface basalts of Khankah, north of Cairo, are the result of the water reaching the heated strata below, thus causing both a volcanic

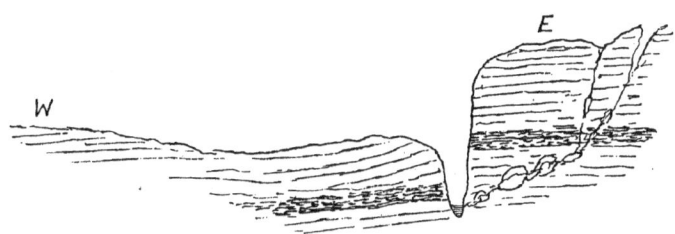

FIG. 2.—Diagram of great fault, eroded into a gorge, fed by water-tunnelled caverns in the cliffs.

eruption, and also the hot springs which silicified the sandstone of Jebel Ahmar, and the trees of the petrified forests, all in this same region. For the geological periods of the great changes see Professor Hull (in Journal of Victoria Institute, 1890).

Some sinking of the land seems to have occurred, by which the bottom of this gorge was brought under sea level, and so became choked with débris (Fig. 3). There

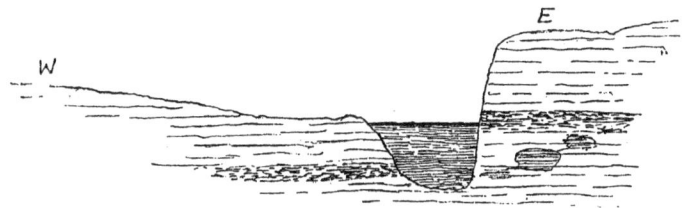

FIG. 3.—Diagram of gorge filled with débris, forming present Nile bed.

is evidence that the gorge was two or three hundred feet deeper than the present valley, as large caverns have collapsed at some hundreds of feet below the present

Nile (Fig. 4), but it became choked before the side valleys were cut very far. Then for a long period the land was

FIG. 4.—Diagram of a collapsed cavern, showing features actually observed above Nile level, and inferred below Nile level. Scale 1 inch to 800 feet.

denuded, and the present side valleys were entirely cut out, almost as we now see them. The climate was during all these ages quite as moist as that of the

FIG. 5.—Cliffs channelled by rainfall, looking through the mouth of a channel, Valley of Tombs of Kings, Thebes.

Mediterranean at present. The rainfall was heavy and continuous, as shown by the severe denudation (Fig. 5); and there can be no doubt that the country was wooded, as in all other wet climates. The cause of the present dryness of Egypt is that it is surrounded by higher lands on all sides but the north, and the north wind must become heated in blowing south, and cannot lose any moisture. The only rain now precipitated is that brought over the low land west of Egypt by cyclonic action from the Mediterranean, and hence the curious sight of heavy rains from the south-west, which is entirely desert. On the south and east the higher mountains drain the air of all the moisture it can part with. From the full rainfall, which extended down almost to historic times, it may be concluded that the western desert was largely a bay of the Mediterranean until the final elevation of the land to its present level.

FIG. 6.—Palæolithic flint, water-worn. Esneh. (Brit. Mus.)

The earliest trace of man yet known in Egypt is of the period of a great submersion of the land in the Pliocene or Pleistocene period, which followed on the carving of its present surface. Deposits on the hills show that the sea extended to at least five hundred feet above the present level; and to this age must be attributed the river-worn flint of the usual palæolithic type, found high up on the hills behind Esneh (Fig. 6).

That this is really river-worn, and not polished by sand action, is shown by the wear being no more on the top surface—as it lay on the ground—than below. On the contrary, the under side was the more worn, owing to its being rather softer; and it is impossible that the wear occurred in the position where it was found.

The prominent sign of this submergence may be seen in the great foot-hills of débris which lie at the lower side of the mouth of each valley; from their forms, their material, and their height, they must have been deposited in fairly deep water. Worked flints have also been found in the bedded detritus washed out of the Valley of the Tombs of the Kings at Thebes. This material must have been deposited under water; but as it is coarse, and not uniform, the water level had probably receded from the full height, and was about fifty or a hundred feet above the present, so that the stream would have enough velocity in the shallow water to bear forward this gravel. Since the river fell still lower, the occasional torrents have cut a bed through the old detritus, and so exposed the flints.

As beds of Nile mud exist twenty or thirty feet above the present high Nile, we learn that a dry climate had set in (owing to the elevation and drying of the Libyan Desert) before the land had quite risen to the present extent. The deposit of mud by the Nile is the sign of the flatter gradient of the lower part of its course, and of the reduction of the volume of the stream (and its consequent carrying power), owing to its evaporation and absence of affluents.

The lowest level of the Nile appears to have been shortly before the historical period. It was still falling when the mud began to be deposited, and it continued to fall until it was at least twenty feet lower than at present. Since then it has gradually risen by the silting up of the bed. From various concordant data this appears to proceed at the rate of four inches a century, or a metre in a thousand years. Hence in six thousand years, which is about the historical period in Egypt, the rise by deposits must have been twenty feet.

PREHISTORIC EGYPT

The Delta was very different in appearance in the early times. There are still many sandy rises in it; but these must have been far larger and more numerous, before they were buried in twenty feet of deposits, and before they were ploughed down by the wind, which has removed probably an equal amount of their height. The Nile then ran between desert hills of sand, in valleys more or less wide; now every part is nearly reduced to a dead level. There has been some upheaval of land at the Suez region, cutting off the sea communication with the Bitter Lakes; and, on the contrary, some depression north of this, on the coast, flooding Lake Menzaleh, which was a most fertile district at the Arab conquest.

Beside the worked flints, whose position indicates their age, large quantities of flint flakes and scrapers are to be found lying about on the surface of the desert. These must not be supposed to be prehistoric in all cases, or perhaps in any case. Flints were used side by side with copper tools from the fourth to the twelfth dynasty (Medum and Kahun) (Fig. 7); they were still used for sickles in the eighteenth dynasty. (Tell el Amarna); and large quantities of flint flakes lie mingled with Roman pottery and glass around the tower south of El Heibi. Hence the undated sites of flint flakes must be of small historical value. Large quantities of worked flints, mostly small flakes, sometimes chipped at the edge, have been found at Helwan. Many occur at Gizeh, and at the back of the Birket Qurun (P.K. 21, xvi.) and Medinet Mahdi (B.A.G. 16 Nov. 1889) in the Fayum; at Tell el Amarna on the top of the desert plateau, where are rudely chipped pebbles, which from their extreme weathering may be even palæolithic; on various parts of the foot-hills along the Nile, at Abydos (B.A.G. 16 Nov. 1889), at Qurnah (J.A.I. iv. 215; A.Z. viii. 113), at the south of Medinet Habu, and at El Kab (B.A.G. 16 Nov. 1889) are places where the ground is strewn with flint flakes and imperfect tools. The finest examples of flint working are the magnificent knives, chipped with exquisite regularity, in a smooth horny flint (see Brit. Mus., Prehistoric, Ashmolean, and Anthrop. Mus. Oxford). These are found in tombs at Abydos; but all of them have been plundered by natives, and no record exists of their age. They are perhaps a priestly survival, for funeral purposes, of the flint working of the XIIth dynasty, lasting perhaps till the XVIIIth. The most distinct use of flints was

FIG. 7.—Flint implements. Kahun. XIIth dynasty.

for sickles; particular forms were made to fit the curves of the sickle, and were notched to cut the straw. Such flints can be recognised by the polish on the saw edge, while the rest is dull, or even retains some of the cement by which it was fastened in the wooden sickle-back.

Of other remains of prehistoric man no trace has been found in Egypt. His dwellings would be upon,

PREHISTORIC EGYPT 9

or close to, the Nile soil; and as now more than twenty feet of deposits overlie the level of that age, it is hopeless to search there for any traces of his works.

The Egyptians — like many other peoples — constructed a mythical period of gods to fill the blank of prehistoric times. The series of names in the lists was probably not arranged thus until a late age, perhaps the XIXth dynasty. In early times there is no sign of a definite and systematic chronology; and such a series of names and periods shows every sign of artificiality. The list given by the Memphite school, in the most complete form (L.K. I. Taf. iii.), is as follows, with slightly different reckonings:—

DIVINE DYNASTY I. 7 GODS.

			Years.	Years.
Hephaistos	= Ptah		9000	9000
Helios	= Ra		992	1000
Sôs	= Shu		700	700
Kronos	= Geb		501	500
Osiris	= Asar		433	450
Typhon	= Set		359	350
Horos	= Har	(100)	300	300
			12,285	12,300

DIVINE DYNASTY II. 9 GODS.

			Years.	Years.
Ares	= Anhur	(92)	276	280
Anoubis	= Anpu	(68)	204	200
Herakles	= Khonsu	(60)	180	180
Apollo	= Harbehdet		100	100
Ammon	= Amen		120	120
Tithoes	= Tahuti		108	100
Sôsos	= Shu		128	120
Zeus	= Amen Ra		80	100
(Four other Gods				370)
			1196	1570

MYTHICAL DYNASTY III. 30 DEMI-GODS.
(No names given, average 121·7) 3650 years.
MYTHICAL DYNASTY IV. 10 KINGS.
10 Kings of This, 350 years.

Here the numbers have been arranged by the different authors who have transmitted these lists, so as to bear a relation to the Sothis period of 1460 years. Thus $12,300 + 1570 = 13,870 = 9\frac{1}{2}$ Sothis periods; or $12,285 + 858$ (another version of Dyn. II.) $= 13,143 = 9$ Sothis periods; $3650 = 2\frac{1}{2}$ Sothis periods, or 30 Sothis months for 30 demi-gods: this evidently artificial arrangement shows nothing but the uncritical ingenuity of the writers. The Heliopolitan origin of the series of gods has been treated by Maspero (S.B.A. xii. 419), who regards the numbers as of months instead of years.

The one point of importance, as a tradition, is that ten kings are said to reign at This (near Abydos) before the foundation of the regular monarchy. Another tradition which may have a basis is that of the followers of Horus (Har·se·ast), the *Shemsu-har*, and the followers of Har-behdet, the *Mesniu* (Maspero in A. 1891). These probably embody the same idea, that a ruler was accompanied by a body of servants or followers. But in the Turin papyrus the *Shemsu-har* are entered as ruling for 13,420 years (or a trifle more which is lost); and this shows that they are regarded there as a long successive series of rulers.

FIG. 8.—Aquiline type, upper part of diorite statue of Khafra, IVth dynasty.

Here, before considering the dynasties, we may briefly consider the question of race. That two or three different races occupied the country in the earliest historic times, is probable. The diversity of features on the earliest monuments, the presence of the aquiline race (such as Khafra) (Fig. 8); of the snouty race (often drawn for the lower classes) (Fig. 9), and of the large-eyed race (as Mertitefs) (Fig. 10) is irreconcilable with a single source for the people. The difference of burial customs in the

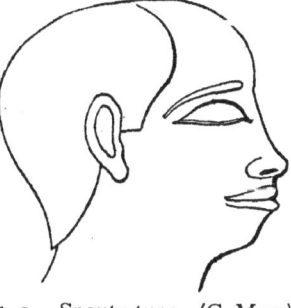

FIG. 9.—Snouty type. (G. Mus.)

FIG. 10.—Large-eyed type, upper part of statue of Mertitefs, IVth dynasty.

earliest interments points to a diversity of beliefs, again showing more than one race. We have then probably an indigenous race and an invading race; or perhaps even two invading races in succession, the large-eyed race preceding the aquiline.

Whence then came the invading race—the high caste race—who founded the dynastic history? The ancient writers consider them as Ethiopians, *i.e.* that they came from the south; and certainly in no other quarter, Libyan, Syrian, or Anatolian, can we find an

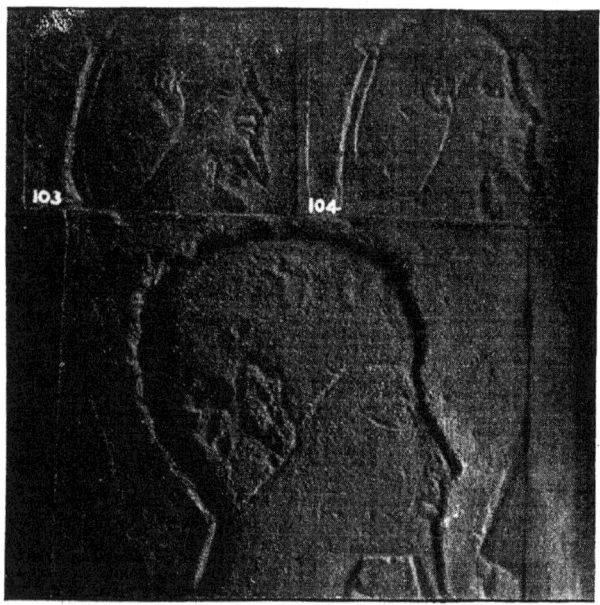

Fig. 11.—Men of the land of Pūn.

analogous people. But Ethiopian was always a wide term, and may cover many different races. On looking to the Egyptian representatives of the various races known to them, we see but one resembling the Egyptian high class race. The people of Pūn (Fig. 11), so admirably sculptured on the temple of Hat·shepsut, are very closely like the high Egyptians. Further, the Egyptians called Pūn "the land of the gods"; and they do not appear to have made war on the Pūnite race, but only to have had a peaceful intercourse of embassies and commerce. It appears that Pūn, or Pūnt, was a district at the south end of the Red Sea, which probably embraced both the African and Arabian shores. The name is connected with the Pœni, or Phœnicians, who appear to be a branch of that race. The Egyptians may then be another branch of the Pūnite race, and their earliest immigration into Egypt confirms this. Before Menes comes a dynasty of kings of This, and Menes is the Thinite who led his people to a new capital at Memphis. If the invading race had come in from the north, or from Suez, Memphis would have been naturally reached first, and their establishment so high up as This would be less likely. But the monarchy starting at This, in the middle of Egypt, points to the race having come into Egypt by the Kosēr road from the Red Sea. They must further have come from the middle or south end of the Red Sea; as, if they were from the north end, they would have entered at Memphis. The first settlement being at This points then to an origin in the southern half of the Red Sea. That this, on the African side, was what was intended by the Ethiopia of the classics, is suggested by the classical record of the gods dwelling with the blameless Ethiopians, which is the Egyptian idea of the "land of the gods," that is, the land of Pūn.

So far we have dealt with the probabilities of the case on the well-known facts; but a crucial test of these views was made by clearing out the temple of Koptos in search of any prehistoric remains. I there found portions of three colossal statues of Min, all of very rude work, but showing a gradation of skill. Upon each statue are some surface sculpturings, one of which is here reproduced (Fig. 12). Not only are these statues (which are of an earlier style than any yet known) found where we presume that the earliest settlers entered the Nile valley, but these statues bear the figures of the shells (*Pteroceras*), sawfish, ostrich, and elephant, which all agree to these immigrants having come from the Red Sea, and rather from the south than the north. The symbols show apparently the fetish pole of Min decorated with a feather and garland of flowers, and hung about with sawfish and shells, like a modern *derwish* pole. The long period required for three varying statues, the difference of attitude from the historical statues of Min, the hieroglyph of Min shown to be originally the garland on a pole, and the style of the work, all point to these sculptures being of the prehistoric age, and not due to any later irruption of a barbarous tribe.

FIG. 12.—Sculptures on statue of Min, Koptos.

If, then, we accept the probability of the dynastic Egyptians having come from Pūn, they would have been a kindred race to the Phœnicians, or Pūn race, whose farthest and latest great colony, in the Mediterranean, was known as Punic. And we see the sense of the kinship stated in the tenth chapter of Genesis between Misraim (Egypt), Caphtorim (Keft-ur = greater Phœnicia, on the Delta coast), and Philistim (or the Phœnicians in Syria). As we have seen it probable that the dynastic Egyptians reached the Nile valley by Kosēr, so the reputed Phœnician settlement at Koptos —the town of the Keft, or Phœnicians—may show the continuance of this immigration, or even perhaps the memory of the first place reached on the Nile by the invaders, as Koptos was the early terminus of the Kosēr road. The racial portraits lend force to this Philistine (Fig. 13) kinship of the Egyptians, as the

PREHISTORIC EGYPT 15

resemblance in features shows that they may well be of the same race.

So far, then, as we can yet gather, it appears as if the Phœnician races, who are at present generally supposed to have had their first home on the Persian Gulf, had thence settled in South Arabia and Somali land; and then, freshly swarming still farther round the Arabian coast, they passed up the Red Sea, crossed the desert into Egypt, followed by fresh swarms which went still

FIG. 13.—Philistines (Medinet Habu).

farther round the coast up into Palestine, and colonised Phœnicia and Philistia; yet farther they pressed on along the African coast, and settled in Carthage, and lastly in Spain. In all their historic period they were a coast people travelling westward, and their prehistoric wandering seems to have been of the same nature, following the lines of water communication by sea or river.

CHAPTER II

THE FIRST THREE DYNASTIES

THE great founder of the Egyptian monarchy is always reputed to be Mēnēs. In all the classical accounts, in the Turin papyrus, in the list on the temple of Abydos, Mena is always the starting-point of history. But this does not in the least imply that contemporary records begin with Mena, or the first dynasty; any more than such records begin in Greece at 776 B.C., because that is the first Olympiad, or begin in Rome at 753 B.C., because that is the date of its foundation.

The first three dynasties are a blank, so far as monuments are concerned; they are as purely on a literary basis as the kings of Rome or the primeval kings of Ireland. And a people who could put into regular chronologic order, as rulers of the land, the lists of their gods, were quite capable of arranging human names as freely and as neatly.

On what, then, do these first three dynasties, and their lists of twenty-six kings, really rest? How far do they embody history? These are the first questions before us.

The authority for the dynastic lists is twofold: classical writings, more or less corrupted by will and by chance; and the papyri and monuments. The classical authority for these lists is all derived from various copyists and extractors who worked on the great Ptolemaic compilation of Manetho. The monumental

THE FIRST THREE DYNASTIES

lists are four: (1) The table of kings (Fig. 14) adored by Sety I. and Ramessu II. in the temple of Abydos, and a duplicate of a portion of it from the smaller temple of Abydos by Ramessu II. (now in the British Museum); (2) the list of the tomb of Thunury at Sakkara (now in

FIG. 14.—List of kings on the Table of Abydos.
Sety I., XIXth dynasty.
A—B I-IVth dynasty.   B—C IVth-VIth dynasty.
C—D VIth-XIth dynasty.   D—E XIIth-XIXth dynasty.

the Ghizeh Museum); (3) the Turin papyrus (Fig. 15), a list of kings, now in a terribly mutilated and fragmentary state,—all of these agree in the order of the kings; (4) the list of the temple of Tahutmes III. at Karnak (now in Bib. Nat., Paris), which shows hardly any order.

Many short lists exist, of one or two dynasties of historic times; but the above great lists are the only authorities for the early period.

What is the value of these lists? They all agree very closely, excepting the last; and stress has been laid on this agreement as being something which

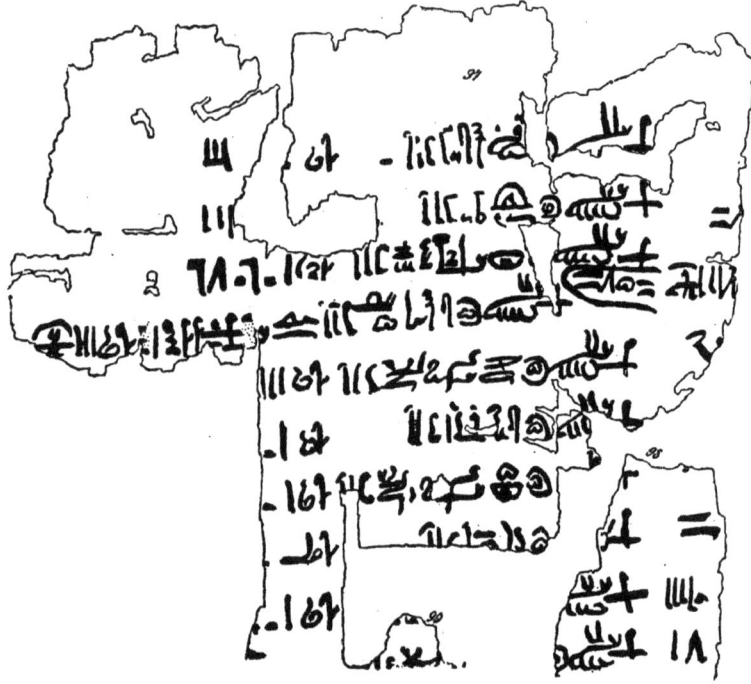

FIG. 15.—Portion of the Turin papyrus, showing three kings of the XIIIth, and the beginning of the XIVth dynasty.

proves their value; also it has been truly said that, so far as the monuments go, they corroborate these lists, and show no discrepancies. But the monuments tell us nothing of the first three dynasties; they therefore cannot corroborate that portion of the lists.

Now all these lists—except that of Tahutmes III.—

THE FIRST THREE DYNASTIES

come from one period, the reigns of Sety I. and his son Ramessu II. The tomb of Thunury is but an excerpt of the list of Abydos, the Turin papyrus is only another edition of the same age, and Manetho's work was doubtless compiled from papyri no older than this (more than a thousand years before him), and probably from documents much more near his time. There is, then, no authority for these lists of the first three dynasties, earlier than the XIXth dynasty; that is to say, the lists are of an age as long after the kings they record, as we are after these lists of the XIXth dynasty.

Were these lists actually compiled, then, in the XIXth dynasty, or are they copies of earlier historical works? Doubtless historical lists were incorporated with them; but when we look at the earlier list of Tahutmes III. at Karnak, it appears as if no such state history had existed when that was carved. The designer has had no regular material to work from; fragmentary statements and half-remembered names seem to be all that was available for making a national monument in the XVIIIth dynasty. The same conclusion is indicated by all our copies of the lists being of one age: the two lists of Abydos, the list of Sakkara, and the Turin papyrus all belong to the same time, and indicate a special taste and fashion for the subject at that epoch. These results, then, —the absence of all early examples of this recension,— the confusion of the list of Tahutmes III.,—and the exact agreement of all four lists, that appear together under Sety I.,—indicate to us that it was Sety I. who ordered the compilation of a national or state history, and that before his time no such regular record was to be had. We cannot, then, regard the first three dynasties as anything but a series of statements made by a state chronographer, about three thousand years after date, concerning a period of which he had no contemporary material.

What material, then, lies behind these lists? The short allusions to events during the various reigns are of a brief and traditional cast: plagues and earthquakes;

the beginnings of the literature, religion, laws, and architecture; and marvels, as the sweetness of the Nile, and an increase of the moon. Of the sources of such notes we see somewhat in the Westcar papyrus, written in the XIIth dynasty, or earlier, and embodying the traditional tales about the early kings—tales of magic and a tale explaining the origin of the dynasty of Ra. This is probably a sample of the material out of which the lists of early kings were constructed. We shall deal with these materials in detail, after the lists of kings; but it is best to treat of each of the sources of information separately, as each class stands or falls, as a whole, according to its general character of trustworthiness.

In the following table, under "Manetho," is given the best reading that can be selected from the varying texts; under "Lists" are given the various readings of the lists marked as *A*. Abydos, *T*. Turin Papyrus, *S*. Sakkara (Thunury); under "Monuments" are given the names found in monuments and papyri, probably none contemporary; under "Years" are the numbers given by Africanus in his edition of Manetho in the third century A.D., which is the only complete copy of the lengths of the reigns :—

	Manetho.	Lists.	Monuments.	Years.
	Ist Dynasty (about 4777–4514 B.C.).			
1	Mēnēs . . .	Mena *A*. Mena *T*.	Menai.	62
2	Athōthis . .	Teta *A*. A...... *T*.		57
3	Kenkenēs . .	Ateth *A*.		31
4	Uenenfēs . .	Ata *A*. ......a *T*.		23
5	Usafais . . .	Hesepti *A. T*.	Hesepti	20
6	Miebis . . .	Mer·ba·p *A*. Mer...pen *T*. Mer·ba·pen *S*.		26
7	Semempsēs .	Sem·en·ptah A.		18
8	Bienekhēs . .	Kebh *A*. Kebhu *S*. ...bh *T*.		26
				263

THE FIRST THREE DYNASTIES

	MANETHO.	LISTS.	MONU-MENTS.	YEARS.
	IInd Dynasty (about 4514-4212 B.C.).			
1	Boëthos . .	Be·za·u A. Neterbau S.		38
2	Kaiechōs . .	Ka·ka·u A. S. ....ka . T.		39
3	Binōthris . .	Ba·neter·n A. S. ..neter·n T.		47
4	Tlas	Uaznes A. S.		17
5	Sethenēs . .	Senda A. Send S. T.	Send.	41
6	Khairēs . . .			17
7	Neferkherēs .	Neferkara S. Neferka... T.		25
8	Sesōkhris . .	Sekerneferka S. T.		48
9	Khenerēs . .	Zefa... S. Hezefa..p T.		30
		Zazai A. Beby S. Zaza T.		...
				302
	IIIrd Dynasty (about 4212-3998 B.C.).			
1	Nekherofēs .	Nebka A. T. (Neb·ka·ra S.)	Neb·ka.	28
2	Tosorthros .			29
3	Tyreis . . .	Zeser·sa A. Zeser S. Zesera.. T.	Zeser.	7
4	Mesokhris . .			17
5	Sōufis . . .			16
6	Tosertasis . .	Teta A. Zeserteta S. Zeserti T.		19
7	Akhēs . . .	(Neb·ka·ra S.)		42
8	Sēfuris . . .	Sezes A.		30
9	Kerferēs . .	Nefer·ka·ra A. Heni S.	Heni.	26
				214

There is some uncertainty about the adjustment of the lists of Manetho and Abydos, etc., between Neferkheres (II. 7) and Tosertasis (III. 6). They are otherwise arranged with Nekherofēs to Zazai, or to Sekerneferka. The list of Sakkara places Neb·ka·ra after Zeserteta; but from the other lists he is probably the same as Nebka, Nekherofes. The tales of the Westcar Papyrus gives the order of kings as Zeser, Nebka, Sneferu, Khufu; and in the Prisse papyrus, Heni is the predecessor of Sneferu. These agree better to the arrangement of the Sakkara table.

The fragments of history embodied in the lists are of much value, as showing the kind of tales current about these kings; and whatever credit we may give to the lists, the statements are at least a tradition of facts.

I. 1. Menes is the "Thinite," who—coming from the previous Thinite dynasty—founded Memphis, according to Herodotus and Josephus. His successors of this dynasty are stated to be his sons; and the statement of the establishment of female succession under Binothris (II. 3) agrees with this detail being noted.

I. 2. Athothis is said to have built at Memphis; and to have written medical works, perhaps a conclusion from his name being confounded with Thoth by the Greeks.

I. 4. Uenefes was troubled with a great plague throughout Egypt, and he is said to have built the pyramids near Kōkhōmē. This statement has been often quoted as referring to the step pyramid of Sakkara, Kokhome being referred to *Ka kem*, "the black bull," the name of a district of Sakkara (B.G. 836). There is also another site that is possible for this name: it may as well be read "the village of Kō," in which sense it is taken in the Armenian version. The modern town of Qau was named Quu in demotic, and Kōou in Coptic, and it might therefore well be written as Kōkhōmē. This neighbourhood should be carefully searched, as it is not an unlikely district for the early kings, between Abydos and Asyut.

I. 7. Semempses is noted as having many wonders in his reign, and a great pestilence.

II. 1. Boēthos begins the second dynasty. In his reign a chasm opened near Bubastis, and many persons perished. This is near the region of plutonic action, at Abu Zabel, and the statement has therefore probably a solid basis.

II. 2. Kaiechōs established the worship of the sacred bulls, Apis in Memphis, and Mnevis in Heliopolis, and the sacred goat (or rather ram) at Mendes. His name, which may be "Bull of bulls," obviously points to this worship, which perhaps was attributed to him afterwards on the ground of this very name.

THE FIRST THREE DYNASTIES

II. 3. Binōthris established the lawfulness of female succession to the throne.

II. 7. Neferkherēs is said to have had the Nile flowing with honey for eleven days in his reign.

II. 8. Sesōkhris is noted for his height of 5 cubits 3 palms, or slightly over 8 feet.

III. 1. Nekherofēs brought in the third dynasty, and under him the Libyans revolted, but submitted through fright at an increase of the moon, apparently after an eclipse.

III. 2. Tosorthros was a great physician, and built a house of hewn stones, and forwarded literature.

Such are the fragmentary tales embodied by Manetho and copied by his abbreviators. We can learn but little from them; but it is noticeable that sacred animals are not supposed to have been worshipped in the first dynasty, and buildings were probably of wood until the third dynasty, when a house of hewn stone is specially noted. This may be the age of the transference from modelling in clay (found at Koptos) to carving in stone. On the monuments we have but few traces of all these kings. The priesthoods of the deceased kings are about the only source of their names in stone.

Of Mena there is a priest Senb·f of the XXVIth dynasty (see L.D. iii. 276 b); also another, Un·nefer, of Ptolemaic time (Serapeum stele, 328).

Of Teta there is the same priest.

Of Send there is the priest Shera or Shery, whose tomb is now dispersed to Oxford, Florence, and Ghizeh. Also Aasen and Ankef, priests on a stele (Aix, Provence, S.B.A. ix. 180). Also a bronze statue made in the XXVIth dynasty (Berlin).

Of Perabsen, the same priest Shera. This king is quite unknown otherwise, but is probably of an early date.

Of Nebka, a priest whose tomb is at Abusir (Berlin).

Of Zeser, a statue of Usertesen II. adoring him (Berlin), and a priest of his, Senb·f, in the XXVIth dynasty (see L.D. iii. 276 c). And a chief of workmen, Khnum·ab·ra, of the Persian period (L.D. iii. 275 a), begins a genealogy from the time of king Zeser.

There are also many late priesthoods of succeeding historical kings. The priest therefore was by no means necessarily of the same period as the king. The tomb of Shera has been taken to belong to the IInd dynasty, solely because he is priest of a king of that time. Doubtless it is a very old tomb, but its style scarcely differs in any way from that of the tombs of Medum, and it probably belongs to the end of the third, or beginning of the fourth dynasty.

In the papyri mention is made of several early kings, usually in attributing the discovery or composition of the document to their time; but as none of these papyri are earlier than the XIIth dynasty, the evidence is worth very little.

Teta is mentioned in Medical papyrus, Ebers; but it may be the king of the VIth dynasty.

Hesepti is in the Medical papyrus, Berlin. The 64th or 130th chapter of the Book of the Dead is said to have been discovered in his time.

Send is named in the Medical papyrus, Berlin.

Nebka is the king of a tale in the Westcar papyrus.

Nebka·n·ra (possibly the same) is the king of the tale of the Sekhti, which would rather place him in the IXth or Xth dynasty.

Zeser is the king of another tale in the Westcar papyrus, and a rubric begins his titles in the Turin papyrus.

Heni is in the Prisse papyrus, next before Sneferu, and is supposed to be the same as Nefer·ka·ra, but of this the sequence is the only evidence.

Of scarabs and small objects there is no trace until we reach the end of the third dynasty. Those with the name of Mena (Fig. 16) (scarabs Ra mena, Ra menas, Menas) are certainly of a date long subsequent to the king's reign, as well as earrings and necklace with name of Mena

FIG. 16.—Late Scarabs of Mena.

(in Abbott Coll. New York). There are reputed objects of Sem·en·ptah, but there is nothing to prove their

THE FIRST THREE DYNASTIES

age being before the historic times, and they may belong to any high priest (*sem*) of Ptah. Not until we

FIG. 17.—The step pyramid of Sakkara.

reach Nebka of the third dynasty can any scarabs be supposed to be contemporary. There are two of Neb ka, and seven of Nebka·ra, which may be as early as this age. Lastly, there is one of Nefer·ka·ra, which may well be of the last king of the IIIrd dynasty.

Of actual monuments that may be attributed to an age before the IVth dynasty there are but few. The step pyramid of Sakkara (Fig. 17) contained a doorway of glazed tiles (now at Berlin), which have been supposed to give the titles of an early king.

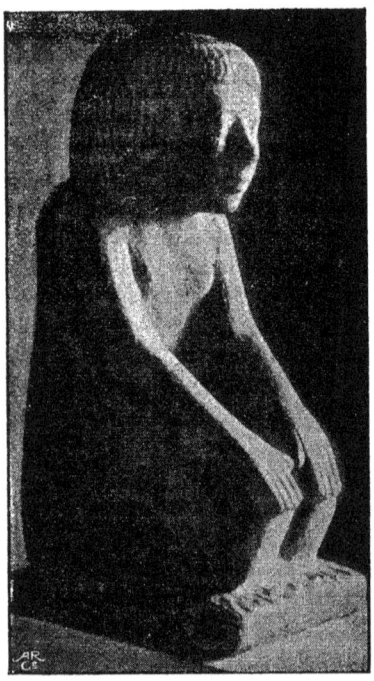

FIG. 18.—Granite statue, Memphis.

From a tablet of the Serapeum (P. Mus.), it would seem that these are the divine titles of the Apis bull, and only show that such bulls were buried in this pyramid. On the other hand, the *ka* name, *khe neter*, has been found apparently on the Sinai rocks, near the names of the IVth dynasty, and if so, would show this to be the name of an early king (Rec. xvi. 104); and the late tablet of Sehel would be confirmed in giving this *ka* name to king Zeser. We shall consider this pyramid further, with that of Sneferu.

Of lesser remains there is the very primitive statue from Memphis, (Ghizeh 6161), with *ka* names of kings on the shoulders, Neter·n, Ra·neb, and Hotep·ankh·menkh, all as yet unknown (Fig. 18); the tombs of Mery in the Louvre, of Seker·kha·bau at Ghizeh, and of Akhet·hotep at Sakkara; the wooden panels of Hesy at Ghizeh (Figs. 19, 20), and the statues of Sepa and Ra·sankh in the Louvre, which all show signs of a greater age than the works of Sneferu.

THE FIRST THREE DYNASTIES

How, then, do these actual remains accord with the state history drawn up in the lists. We are asked to believe that twenty-seven kings reigned during a space of 779 years, and yet we cannot find more than half a dozen tombs that can be attributed to this long period; while ten or twenty times this number could be assigned at once to either of the succeeding dynasties. We have no right to assume that there perished a larger proportion of tombs belonging to one period than to

FIG. 19.—Wooden panels of Hesy (G. Mus.).

another. If we cannot find a fiftieth of the proportion of tombs before the IVth dynasty that we find so soon as dated monuments arise, the inference is that there never existed any much greater number, and that therefore they should be attributed to a far shorter time. If we consider that actual remains begin with the middle of the third dynasty, we have a far more consistent result.

Another criterion also comes in. At Medum in the
beginning of the IVth dynasty there were two entirely
different customs of sepulture, indicating different
beliefs and ideas. Yet in other cemeteries later on
in the various succeeding dynasties such differences
are not observed. Are we to believe that the dynastic
Egyptians had been 800 years in contact with the

FIG. 20.—Head of Hesy.

aborigines without a change of customs or a mixture
of races, and that the change then came about suddenly
in one or two centuries? This at least is improbable.
Without wishing to dogmatise, we may say that the
conclusion that seems at present most probable from
the scanty inferences we can draw is as follows :—

For a few centuries before the IVth dynasty (or from
about 4500 B.C.) the dynastic Egyptians had been filter-

ing into the Nile valley through the Kosēr road ; they had early pushed down to Memphis and got a footing there. Various rulers had arisen in different districts, who were remembered mainly by tradition. About a century before the IVth dynasty, they consolidated their power; tools of copper were introduced, workmen were organised, and they began to use stone architecture, which was a novelty, all previous work having been in wood. The traditional tales about these kings were written down as popular stories, such as the Westcar papyrus. Lastly, in the XIXth dynasty these floating tales and traditional accounts were collected, and a continuous list of kings made out from them, all in consecutive order.

CHAPTER III

THE FOURTH DYNASTY

Manetho	Lists.	Monuments.	Years.	B.C. about
				3998
1 Sōris	Sneferu	Sneferu	29	
				3969
2 Sūfis	Khufu	Khufu	63	
				3908
3 Sūfis	Kha·f·ra	Kha·f·ra	66	
				3845
4 Menkherēs	Men·kau·ra	Menkaura	63	
				3784
5 Rhatoisēs	Ra·ded·f	Radedf	25	
				3759
6 Bikheris	Shepses·ka·f	Shepses·ka·f	22	
				3737
7 Seberkherēs	Sebek·ka·ra	...	7	
				3730
8 Thamfthis	...	Aimhetep	9	
				3721
	Total stated 277, actually		284	

In this list the order of Manetho is followed; but it does not always accord with that of the monumental lists. At Abydos Ra·ded·f is placed between Khufu and Khafra, but this is unlikely from the succession stated on the statue of Mertitefs. In the list of Sakkara, Sebek·ka·ra is placed between the end of the VIth or VIIth dynasty, and the end of the *inverted* XIIth dynasty. As there is not another instance of the names Seberkherēs or Sebek·ka·ra in any place, it seems possible that the designer of the Sakkara list in his evident confusion (inverting a dynasty) brought in Sebek·ka·ra in the place of Sebek·neferu, who should hold that position at the end of the XIIth dynasty next to Amenemhat IV. The name Aimhetep is reasonably an origin for the form Thamfthis of Manetho; but his inscription in Wady Hammamat (L.D. ii. 115 h) does not perhaps seem so early as the end of the IVth dynasty: his name may therefore have been accidentally transferred from the end of the Vth to the end of the IVth dynasty, by Manetho or a copyist. The list of Abydos is more complete than that of Sakkara, which only gives the kings 1, 2, 3, and 5. No names remain in the Turin papyrus; for the numbers of frag. 32, usually set to this dynasty, have no connection with it; not a single reign corresponds with Manetho, and a name ending in . . . zefa shows it rather to belong to the XIVth dynasty.

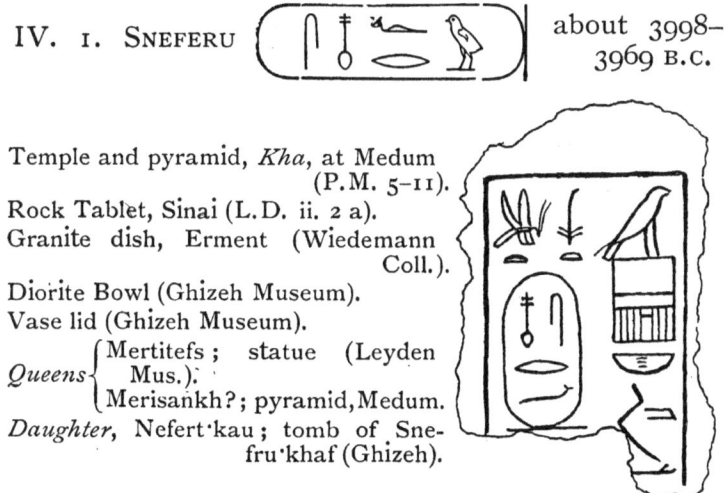

IV. 1. SNEFERU about 3998–3969 B.C.

Temple and pyramid, *Kha*, at Medum (P.M. 5–11).
Rock Tablet, Sinai (L.D. ii. 2 a).
Granite dish, Erment (Wiedemann Coll.).
Diorite Bowl (Ghizeh Museum).
Vase lid (Ghizeh Museum).
Queens { Mertitefs; statue (Leyden Mus.).
Merisankh?; pyramid, Medum.
Daughter, Nefert·kau; tomb of Snefru·khaf (Ghizeh).

FIG. 21.—Vase lid of Sneferu (G. Mus.).

With the reign of Sneferu we reach firm ground historically, his own monuments and those of his subjects being well known. The royal domains seem to have lain about forty miles south of Cairo, at Medum, as the pyramid is there, and near there was the town Ded-Sneferu. The pyramid of Medum has been the subject of strange suppositions,—that it was a rock cut into shape, that it had no passages, that it was externally a step pyramid, etc. The tombs near it have been assigned to the XIIth dynasty, in spite of the most obvious resemblances to the earliest work of the IVth dynasty. Recent researches have cleared away such speculations (P.M. 5–11).

The primitive form of the sepulchre of Sneferu was a square *mastaba* (Fig. 22), that is, a mass of masonry, flat-topped, with sides slanting inward at about 75° or

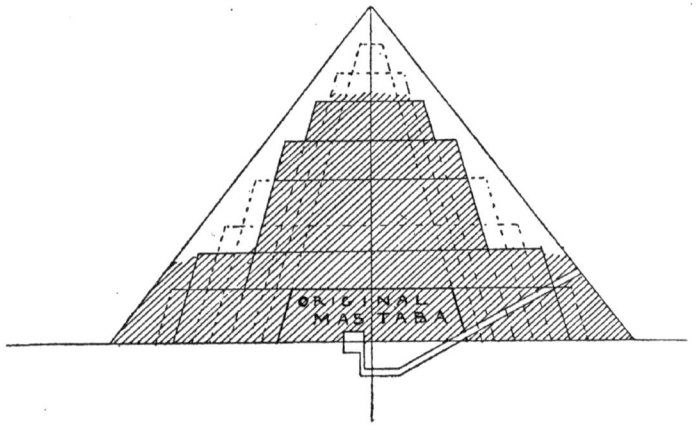

FIG. 22.—Section of pyramid of Medum. Scale, 1 inch to 200 feet.

1 in 4. The entrance was in the lower part of the north face. To enlarge this tomb a coating of masonry was put over it, as was often done in brick to the tombs of this age. The original mass was also carried upward, and thus a step resulted on the outside. This same process was repeated seven times, resulting in a compound pile, of which the top surface of each coat formed a great step on the outside. The outline thus became pyramidal, and the last process was to add

one smooth casing in one slope from base to top, and so carry it up to a point at the pyramid angle 14 on 11 (Fig. 23). Two of the casings having been partly removed for stones, have left the mass inside of them standing up in a towering form. This is the earliest pyramid known, as the step pyramid of Sakkara is not a true pyramid, but a mastaba which was repeatedly enlarged; and was never coated over in one slope; thus it was never finished into a pyramid like that of Medum.

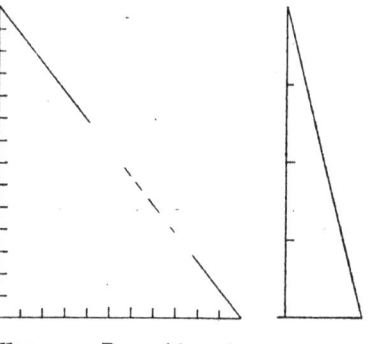

FIG. 23.—Pyramid angle, 14 on 11; mastaba angle, 4 on 1.

The successive enlargements of the pyramid of Medum have led to a theory being started, that all pyramids were similarly enlarged by coats during the kings' lives; but no other pyramid has this peculiarity. That of Menkaura at Ghizeh has once been enlarged before it was finished, but no such system of building was followed, and in several cases the details of arrangement prove that the full size was planned from the first.

The interior of the Medum pyramid is reached by a long passage sloping down from the north face; in the rock under the centre it runs horizontal for a short way, and then turns upward as a vertical shaft, opening into the floor of the sepulchral chamber. This chamber is built on the surface of the rock, and is roofed by nine overlapping courses of stone. In the chamber, and the passage beneath it, were found pieces of the wooden coffin and a wooden jar, all broken and wrenched into splinters (F.P. Coll.). The wooden beams supporting the shaft lining are still sound and firm, being saturated with salt from the rock.

Outside of the pyramid, against the middle of the eastern face of the casing, was built a courtyard and chambers, forming a small temple. In this courtyard stood an altar for offerings, between two tall steles, without any inscription. On the temple walls were graffiti dating from the old kingdom to the XVIIIth dynasty; five of these mention Sneferu as the king to whom this pyramid was attributed. And the styles of the pyramid, the temple, and the tombs are in every respect distinctly more archaic than the works of any later period, so that there is no possible ground to throw doubt on this repeated testimony. The temple is as plain as possible (Fig. 24); no stone is used but limestone, and there is not the slightest ornament or decoration in any part of it. The walls were built in the rough, and trimmed down afterwards. A peribolus wall enclosed the pyramid and temple; the entrance to it was on the east side, leading to the temple; and the approach to it was by a causeway, walled on either hand, leading up from the plain.

FIG. 24.—Pyramid temple of Medum, drawn from measurements.

It appears that Sneferu had two pyramids; at Dahshur is the tomb of certain keepers of his pyramids; Dua-ra, keeper of the two pyramids named *Kha*; and also Ankh·ma·ra, keeper of the two *kha* pyramids of Sneferu (M.A.F. i. 190), one being distinguished as the south *kha* pyramid.

The worship of Sneferu was maintained constantly. His priests and adorers were :—

Methen	Early IVth dyn.	Tomb, Abusir (Berlin, L.D. ii. 5)
Dep·em·ankh	Vth ,,	Tomb, Sakkara (M.M. 198)
Thentha	Vth? ,,	Tomb, Dahshur (M.A.F. i. 191)
Dudu	XIIIth ,,	Dedication on base (M.A. 587)
. . . .	XVIIIth ,,	Stele, Leyden
Ankh hapi	Ptol.	Coffin, Louvre (B.T. 1256)

B.C. 3998–3969.]   SNEFERU   35

The only great royal inscription is that of the tablet in Sinai. It is headed by a cartouche containing the whole of the royal titles and name : the order of which differ remarkably from later usages, reading "(The King of Egypt, lord of the vulture and uraeus, *Neb maāt*, the Golden Horus, Sneferu). The Horus *Neb maāt* (*ka* name) Sneferu, great god, giving all power, stability, life, health, expansion of heart, for ever. Subduing the countries." The king is seizing on a Bedawi (marked by his thin, narrow beard), and preparing to smite him with a mace. A scarab of Sneferu in lazuli (M. Coll.) is probably of the XXVth dynasty, from the material and style.

Although it is doubtful if Khufu was the son of Sneferu (and De Rougé has remarked that none of the early kings appear to be sons of their predecessors), yet the family of Sneferu continued to the fourth generation. At Gizeh, on the hill-edge south-east of the pyramid of Khufu, is a tomb of Sneferu·khaf, whose father, Nefer·maāt, was son of Nefertkau, the daughter of Sneferu. A queen of Sneferu was named Mertitefs ; her statue is at Leyden, and a tablet of hers was found at Gizeh (M.M. 565). The type of face is very curious (see Fig. 10), belonging to a very marked race, to which may also be referred two early statuettes at Gizeh, and the scribe of the Louvre. Thus a royal wife might be of the inferior race, and not of the high type. Her inscription helps in determining the succession, as she was a favourite of Sneferu and of Khufu, and attached to Khafra in her old age. Hence there is no room for Radadef between these kings ; and he must have been either a co-regent or a successor. Another queen is named, apparently as a wife of Sneferu, at Medum in a temple' graffito of the XVIIIth dynasty (P.M. 40). Her name, Meri·s·ankh, is usually attributed to a queen of Khafra ; but it is only stated as the name of a royal wife in the tomb of her son, the Prince Neb·em·akhet (Gizeh). If she were a wife of Sneferu in the end of his reign, her son might not be older than the reign of Khufu, and in his old age might therefore easily engrave in his tomb farm names compounded with the name of Khafra, which are the only indication of date in it. Thus it would not be at all impossible for her to be the wife of Sneferu. Or, again, she might have passed on to the harem of Khufu, as did Mertitefs, and her son Neb·em·akhet may not have been born till twenty years of the reign of Khufu had passed. There is therefore no sufficient reason to deny the accuracy of this statement of the XVIIIth dynasty graffito.

The private tombs of Medum probably belong to this reign. The principal persons buried there were two royal sons, Rahotep, with his wife Nefert, and Nefermaāt, with his wife Atet. Though entitled royal sons, they may not have been the immediate sons of Sneferu, but only descendants of some king. The only absolute sign of the age is in the name of a farm of Nefermaāt, which is called Menat-Sneferu; but the whole style of these tombs is most closely related to the tomb of Methen (at Berlin), and the tomb of Merab (at Berlin), which are both undoubtedly of the beginning of the IVth dynasty.

Rahotep and Nefert are well known from their incomparable statues in the Ghizeh Museum (Fig. 25). These statues are most expressive, and stand in their vitality superior to the works of any later age in Egypt. They were found in the tomb chamber, which—inviolate when discovered in 1871—is now much injured. The sculptures on the walls are quite worthy of a place by the side of the statues. The scenes (P.M. ix.-xiv.) are drawn with more vivacity and expression than in any tombs of succeeding dynasties. The tomb of Nefermaāt (P.M. xvi.-xxvii.) is peculiar for a special experiment of his own; all the hieroglyphs and figures are deeply incised, and filled with coloured pastes, secured in place by undercutting and keying carved in the hollows. The details of faces were worked in the colours. The inlaying, however, is soft, and soon perishes by exposure, and by salt efflorescence. The drawing is very good, but lacks the expression of detail in the faces which are so finely rendered in the reliefs of Rahotep. The signs carved in these tombs are among the earliest known; and they are of great value as pointing to the origin of the hieroglyphs, and to the state of civilisation in which they were adopted. The advanced state of architecture shown in the forms figured there is very remarkable; but it appears to be mainly taken from wooden forms, and illustrates the lateness of the adoption of stone building.

FIG. 25.—Rahotep and Nefert, painted limestone (G. Mus.).

The cemetery of Medum has also provided many examples of a different mode of burial from that of the well-known Egyptian method. Instead of full-length burial, with coffins, head-rests, vases, and provision for a future life, the more usual method of burial at Medum is lying on the left side, with the knees drawn up, facing the east, and without any vases or other objects. This shows a diversity of beliefs, and probably also of races, at this period (P.M. 21).

IV. 2. Khufu  about 3969–3908 B.C.

Temple and pyramid, *Akhet*, at Gizeh (P.P.).
Rock tablet, Sinai (L.D. ii. 2 b).
Block, Bubastis (N.B. viii.).
Tablet, *Hat-nub* quarry (P.A. xlii.).
Alabaster vases (Liverpool, L.D. ii. 2; Posno Coll.; F.P. Coll.).
Diorite bowl, *ka* name, Gizeh (F.P. Coll.).
Plummet, Gizeh (F.P. Coll.).
Weight (H.P. Coll.).
Scarabs. Plaque (see side).
Daughter, Henutsen. Tablet of Pasebkhanu (M.D. 53).

Fig. 26.—Plaque (F.P. Coll.).

The great pyramid of Gizeh has made the name of Khufu, or Kheops, better remembered than that of any other king of Egypt; a fact which reverses the thoughtless verdict that pyramids are monuments of senseless ambition, and contradicts Sir Thomas Browne in his sentence that "to be but pyramidally extant is a fallacy of duration." Khufu has provided the grandest monument that any man ever had, and is by this means better remembered than any other Eastern king throughout history.

The great pyramid was set out from the first upon a vast scale, larger than any other pyramid; and it contains more stone than probably any other single building ever erected. Its base is far greater than the whole area of the great temple of Karnak, from Amenemhat to Ptolemy; its height is greater than any other building, except two or three slender towers of this century. Yet it stands as one of the earliest structures of the world (Fig. 27).

That it could not have been designed of any much smaller size is shown conclusively by the internal passages. The entrance to these would have been quite impracticable in design on any size of building not much over two-thirds of the present base. The actual size, moreover, shows that both this and the pyramid of Medum were designed to an exact dimension. The most probable theory of its construction is that it was of such an angle that the height was the radius of a circle equal to the circuit of the base. This is so exactly the case, that it can hardly be questioned; and as the earlier pyramid of Sneferu has the same angle, it is evident that some attention was given to it. This angle is practically a rise of 14 on a base of 11 (as the ratio of radius to circle is closely 7:44); and hence the height of the pyramid should be divisible by 7, and the base of the side by 11. On looking at

FIG. 27.—The Nine Pyramids of Gizeh from the south.

these two pyramids, we see that they were set out by a modulus of an even number of cubits. They measure—

Heigh . . 7⎫
Base t . . 11⎭ × 25 cubits in Sneferu's pyramid.

Height . . 7⎫
Base . . 11⎭ × 40 cubits in Khufu's pyramid.

Such a simple and direct application of a similar design to each of these pyramids makes it very improbable that they had been enlarged hap-hazard to their final size without a clear design before arranged.

The pyramid was built of stone from the quarries on the opposite side of the Nile; both the fine casing and the rough core must have come from there, as no such stone, and no equivalent quarries, exist on the west bank. The tradition recorded by Herodotus as to the labour employed, is so entirely reasonable for the execution of such a work, that we cannot hesitate to accept it. It is said that a hundred thousand men were levied for three months at a time (*i.e.* during the three months of the inundation, when ordinary labour is at a standstill); and on this scale the pyramid-building occupied twenty years. On reckoning the number and weight of stones, this labour would fully suffice for the work. The skilled masons had large barracks, now behind the second pyramid, which might hold even four thousand men; but perhaps a thousand would quite suffice to do all the fine work in the time. Hence there was no impossibility in the task, and no detriment to the country in employing a small proportion of the population at a season when they were all idle by the compulsion of natural causes. The training and skill which they would acquire by such work would be a great benefit to the national character.

The workmanship greatly varies in different parts. The entrance passage and the casing are perhaps the finest; the flatness and squareness of the joints being extraordinary, equal to opticians' work of the present day, but on a scale of acres instead of feet or yards of material. The squareness and level of the base is brilliantly true, the average error being less than a ten-thousandth of the side in equality, in squareness, and in level. The Queen's chamber is also very finely fitted, the joints being scarcely perceptible. Above that the work is rougher; the grand gallery has not this superlative fineness, and the construction of the King's chamber is flagrantly out of level, though its granite courses are fairly well wrought. A change of design is also shown by the shaft which has been cut through the masonry from the grand gallery to the subterranean parts; and also by the unfinished rough core masonry left for the floor of the Queen's chamber. Apparently the architect who designed and insisted on all the fine work, died during its progress, and far less able heads were left to finish it.

That the entrance was closed by a hinging trap-door of stone is evident from the account of Strabo, and the remains of such a door to the south pyramid of Dahshur. The interior is so familiar in many books that it is needless to describe it here. The arrangement and number of chambers is entirely different from that known in any other pyramid; but from our ignorance of their former contents, it is almost useless to speculate about their purpose. The granite box-coffin in the King's chamber seems to point to that as the sepulchral chamber, especially as the great subterranean chamber in the rock was abandoned before it was cut out. The second high-level chamber, called the Queen's chamber, is said by Edrisi (1236 A.D.) to have contained then a second coffin; but no trace has since been seen of it. The great niche or recess in the east wall of the chamber seems as if it might be for the *ka* statue of the king.

The name of the king is found repeatedly written in red paint, among the quarry marks, on the blocks of masonry above the King's chamber; this establishes the traditional attribution of the pyramid. The chips and waste of the masons were thrown out around the pyramid to extend the platform on which it stands, thus forming extensive banks lying against the cliff, and stratified at the angle of rest. From these strata pieces of pottery, charcoal, and thread may be obtained.

Outside of the great pyramid extended a wide pavement of limestone, which on the east side stretched out to a temple which stood there. Of this temple no walls remain; but there are portions of a pavement of brown basalt, 190 feet long and 80 feet from east to west. Outside of this pavement are three deep trenches cut in the rock; these were lined with blocks of fine stone, and must have been originally about 160 feet long, 20 feet deep, and not over 5 or 6 feet wide. The purpose of such trenches is quite unknown; but there may have been some system of observing azimuths of stars by a surface of water at the bottom, and a cord stretched from end to end at the top; by noting the moment of the transit of the reflection of the star past the cord, an accurate observation of azimuth might be made, and opposite azimuths of two stars (a polar and an equatorial) could be noted by an observer at each end of the cord. This is only a surmise; but it is one which would be in agreement with the accuracy of star observation shown by the orienting of the pyramid, and it would explain the peculiar form of these trenches. A fourth trench in the rock is but shallow, and has a steady fall down to the cliff edge. As it is worn by water, it was doubtless a drain for the washing of the pavement.

The worship of Khufu was maintained till a late period. The priests and keepers of the pyramid recorded are—

Merab	Early IVth dyn.	Tomb,	Gizeh (Berlin),	L.D. ii. 22 c
Ka·em·nefert	,,	,,	Tomb,	Gizeh,	. L.D. ii. 16
Khufu·ka·aru	,,	,,	,,	,,	. L.D. ii. 17 d
Khemten	,,	,,	,,	,,	. L.D. ii. 26
Ka·y	,,	,,	,,	,,	. L.D. ii. 34 b
Thentha	,,	,,	,,	Sakkara,	. M.M. 89
Hetep·hers	,,	,,	,,	,,	. M.M. 90
Aimeri	Vth	,,	,,	Gizeh,	. L.D. ii. 50 b
Shepses·kaf·ankh	,,	,,	,,	,,	. L.D. ii. 53 a
Ptah·bau·nefer	,,	,,	,,	,,	. L.D. ii. 55
Dep·em·ankh	,,	,,	,,	Sakkara,	. M.M. 198
Snezem·ab·Antha	,,	,,	,,	Gizeh,	. L.D. ii. 76
(Unknown)	VIth	,,	,,	Shekh Said,	. L.D. ii. 112 a–c
Ra nefer ab	XXVIth	,,	Ring, Abbott Coll., New York
Psemtek menkh	,,	,,	Serapeum stele 314, Louvre

The only great royal inscription, like that of Sneferu, is on the rocks of Sinai. There are two tablets: one with name and titles of Khufu, the other with the king smiting an enemy, and the name Khnum Khuf (L.D. ii. 2, b, c.). This raises a difficult question, to which no historian has yet given a satisfactory answer. Who was this person designated as Khnum Khuf? Was he the same as Khufu, or an associated king? That he was not a successor is evident by the name being used indifferently with that of Khufu, in the quarry marks inside the pyramid (L.D. ii. 1), and by his not appearing in any of the lists. The name is found in five places—the pyramid quarry works (L.D. ii. 1), the tablet of Sinai (L.D. ii. 2), the quarry of *Hat-nūb*, the tomb of Khemten at Gizeh (L.D. ii. 26), and two farm names of Shepseskafankh in Vth dynasty (L.D. ii. 50). In each of these places the normal cartouche of Khufu also occurs, except in the quarry; and the second cartouche differs in never being written with the two *u*

FIG. 28.—Rock tablet of Khufu, Wady Maghara.

signs; it is always Khnum-khuf, while the other name is Khufu. The addition Khnum cannot be merely a flight of orthography, as on the tomb of Khemten we read, "Lord of vulture and uraeus, Mezed (*ka* name of Khufu) (Khnum·khuf) Khent (Khufu)..." The two names being thus placed in succession in one inscription cannot be mere chance variants of the same. Either they must be two distinct and independent names of one king, or else two separate kings. If they were two separate kings, Khnum Khuf must have been the more important (his name being first, and being that of the royal figure at Sinai); he must have lived through the greater part of Khufu's life (as the name was used in quarries when the pyramid was four-fifths built); and he must have died before him (as the name never occurs except with Khufu's). On the whole, it appears rather more likely that this was a second and wholly separate name of Khufu.

Another debatable question with regard to this reign is the tablet containing a reference to the sphinx, which has been often published and commented on (M.D. 53). The work of the tablet is wholly unlike that of the IVth dynasty; and it is generally agreed that it was executed in a late period. It was found in the small temple beyond the small pyramid south-east of the great pyramid. This temple was built by Pasebkhanu of the XXIst dynasty; and this tablet was carved probably under him, or some successor of his. The whole value of it turns on the question, then, whether it is an exact copy of an earlier tablet engraved by Khufu. This can only be judged by the character of it. In the first place, we have no such series of figures of gods on any existing monuments of the old kingdom; and Osiris, Isis, and the child Horus, which are mainly figured on this tablet, are rarely mentioned in early times, but are very common later. Osiris is called "lord of Rustau," a title not found in early times, but used by Pasebkhanu in this temple; and the tablet is full of instances of late writing, such as serpent determinative, *nen*, etc., which are unknown in early use, but are common later on.

The subject of the inscription, a statement of the searching for, or discovery of, certain buildings by Khufu, is suspicious. It is just what would be very likely to be put up in order to attach a credit and a history to those temples—like the common recital of the discovery of papyri under early kings. Moreover, we have seen that it is very doubtful if any masonry existed in Egypt before Tosorthros, "who built a house of hewn stones" in the IIIrd dynasty. And how then could Khufu have needed to search for buildings erected not long before his time? Also, it is implied that there were temples of Osiris and Isis here before Khufu, which is very improbable, as there is no sign of earlier remains at Gizeh before Khufu selected this site of open hill-desert, Sneferu having built far away from Gizeh. Again, the figure and mention of the Sphinx and its temple is prominently introduced; whereas there is no other trace of the Sphinx, or any temple or worship connected with it, among the dozens of various priesthoods, or the hundreds of tombs, of the old kingdom. Further, what chance was there of such a tablet of Khufu remaining until the XXIst dynasty to be copied, and yet not being itself set up in the temple? In every direction, then,—style, figures, and subject,—there are very suspicious details about it; and it is impossible to accept this as certainly an exact copy of a work of Khufu. The references to the positions of buildings, then, have no higher authority than the beliefs of the XXIst dynasty. The localities stated are a temple of Isis near the pyramids of Khufu and his daughter Henutsen, a temple of the Sphinx south of that, and a temple of Osiris south or south-east of the temple of the Sphinx. The temple of Isis would seem by the position to be the place of the temple of Pasebkhanu where this tablet was found, and the reason of carving such a tablet, to give a credit of great antiquity to the place, is obvious. Of the temples of Osiris and of the Sphinx nothing whatever is known. The granite temple is clearly as late as Khafra,—as we shall see presently,—and hence could not possibly be a temple found by Khufu. The only point that can be identified is the very place at which this tablet was required to give the sanctity of age to a new building.

The need of fine stone for the advancing luxuries of architecture led to the discovery and working of the alabaster quarry, as much as ten miles from the Nile, behind Tell el Amarna. There Khufu began by cutting a wide, gently-sloping road, descending into the plateau, to reach the rock-masses of alabaster; and the cartouche *Khnum Khuf* and *ka* name, cut as his sign of possession on the rock, have stood open to the day ever since. This quarry was that well known as Hat-nub in the later inscriptions; it was used during the old kingdom, and was probably the source of all the alabaster building and vessels of that age. In the middle kingdom an adjacent quarry was opened, and others during the empire. Alabaster vases of Khufu are known (Liverpool and Posno Coll.), and a piece of one was found at Koptos (F.P. Coll.).

At Bubastis, a granite block with a largely sculptured *ka* name of Khufu points to his having executed some great building here; and this early work is confirmed by an adjacent block of Khafra.

It has been stated that Khufu erected an obelisk (W.G. 178, 185), but this is a mis-reading. The real passage is, that Merab (L.D. ii. 22 c) was *Ur maa*, or high priest, of Heliopolis (as Rahotep was at Medum, P.M. xiii.), and also priest of Khufu; the obelisk, or rather column, merely occurs here as a sign in writing the name of Heliopolis, and has nothing to do with Khufu.

There are many tombs of great persons with the title " king's son," some being grandsons of kings, as Merab (L.D. ii. 20, 21), whose mother was a king's daughter, but not a king's wife. Hence it is impossible to settle the parentage of these persons, or to which king they should be referred. These being, then, without direct historical connection, we cannot here refer to them, except when they held royal priesthoods or other such offices. A weight bearing the name of Khufu carries back the gold standard of 200 grains to his time (H.P. Coll.).

The scarabs of Khufu are not very rare; from their workmanship, they are probably contemporary, excepting one of pottery made under Amenardus (G.M.). The plaque at the heading of this reign bears the earliest example of the winged disc (F.P. Coll.).

IV. 3. KHAFRA  about 3908-3845 B.C.

Temple and pyramid *Ur*, at Gizeh (P.P.).
Granite temple and causeway (P.P.).
Great statue and others, granite temple (G. Mus.).
Alabaster statue, Sakkara (G.Mus.).
Block, Bubastis (N.B. xxxii.).
Name from a bowl, temple of pyramid (B.M.).
Names on mace-head   ,,   (F.P. Coll.).
Scarabs (B.M., etc.) Cylinder (F.P. Coll.).

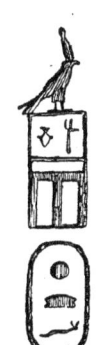

FIG. 29.—Names of Khafra from a statue.

The pyramid of Khafra stands near that of Khufu, on the south-west. It has always been attributed to him by Herodotus and Diodoros, and by modern writers. The only monumental evidences are the pieces of a bowl and a mace-head with his name, found in the temple of this pyramid. But the sequence of position between the first and third pyramids makes this attribution unquestionable.

The pyramid is rather smaller than that of Khufu, inferior in accuracy, and of a worse quality of stone, both for core and for casing masonry. The lowest course, however, was of red granite, which did not appear on the outside of Khufu's pyramid; the entrance passage is also of granite. The site of the pyramid has been levelled considerably. At the south-east it is built up of blocks of rock; at the west and north it is deeply cut into the rock hill, leaving a wide space around the sloping mass of the sides, with a vertical boundary facing the pyramid. The lower part of the pyramid on these sides is undisturbed rock cut into shape; upon that lie a few courses of enormous rock blocks, cut out from the rock clearance around the pyramid, and above that comes building of smaller blocks brought from the east cliffs. The casing still remains upon the top of this pyramid.

It had originally two entrance passages, one high on the face; another leading out in the pavement in front of the face; this was, and still is, blocked with masonry. The chamber is on the ground level, sunk in the rock, but roofed over with slanting beams of stone. The sarcophagus is of granite; the lid was secured by under-cut grooves in which it slid, and was held from being withdrawn by bolts (of copper?) which fell into holes, and were secured by melted resin, which still remains. The sarcophagus was sunk into the floor when Belzoni found it, and its lid lay over it, displaced: now the floor is all destroyed.

On the east side of the pyramid stood a temple. The vast blocks of rock which formed the core of the walls still remain; and some of the granite casing of the interior is yet in place. It is encumbered with masses of chips, among which are pieces of the furniture of the temple, statues, vases, etc.

From this temple a causeway led down a line of the rock plateau, where a gradual and easy slope could be laid out. It is evident that this is a road of convenience, made exactly where it could be laid out with the best gradient, and distinctly not square with the pyramid or the temple, being about 15° south of east. It was doubtless the road up which all the material was brought for the building of the pyramid and the temple, like the roads belonging to the other pyramids. It was paved with fine stone, recessed into the rock bed.

This road led down to the plain, and must have been open at the end when the material was being taken up it. After the pyramid and its temple were finished, the road was utilised as a junction between the pyramid-temple at the top of it, which was built square with the pyramid, and another temple at the foot of it, which was built with a skew entrance in continuation of the road (Fig. 30). This is a point of great importance as proving the age of the granite temple. Both of these temples are oriented square to the points of the compass; but the road between them is askew for reasons of its construction, and the lower temple passage is all one with the line of the skew road. This skew passage has never been altered or adapted to the road after the rest of the temple was built; for there are no signs of any reconstruction, and the doorway in the corner of the great hall is askew in the wall, so that it could not have been altered without pulling down all that end of the building. The courtyard on the top of the temple, and the stairs of access to the top, are also dependent

FIG. 30.—West side of granite temple, showing passages and causeway leading askew up to temple of second pyramid.

on this skew passage, which is built in one compact mass with the whole body of the temple. Hence the granite temple must be subsequent to the roadway and to the building and finishing of the pyramid and temple of Khafra; and as his statues were found in this temple, the building of it may be almost certainly attributed to Khafra.

This granite temple—often misnamed the temple of the Sphinx—is really a free-standing building on the plain at the foot of the hills; but it is so much encumbered that it is often supposed to be subterranean. The upper part of it now consists only of the great blocks of inferior rock which formed the core of the

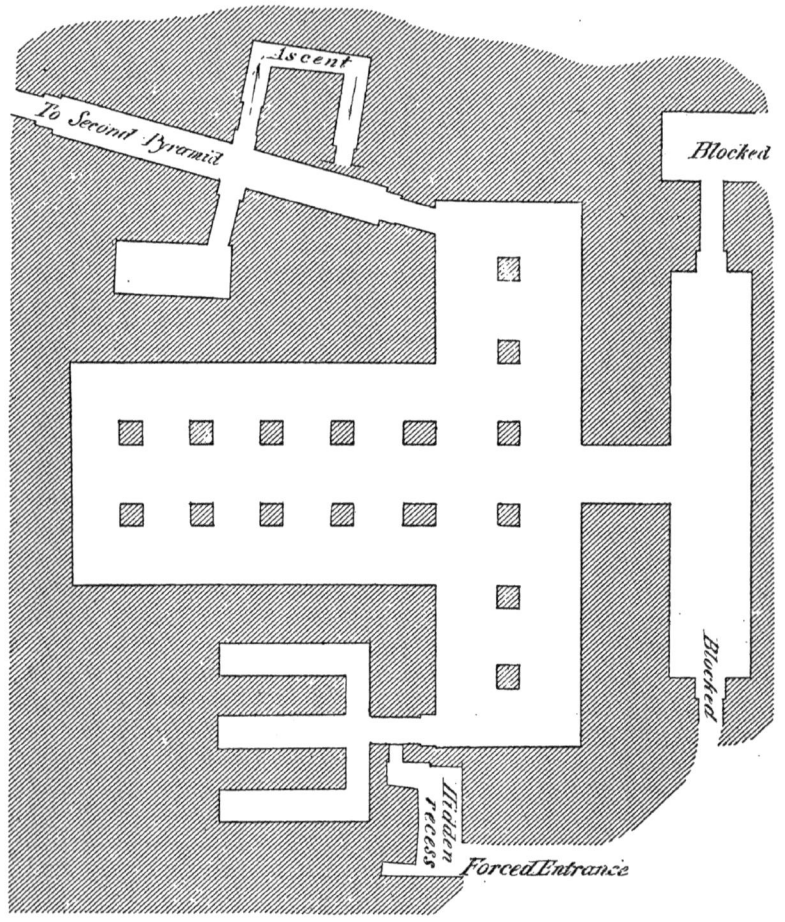

FIG. 31.—Plan of granite temple. Scale $\frac{1}{400}$.

walls; but the lower storey of it inside is perfect, and outside of it the casing still remains, showing that it was decorated with the primitive pattern of recessing.

The origin of this pattern is unknown; probably it is derived from brick decoration, as it is found equally in the earliest brickwork in Egypt (Medum) and in Babylonia (Wuswas; see Loftus, *Chaldea*, 172–179). The whole of the surfaces inside are of red granite, or white alabaster (Fig. 31). The essential parts of it are a T-shaped hall with the stem toward the pyramid, and a long hall parallel with, and adjoining, the head of the T. From the T-hall opens a chamber with three long recesses, each divided into an upper and lower part by a thick shelf. These recesses are of alabaster, and from their form probably contained sarcophagi. This chamber, and one opening from the entrance passage, retain their roofs complete, with ventilating slits along the top of the wall. Over the T-hall was an open court, reached by a sloping way, which turns in the thickness of the wall, from the entrance passage. The long hall is higher than the T-hall, and had a large recess above each of the doors which occupy the ends of it. These recesses seem as if they might be for statues, as there is no access to them, and they were closed at the back, and so could not be for windows. The diorite statue of Khafra was found in this hall, thrown into a well, or subterranean chamber. This is now filled up, and no proper account was ever given by the explorers. The east side of the temple has not been cleared, and the structure of it further in this direction is yet unknown.

Near this temple stands the Sphinx (Fig. 32); and as there is no evidence of its age, we may consider it here owing to its position. Its whole mass, lion's body and man's head, is entirely carved in unmoved native rock, although the weathering lines give the head the appearance of built courses. The body has been cased with stone, and the paws of it are built up with small masonry, probably of Roman age. It must have been a knoll of rock, which ran out to a headland from the spur of the pyramid plateau; and the hardness and fine quality of the mass now forming the head had doubtless preserved it from the weathering which had reduced the soft strata below that. When then was this knoll of rock so carved? And by whom? A later limit is given by the stele of Tahutmes IV. placed between its paws, which records a dream of his, when taking a noonday siesta in its shadow. It must then be much older than his time. On the other hand, it has been supposed to be prehistoric. But there is some evidence against that. In the middle of the back is an old tomb shaft; such would certainly not be made at a time when it was venerated, and it must belong to some tomb which was made here before the Sphinx was carved. And no tombs at Gizeh are older than Khufu, nor are any in this part of the cemetery older than Khafra. We may see this on looking at the wide causeway in the rock up to the second pyramid. On either hand of that is a crowd of tomb shafts, but not one is cut in the whole width of the causeway. In short, the causeway of Khafra precedes the tombs in the neighbourhood; but the Sphinx succeeds these tombs. Another consideration points to its being later than the old kingdom; there is no figure or mention of the Sphinx itself on a single monument of the old kingdom, nor do any priests of his appear. On the stele of Tahutmes IV. Khafra is alluded to, perhaps as the maker of the Sphinx; this connection was easily suggested by its nearness to his pyramid and temples. But how much Tahutmes knew of Khafra, or cared to

FIG. 32.—The Sphinx, side view.

honour him, is shown by the material he selected for his tablet. It is carved on a grand door lintel of red granite, which almost certainly was robbed from the adjacent granite temple of Khafra. The devotion of Tahutmes to his predecessor was a fiction, and no more; and how much he knew of the works of Khafra may well be doubted. The real period of the Sphinx may be between the old and middle kingdom, to which age it now seems that we must assign all those sphinxes formerly attributed to the Hyksos.

The front of the Sphinx was a place of devotion in Roman times; and great brick walls were built to hold back the sand on the side next the granite temple. A wide flight of steps leads down to the front, where a Roman altar of granite stood before the shrine between the paws, which was formed of tablets of Tahutmes IV., Ramessu II., etc. This front of the Sphinx has been cleared three times in this century; but the back of it, and lower part of the sides, have never been examined.

Khafra was worshipped till late times, like the other great kings of this age. His priests and keepers of the pyramid were—

Thetha	IVth dynasty	(L.A. 8, a, d)
Uash (his son)	,, ,,	(L.A. 8, b, c)
Khafra·ankh	,, ,,	(L.D. ii. 8, 10, 11)
Nefermāat	Dahshur	(M.A.F. i. 191)
Ka·em·nefert	Vth dynasty	(M.M. 248)
Dep·em·ankh	Vth dynasty	(M.M. 198)
Psamtek·menkh	XXVIth dynasty	(Serapeum stele, 314)

Apparently some other great building of Khafra existed to the south of the Memphite cemeteries; for in the construction of the south pyramid of Lisht are built in some fragments of a lintel and walls, bearing the name of Khafra.

The statues of Khafra have brought us face to face with him, and caused his features to be almost as well known in our times as in his own reign (Fig. 33). The great diorite statue is a marvel of art; the precision of the expression combining what a man should be to win our feelings, and what a king should be to command our regard. The subtlety shown in this combination of expression,—the ingenuity in the overshadowing hawk, which does not interfere with the front view,—the technical ability in executing this in so resisting a material,—all unite in fixing our regard on this as one of the leading examples of ancient art. Six other

FIG. 33.—Khafra. Diorite statue. (G. Mus.)

statues of lesser size were also found in the granite temple, carved in diorite and green basalt. A smaller statue of fine work in alabaster was in the group of early statues lately found at Sakkara. All of these are now in the Ghizeh Museum. Fragments of diorite statues occur in the mounds of chips over the temple of the second pyramid. From this same place come a piece of an alabaster bowl with his cartouche

(B.M.), and a piece of a mace-head in hard white limestone, with *ka* name and cartouche (F.P. Coll.). A block of granite with the names of Khafra was found at Bubastis (N.B. xxxii.), showing his activity in the Delta. The earliest dated cylinder is of the reign of Khafra; it is rudely cut in greenish steatite, with a variant of the name "(Ra·en·khaf), loving the gods" (F.P. Coll.). His scarabs are not very rare.

IV. 4. MEN·KAU·RA 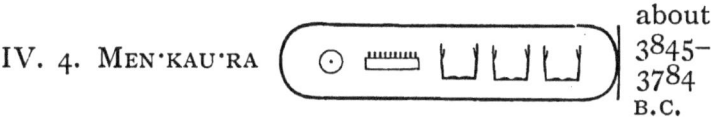 about 3845-3784 B.C.

Temple and pyramid, *Her*, Gizeh.
Pyramid, *Neter*, Abu Roash.
Small pyramid by *Her* pyramid, Gizeh.
Diorite statue, Sakkara (G. Mus.).
Scarabs (B.M., etc.); cylinder (see side).

FIG. 34.—Steatite cylinder. ½ scale. (F.P. Coll.)

As in the case of Sneferu, we again meet with the strange occurrence of a king having apparently two pyramids. In the tomb of Urkhuu, at Gizeh, we find that he was priest of Menkaura, and keeper of a place belonging to the pyramid *Her* (L.D. ii. 43 d, 44 a). And Debehen, who was a high official of Menkaura, also mentions the pyramid *Her* (L.D. ii. 37 b, 1st col.), so that it is always recognised by historians as his pyramid. But Debehen goes on to say that he inspected the works of the Menkaura pyramid *Neter* (2nd col.). And Uta in the IVth (G. Mus.) and Dep·em·ankh (M.M. 198) in the Vth dynasty were priests of the Menkaura pyramid *Neter*. Hence it is probable that there were two pyramids; and they cannot belong to different kings called Menkaura, as Debehen names them together in his inscription, and both cartouches are Ra·men·kau, thus excluding Ra·men·ka (singular), *i.e.* Netakert of the VIth dynasty.

This mention of two pyramids exactly accounts for the name being found at two places. The third pyramid of Gizeh has been attributed to Menkaura by Herodotos and Diodoros, and his name is found in one of the small pyramids by its side. But also a piece of a diorite statue—like those of Khafra—was found at the hill pyramid of Abu Roash, with part of the cartouche Ra·men.....; and the casing and passage lining of the Abu Roash pyramid with granite was closely like the casing and lining of Menkaura's Gizeh pyramid with granite. The style of the statue and of the casing link the pyramid of Abu Roash to the middle of the IVth dynasty. Which of the pyramids was the final sepulchre we may guess; that of Gizeh is evidently in sequence with those of Khufu and Khafra, and was probably built first. But it was enlarged in course of building, and yet the casing is left unfinished. Finally, seeing that it was hopeless to rival the great structures of his predecessors, Menkaura seems then to have selected a new site at Abu Roash, where, on the highest hill of the western cliffs, a small pyramid might show with advantage. At Abu Roash it is that the funeral statue was placed, together with a granite sarcophagus, which has been destroyed. Following the sequence thus indicated, it seems that *Her* was the earlier pyramid—that of Gizeh; for there is no priest of the pyramid *Her*, and it is mentioned by Debehen before the pyramid *Neter*. On the other hand, Debehen names the pyramid *Neter* later, and there were priests of it in the IVth and Vth dynasties. *Neter* seems then to have been the actual sepulchre, and would therefore be the later pyramid—that of Abu Roash.

The pyramid of Menkaura, at Gizeh, is far smaller than those of his predecessors; and it is also far inferior in accuracy. But the masonry is good, and it is built in a more costly manner. The lower sixteen courses were cased with red granite, most of which still remains; the upper part was of limestone, of which heaps of fragments now encumber the sides. The granite casing was quarried and brought to Gizeh with an excess of several inches' thickness on the face, the building joint-line being marked by a smoothly-worked slanting strip down the side of the stone, beyond which it rounds away. This excess has never been removed from the faces, and the pyramid was never finished. The interior differs from that of the other pyramids (Fig. 35). The present entrance is

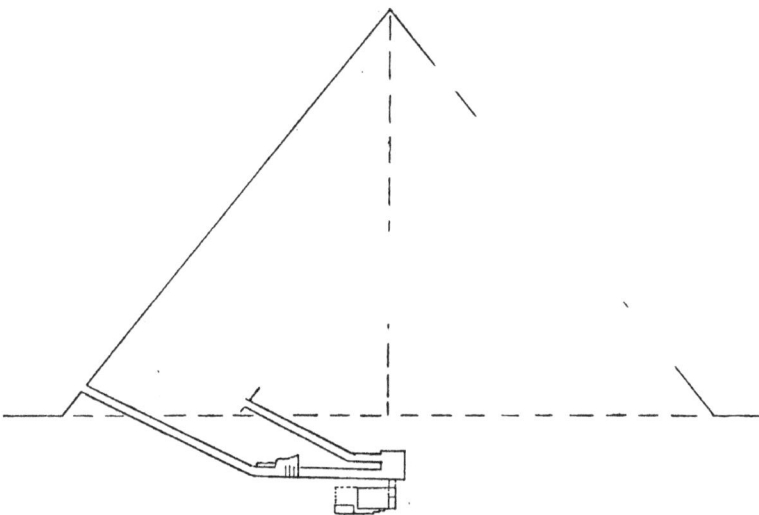

FIG. 35.—Section of the pyramid of Menkaura.

lower than the line of an earlier passage, which was disused when the pyramid was partly built. The early passage now opens on to the great chamber at a higher level than the present door, and it runs northward in the masonry until blocked by the outer part of the building. The lower passage is lined with red granite down to the rock, like the entrance of Khafra's pyramid. In the horizontal part in the rock are several portcullises, and a small chamber, or enlargement of the passage, decorated with the early recessed pattern.

Beyond all this the large chamber is reached, entirely cut in the rock. The doorway of the earlier passage is now high up above the doorway of the later passage. The chamber has a recess in the floor, apparently intended for a sarcophagus; but another short passage descends in the midst of the chamber westward, and opens into a lower chamber in which stood the basalt sarcophagus, decorated with the recessed pattern of panelled doorways. This was removed by Vyse, and lost at sea. The lower chamber is lined with granite, built into a flat-topped chamber cut in the rock. The floor and walls are of granite, and the roof is of sloping granite beams, butting together, and cut out into a barrel roof beneath, like the barrel roofs of some of the early tombs at Gizeh. Some steps descend from the side of the passage to a small chamber with loculi. In the upper chamber was found the lid of a wooden coffin with inscription of Menkaura, and part of a skeleton, probably of a later interment.

From this, and considerations on other pyramids, it has been lately suggested that a great amount of reconstruction of the pyramids took place under the later kings of the renascence,—about the XXVIth dynasty,—and that much of the present arrangements are due to them. This will be the best place to review such a theory. The strong points of it are that the inscription on the wooden coffin of Menkaura has some details which are unparalleled in any inscription so early; hence this coffin is probably a reconstruction. Next, the step pyramid of Sakkara has certainly been largely altered, and new passages made in it, probably more than once; the glazed tiles of the doorway in it are also considered by some to be late in date, but the most distinct point claimed for this is the writing of *maa* with the cubit inside the sickle, yet this is found also on the jar lid of Sneferu (G.M.), which is certainly early. The peculiar form of the granite sarcophagus of the pyramid of Illahun, with a lip around it, and a sloping base, is adduced as a sign that it was let into the floor in the first construction, and that therefore the chamber in which it now stands is a reconstruction. The winding passage of the pyramid of Hawara, and the steps down the entrance passage, are also looked on as a reconstruction, and the original passage is supposed to have been direct from the north side to the middle of the chamber roof, the continuation of the trough in the floor of the upper chamber.

Now, there cannot be any question that there has been a re-use of some of the pyramids for sepulture, the small ushabtis of the XXXth dynasty in the pyramid of Hawara put this beyond doubt. Nor can we doubt that alteration has been made in some cases, as in the many passages of the step pyramid of Sakkara. Nor is it unlikely that the coffin lid of Menkaura is a late restoration, especially as we have seen that it is probable that he was actually buried at Abu Roash. And in some cases it is certain that changes have taken place in course of building, as in Khufu's and Menkaura's pyramids.

The question, then, is one of degree. It can hardly be questioned that the idea of changes having taken place holds good in some cases; but how far have such changes extended? Is it conceivable that any king, for instance, could have made all the winding passages of the Hawara pyramid as a reconstruction? The great length of them, the series of blocking chambers with gigantic trap-doors in the roofs, the long, false passage blocked up, the dumb wells which lead nowhere, all these great works, if subsequent constructions, would have had to be built into a mass of loose bricks and sand, in which it is a great difficulty to run even a small drift-way, to say nothing of the great spaces required for such construction, and for executing work on such great masses. It would be more practicable to take down the whole pyramid before putting in such a mass of heavy masonry, and then re-erect it afterwards. Again, at Illahun, if the sarcophagus were originally let into the floor, the whole granite chamber must be a reconstruction, and a gigantic work of reconstruction it would be, to introduce the whole of this masonry and form a new and secondary chamber beside the main one already existing.

If any such grand works of reconstruction had taken place, to whom can they be attributed? Certainly not to the XVIIIth or XIXth dynasty, for plundering was rather the habit then, as witness the sweeping away of the temple and shrine of Usertesen II. at Illahun by Ramessu II. (P.K. 22). The XXVIth dynasty, with its renascence of the old ideas, is the only likely period for such attention to the older kings, as many priesthoods of those kings were revived then. But if so, how is it that the restorers have not left a single trace of their presence? Over-modesty was not a failing of Egyptian kings in any age; usually they stamped out all remembrance of their forerunners in order to aggrandise themselves. Even the more reasonable kings always put up their names, and a statement of the rebuilding they had done, when they repaired a temple. Is it then possible to suppose that, after doing work comparable with the building of the pyramids, they should have sunk all trace of themselves? Not a hieroglyph, not a graffito, can be seen anywhere associated with these supposed reconstructions. Again, if they had spent such toil and cost upon the hidden interiors of the pyramids from a deeply religious veneration for the ancient kings, and appointed services of priests to adore them,—as we see by the priesthoods,—is it conceivable that they should never have provided any restoration of the old temples in which these priests could worship? Would the external buildings for the honour of the king, and the use of the priest, have been totally neglected, while a lavish grandeur of work was spent on the hidden interior? Yet there is no trace of reconstruction of the pyramid temples. The temples of Illahun were swept away by Ramessu II., as shown by objects of his time, and by his name scrawled on the stones, and no sign of reconstruction is to be found. The priests must have adored at the pyramid in open air, while vast and needless granite work was being made inside the pile. At the temple of Khafrà there is no trace of restoration; but the rubbish now filling it contains the relics of small objects, which would never have remained in use until a restoration three thousand years later. The present ruin must be the first and only one which has overtaken that site.

So far, then, from pushing the theory of reconstruction as far as possible, and explaining every little anomaly and change of design by that means, we meet with such serious difficulties in supposing this reconstruction to be important in either amount or extent, that it is needful to limit it firmly to such cases as are inexplicable on any other supposition. One instance which has not been actually adduced, but which seems at first sight a good case, is the late style of the figure of king Men·kau·hor, on a slab brought from his temple (reworked into the Serapeum), and now in the Louvre. The details of the figure, the vulture flying over it with the ring in the claws, the decoration of the kilt in front, all look certainly of late date, at least of the XIXth dynasty. But sculptures of Antef V. (XIth dyn.) and of Sebekhotep IV. (XIIIth dyn.) bear figures which are almost exactly the same, showing that what seems to be late may be far earlier than we suppose. And, moreover, the slab of Menkauhor has been reworked into a tomb, the hieroglyphs of which are certainly later in position than the figure of Menkauhor; yet these hieroglyphs can hardly be later than the XVIIIth dynasty, and are more probably of the XIIth. Thus in a case which at first sight seems good evidence of restoration by the XXVIth dynasty, we see reasons for setting aside any such hypothesis when we learn more of the facts. This may serve as a useful instance of the risk of rashness in applying theories too widely and generally.

Of the temple of Menkaura, only the outline of core blocks is now known; the granite casing and pillars having been removed·in the last century.

Of lesser remains of Menkaura there is a statuette in diorite found at Sakkara (Fig. 36) (G. M.). The work

FIG. 36.—Statuette of Menkaura.

is not equal to the statues of Khafra, but is better than that of some later statuettes found in the same group. It seems from the diversity and continual deterioration of the work, that these statuettes must have been executed under the kings whose names they bear. Unhappily they were found at Sakkara by Arab diggers, from whom they were bought at a high price for the Ghizeh Museum; and very contradictory statements have been made as to their real source.

The second earliest cylinder known is of Men·kau·ra; it is cut in black steatite, and is of the same work as the small rude cylinders of black steatite which are of

FIG. 37.—Scarab of Menkaura, and restoration by Hatshepsut.

very early date, and appear to be substitutes for funereal steles. This bears the name "(Ra·men· kau) beloved of the gods (Ra· men·kau) Hathor . . ." (F.P. Coll.). The contemporary scarabs of Menkaura are rarer than those of either of his predecessors (Fig. 37); but his name was frequently used in later times. Hatshepsut made scarabs of him, and in the XXVIth dynasty his name is common on scarabs, cylinders, and plaques, found—and probably made—at

Naukratis, Marathus, and elsewhere. It is remarkable how correctly he is entitled on these objects, which appear to have been copied from some real scarabs of his time.

The prince Hordadef is said in the Book of the Dead to be a son of Menkaura; but this is not an earlier authority than the Westcar papyrus, which in one tale names Hordadef son of Khufu. As there is no other person Hordadef known, it is probable that this is a confusion of one person, whose date cannot be settled without contemporary evidence. It is possible that this is the same person as the next king, Ra·dad·ef.

IV. 5. RA·DAD·EF 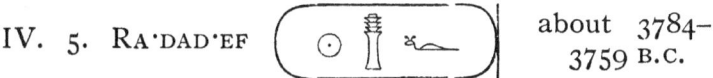 about 3784–3759 B.C.

Scarcely anything is known about this king, and even his historic position is not certain. On the one hand, his name appears in the lists of Abydos and Sakkara, between Khufu and Khafra. But, on the other hand, he is omitted by Mertitefs, who recites her successive connection with Sneferu, Khufu, and Khafra (R.S.D. 37). Psamtek·menkh and Psamtek, his priests in the XXVIth dynasty, give the sequence in both cases as Khufu, Khafra, and Ra·dad·ef (R.S.D. 53). We can hardly refuse to recognise the Rhatoises of Manetho as Ra·ded·f; and here again the name appears after Khafra, and after Menkaura. There is a bronze cylinder of this king in the Poignon Collection (W.G. 187); but there are no other traces of him, except a priest Ptah·du·aau (R.E. 62) at Gizeh, a slab of another priest of his (G. Mus.), and a farm named after him in the tomb of Persen (R.S.D. 53, 54) at Sakkara. His pyramid is unknown.

IV. 6. SHEPSES·KA·F  about 3759–3737 B.C.

Pyramid, *Keb*, site unknown.

Scarab (see side); cylinder (F.P. Coll.).

Eldest daughter, Maāt·kha.

FIG. 38.—Scarab (F.P. Coll.).

The only list containing this king's name is that of Abydos; and in that, and the few other monuments, his name is always thus written, but on a scarab it appears with *ra* added (see above). There may have been two forms of the name, as there were the two forms, Neb·ka and Neb·ka·ra, apparently both belonging to the same king; and at Shekh Said Userkaf has *ra* added to his name, as Manetho also gives Userkheres (*i.e.* User·ka·f·ra) for User·ka·f. The name in Manetho, Bikheris, may possibly be a mutilated form of this name retaining only the *p·ka·ra*. Or else the Seberkheres, the next name on the list, might refer to this king; but as the tomb of Ptah·shepses shows this noble to 'have lived through the reigns of Menkaura and Shepseskaf, it is less likely that the Rhatoises and Bikheris of Manetho should both have to come between those kings.

Most of our knowledge of this king is from the tomb of his son-in-law, Ptah·shepses. He begins his biography by saying that "Menkaura educated him among the royal children, in the great house of the king, in the private apartments; in the *harem* he was precious to the king more than any child. Shepseskaf educated him among the royal children in the great house of the king, in the private apartments in the *harem*; he was distinguished with the king more than any boy. The king gave to him his eldest daughter Maāt·kha as his wife. His majesty desired better to put her with him than with any person. He was precious to the king more than any servant; he entered all the boats, he selected the bodyguard upon the ways of the court to the South in all festivals of appearing. He was secretary of all the works which it pleased his majesty to make, continually pleasing the heart of his lord. He was allowed by his majesty to kiss his knees, and was not allowed to kiss the ground. He pleased the heart of his lord when he entered in the boat 'Which bears the gods,' in all festivals of the appearing, loved by his lord. Satisfying the heart of his lord, loving his lord. Devoted to Ptah, doing the will of his god." He fulfilled many great offices, both priestly and civil; and among these charges we find for the first time priesthoods attached to three obelisks of Ra. These obelisks continued to be worshipped throughout the Vth dynasty: one is named in the phrase "Of Ra · prophet in the Sep-ra," with the obelisk on a mastaba base as a determinative; "of Ra · prophet in the Shepu·ab·ra," with the same determinative; and "of Ra·em·akhti prophet in the Ast·ab·ra," again with the obelisk. On these structures see Sethe (A.Z. xxvii. 111).

Sebek·ka·ra  about 3737-3730 B.C.

This king is only known on the table of Sakkara, and his position there is between the end of the kings after the VIth dynasty, and the end of the reversed order of the XIIth dynasty. No such king is known in other lists at that period, and he agrees well to the Manethonic name Seberkheres. But it is perhaps more likely that Sebek·ka·ra is a mistake of the sculptor for Sebek-neferu-ra, who would occupy that place if inserted at the end of the XIIth dynasty. The sculptor made a mistake close by this of *ma* for *dad*.

IMHOTEP  about 3730–3721 B.C.

This king is only known by an inscription of his in the Wady Hammamat (L.D. ii. 115 h). But there is no indication of his position except the apparent equivalence with Thamfthis in Manetho. As there are no other inscriptions as early as this at Hammamat, it is possible that he has been misplaced in Manetho.

In closing the account of this dynasty we will try to grasp somewhat of its character. The essential feeling of all the earliest work is a rivalry with nature. In other times buildings have been placed either before a background of hills, so as to provide a natural setting to them, or crowning some natural height. But the Egyptian consented to no such tame co-operation with natural features. He selected a range of desert hills over a hundred feet high, and then subdued it entirely, making of it a mere pedestal for pyramids, which were more than thrice as high as the native hill on which they stood. There was no shrinking from a comparison with the work of nature; but, on the contrary, an artificial hill was formed which shrunk its natural basis by comparison, until it seemed a mere platform for the work of man.

This same grandeur of idea is seen in the vast masses used in construction. Man did not then regard his work as a piling together of stones, but as the erection of masses that rivalled those of nature. If a cell or chamber was required, each side was formed of one single stone, as at Medum. If a building was set up, it was an artificial hill in which chambers were carved out after it was piled together; thus a mere hollow was left where the chamber should be, and then it was dressed down and sculptured as if it were in the heart of the living rock.

The sculptor's work, and the painter's, show the same

sentiment. They did not make a work of art to please the taste as such; but they rivalled nature as closely as possible. The form, the expression, the colouring, the glittering transparent eye, the grave smile, all are copied as if to make an artificial man. The painter mixed his half-tints and his delicate shades, and dappled over the animals, or figured the feathers of the birds, in a manner never attempted in the later ages. The embalmer built up the semblance of the man in resins and cloth over his shrunken corpse, to make him as nearly as possible what he was when alive.

In each direction man then set himself to supplement, to imitate, to rival, or to exceed, the works of nature. Art, as the gratification of an artificial taste and standard, was scarcely in existence; but the simplicity, the vastness, the perfection, and the beauty of the earliest works place them on a different level to all works of art and man's device in later ages. They are unique in their splendid power, which no self-conscious civilisation has ever rivalled, or can hope to rival; and in their enduring greatness they may last till all the feebler works of man have perished.

CHAPTER IV

THE FIFTH DYNASTY

	MANETHO.	LISTS.	MONUMENTS.	YEARS.	B.C. about
1	Ūserkherēs	User·ka·f	User·ka·f	28	3721
2	Sefrēs	Sahu·ra	Sahu·ra	13	3693
3	Neferkherēs	{Nefer·ar·ka·ra / Kakaa. A.	{Nefer·ar·ka·ra / Kakaa?	20	3680
4	Sisirēs	Shepses·ka·ra	{Shepses·ka·ra / Suhtes?	7	3660
5	Kherēs	{Nefer·f·ra. A. / Kha·nefer.ra.S.	{Nefer·f·ra / Akauhor?	20	3653
6	Rhathūrēs	Ra·en·user	{Ra·en·user / An	44	3633
7	Menkherēs	Men·kau·hor	Men·kau·hor	T.P. 9 8	3589
8	Tankherēs	Dad·ka·ra	{Dad·ka·ra / Assa?	44 28	3580
9	Onnos	Unas	Unas	33 30	3536
		Total stated 248, actually		218	3503

WITH the fifth dynasty we come to a new family, and to a more marked separation from previous times than has been met before. In the lists of Manetho the previous dynasties were all Thinite or Memphite, but here we meet a sudden change to Elephantine. In the Tales of the Magicians of the Westcar papyrus there is a curiously impossible tale, which evidently embodies some tradition of the change. Hordadef, the son of Khufu, is represented as introducing an ancient magician named Dedi, who tells Khufu that the eldest of three children, yet to be born, shall deliver to him certain documents he desires. Then the birth of the children is described, and the goddesses name them by punning names,—User·ref, Sah·ra, and Kakau, imitating the names of the first three kings of the Vth dynasty. The goddesses also declare of each that it is a king who shall reign over all the land. They then make crowns, and leave them in the house; and a sound of royal festivity emanates from the royal emblems. A maid-servant out of jealousy starts to tell king Khufu of these new claimants, and the tale is here broken off. The confusion of dates in supposing Kaka to be born in the reign of Khufu is obvious, but yet there is no reason to discredit the basis of the tale. The essential points of importance are that these three kings of the Vth dynasty are supplanters, of whom Dedi prophesies to Khufu, "Thy son shall reign, and thy son's son, and then one of them"; that these supplanters are born of the wife of a priest of Ra, who conceives these triplets by Ra; and that the god has promised the mother that they shall reign, and that the eldest of them shall be high priest in Heliopolis. Here, then, the new dynasty starts from a high priest of Heliopolis, and claims divine descent from Ra. Until this tale comes to be considered, it has never been observed that no Egyptian king claims descent from Ra until this Vth dynasty. The earlier kings are always Horus kings, or Horus and Set united; but no king calls himself "Son of Ra" until the new dynasty, who are here stated to be children of the god Ra, and to begin as his high priests at Heliopolis. Thus the claim of the divine descent recorded in this tale precedes, and accounts for, the new title found on the monuments. There is a further possibility of connection with this tale; for it is there said that the wife of the priest who bore these kings dwelt at Sakhebu, a place somewhere in the Delta, probably not far from Héliopolis. Possibly here is the origin of Manetho's calling the dynasty Elephantine; according to the tale they come from ; according to Manetho from Elephan- tine, written a form which might be a corruption of the real name Sakhebu, by substituting for it the better-known name of Elephantine.

Of the order of the kings of this dynasty there is but little doubt. The only questions are concerning the double names that become common with the new race, who probably each had a second name as a son of Ra, a divine name as well as a human name. The list of Abydos and that of Sakkara each omit one king, but the monuments and Manetho leave no doubt as to the true order.

V. 1. USER·KA·F  about 3721–3693 B.C.

Pyramid, *Uab·asut*, Abusir?
Cylinders (M.D. 54 e. B. Mus.).

The position of the pyramid of this king is yet unknown; but as two of this dynasty that have been identified are at Abusir, it seems not unlikely that the others are included among the nine of that group.

FIG. 39.—Cylinder (B. Mus.).

Unas, however, was buried at Sakkara. Besides the pyramid, there was special devotion in this king's reign to the obelisk standing upon a mastaba-formed base, dedicated to Ra, and known by the name of *Ra·sep*. Both *uab* priests and *neter hon* prophets were attached to it. The following are the persons holding sacred offices belonging to the king (K), the pyramid (P), or the Ra-obelisk (R)—

```
K   Pehenuka (L.D. ii. 48).
K   Ur·ar·na (L.D. ii. 112 a).
P   Affa (M.M. 101).
P   Min·hon (M.M. 199).
P   Ra en kau (M.M. 313).
R,P Nen·khetf·ka (M.M. 308).
R,P Ne·ka·ankh (M.M. 311).
R,K Khnum·hotep (M.M. 312).
R,K Ptah·hotep (M.M. 314.  B.R.I. vii. 3).
R,K Sennu·ankh (M.M. 316-319).
R,K Snezem·ab (M.M. 259).
R,P Dep·em·ankh (M.M. 199).
```

Of actual remains of this reign there are but two cylinders; one formerly in the Bulak Museum, stolen in 1878, and one in the British Museum. They both belong to the rude class of these cylinders.

V. 2. SAHU·RA  about 3693-3680 B.C.

Pyramid, *Kha·ba*, Abusir, North.
Sinai, rock stele (L.D. ii. 39 f).
Sill (?) (G. Mus.).
Inscription, Sehel (M.I. i. 88).
Cylinders (B. Mus.; F.P. Coll. See side).

FIG. 40.—Cylinder.
½ scale. (F.P. Coll.)

The pyramid of Sahura is determined to be the north one of Abusir, by the red ochre quarry mark on one of the blocks.

In Sinai he warred on the native tribes, and carved a rock tablet commemorating his smiting the Menthu (L.D. ii. 39 f.) A tablet of an official of this reign occurs at Sehel (M.I. i. 88). The worship of Sahura was largely carried on during this dynasty, and lasted until Ptolemaic times. The priests of Sahura (K) or of his pyramid (P) are as follow—

P Dep·em·ankh (M.M. 198).
K Ankh·em·aka (M.M. 213).
K Ka·em·nefert (M.M. 242).
K Ptah·kha·bau (M.M. 294).
P Nen·khet·ef (M.M. 308).
P Sennu·ankh (M.M. 319).
K Nefer·art·nef (M.M. 324).
K Shepses·kaf·ankh (L.D. ii. 55).
K Ai·mery   (,,   ).
K Ptah·bau·nefer (,,   ).
K Ata (L.D. ii. 59a).
K Unknown, XIXth dyn. (Serapeum stele 427).
K   ,,   ,,   (Sarcophagus 38, Berlin).
K   ..   ,,   (Memphis, B.R.I. iv. 3).
K   ,,   (Serapeum stele 413).

A sill of black granite, apparently from the temple of the pyramid, is in the Ghizeh Museum. Two steatite cylinders are the only small remains of Sahura; one (in Brit. Mus.) gives his *ka* name and cartouche, the other (F.P. Coll.) is figured above.

There are some lists which confirm the order of this dynasty. That in the tomb of Ra-skhem-kha (L.D. ii. 41 a) gives the kings to whom he professes to have been attached; but the range from Khafra to Sahura is so long that it is hard to credit it; the intervening reigns that he mentions are down for 113 years in the lists of Manetho, besides 41 years more of reigns which are presumably interposed, though not mentioned. This might, perhaps, be cut down to 70 years for the named kings by arbitrary retrenchment on Menkaura's reign, but then some years still have to be added for parts of the reigns of Khafra and Sahura, to say nothing of the unmentioned kings between. There is no sufficient proof that a person might not claim to be devoted (*amakh*) to deceased kings (as Ptah·bau·nefer was *amakh* of Khufu) as well as to the living.

The list on a stone in Palermo states the offerings for the feasts of four kings (R.S.D. 74); and the list of priesthoods of Ptah·kha·bau (M.M. 295) gives also four kings in order. Thus we have—

Ra·skhem·ka.	Palermo.	Westcar papyrus.	Ptah·kha·biu.
Khafra			
Men·kau·ra			
Shepseskaf	Shepseskaf		
Userkaf	Userkaf	User·ref	
Sahura	Sahura	Sah·ra	Sahura
	Nefer·ar·ka·ra	Ka·kau	Neferarkara
			Nefer·ef·ra
			Ra·en·user

V. 3. NEFER·AR·KA·RA- 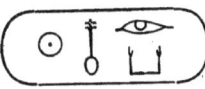 about 3680–3660 B.C.

Pyramid, *Ba*.
Cylinder, formerly Bulak Mus. (M.D. 54 f).

The pyramid of this king was known as *Ba*, but it has not yet been identified; probably it lies at Abusir.

FIG. 41.—Cylinder. ½ scale.

Thy, whose celebrated tomb is at Sakkara, was keeper of this pyramid (R.S.D. 94). The priests of the king (K) and of the pyramid (P) are—

P Thy (R.S.D. 94).
P Akhut·hetep·her (M.M. 340).
P Seden·maāt (M.M. 329).
P Ptah·en·maāt (M.M. 250).
K Snezem·ab (M.M. 258).
K Ata (L.D. ii. 59 a).
K Urkhuu (L.D. ii. 43).
K Ptah·kha·bau (R.S.D. 92).
K Shepses.kaf·ankh ⎫
K Aimery   ⎬ (L.D. ii. 55).
K Ptah·bau·nefer ⎭
K Ptah·ru·en (Louvre stele, c 154).

Offerings to him are mentioned on the Palermo list; and farms are named after him in the tombs of Pehenuka

(L.D. ii. 45), Aimery (L.D. ii. 49), and Semnefer, at Gizeh.

Only one object of his reign is known, a cylinder, formerly in the Bulak Museum, stolen in 1878. (See M.D. 54 f.)

KAKAA. 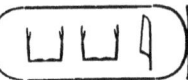 We here come to the most difficult question of the Vth dynasty, the assignment of the double names which several kings then used. Kakaa must be the same as either Nefer·ar·ka·ra or Shepses·ka·ra, as he is placed in the list of Abydos between Sahu·ra and Nefer·f·ra. The Westcar papyrus places him along with the first two kings of the dynasty, and therefore he is more likely to be the same as Nefer·ar·ka·ra; but the matter is not certain. His name occurs in five places, besides a scarab (which may be later than his age by the style), and a fly.

Table of Abydos, after Sahura.
Westcar papyrus, after Sahura.
Quarry works, tomb of Thy (R.S.D. 97).
Papyrus of accounts, Sakkara. (See Assa.)
Name of a queen, Kaka·hekenu, on a vase in tomb of Thy (W.G. 197).
Scarabs (G. Coll.; B. Mus.).
Fly (B. Mus.).

FIG. 42.—Scarab (B. Mus.).

Also in place-names in tombs of Ptah·hotep (M.M. 353) and Snezemab (M.M. 504, 509), and a personal name, Kakaa·ankh (R.E. 4, 62).

V. 4. SHEPSES·KA·RA  about 3660– 3653 B.C.

This king is only found on the table of Sakkara, and on a scarab (G. Coll.). This scarcity of remains agrees with his reign being the shortest of the dynasty. Probably he is the same as king Suhtes of the Palermo list of offerings (A.Z. 1885, 78); as that king succeeds Nefer·ar·ka·ra, and the personal names of the next two kings are both known.

FIG. 43.—Scarab (G. Coll.).

V. 5. NEFER·F·RA 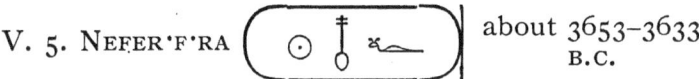 about 3653–3633 B.C.

This king is miscalled Kha·nefer·ra in the list of Sakkara; but the reading of the list of Abydos, given above, is clearly the right one by the monuments.

The pyramid of this king was known as *Neter bau*. Two priests of the pyramid are known, Ra·ankh·em·a (M.M. 283) and Seden·maāt (M.M. 329); and two prophets of the king, Ra·en·kau (M.M. 313) and Ptah-kha·bau (M.M. 295). He is named on a stele of Sen-amen (G.M. See W.G. 198); and a private person is named after him, Nefer·f·ra·ankh (M.M. 335).

HOR·A·KAU is a name only occurring in three farm names, in the tombs of Snezem·ab (L.D. ii. 76), Ptah·hotep (M.M. 353), and Semnefer (L.D. ii. 80 b). As all the succeeding kings of this dynasty occur in these farm names of Snezem·ab, there is some presumption that this was the personal name of Nefer·f·ra.

V. 6. RA·EN·USER 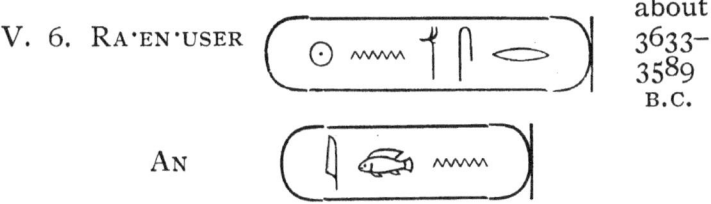 about 3633–3589 B.C.

AN

Pyramid, *Men·asut*, Abusir middle (L.A. 7).
Rock tablet, Sinai (L.D. ii. 152 a).
Red granite statuette (G. Mus.).
Statue (by Usertesen I.), Brit. Mus. (L.A. 9).
Alabaster vase, Berlin (L.D. ii. 39 c).
Scarabs.

FIG. 44.—Scarab (F.P. Coll.).

These two names certainly belong to one king, as they are both given on a statue of king An, made by Usertesen I.; on the belt, and on one side, An is named, and on the other side, Ra·en·user (L.A. 7). The pyramid of this king is at Abusir, the middle one of the group, as shown by red quarry marks on the stones. The name of it was *Men·asut*, and it is repeatedly found named with priesthoods; these are marked (P), and priesthoods of the king (K), in the list here—

    P Ankh·em·aha (M.M. 213).
    P Ka·em·retu (M.M. 175).
    P Snezem·ab (M.M. 258).
    P Seden·maāt (M.M. 329).
    P Ka·em·nefert (M.M. 242).
    P Hapi·dua (M.M. 338).
    P Ptah·kha·bau (R.S.D. 92).
    P Thy (R.S.D. 94).
    P Akhet·hotep (W.G. 199).
    P (?) Nekht·abs, pillar (W.G. 199).
    K Ptah·bau·nefer (L.D. ii. 55).
    K Ata (L.D. ii. 59).

An altar of Ana·ankh (G.M.) belongs also to this reign. A red granite statuette of this king (Fig. 45) was found in the group of early figures at Sakkara, already mentioned (G. Mus.). The alabaster vase bearing the name of Ra·en·user is one of a large class. They are found bearing names of Khufu, Raenuser, Unas, Pepi, and Merenra, and are so much alike that it is hard to believe that they were made during three different dynasties. The original site of them is unknown, but they were probably found all together, as it is unlikely that so many and such thin vases should have survived in the ruins of several temples. They may rather have come from some temple where a king of the sixth or later dynasties had made a set for his predecessors, and several are stated to have come from Abydos. As there are many of Merenra, he is probably their author.

Some scarabs bearing a fish have been attributed to king An, whose name could be thus sufficiently written without the signs *a*, *n*: one scarab with the title *sa ra*, "son of the sun," has a good claim to this attribution, and would be the earliest example of the use of this title claiming descent from Ra.

There has been some uncertainty as to which pyramid belongs to this king, as the name of Ra·user·en has been found at the little pyramid of Riqqah, north of Zawyet el Aryan. As Ra·en·user was a powerful king, with a long reign, it is more likely that the large middle pyramid of Abusir was his rather than that of Riqqah. But in some priesthoods named the pyramid sign is more like an

FIG. 45.—Statuette of Ra·en·user (G. Mus.).

obelisk, which has led to the suggestion that the double slope pyramid of Dahshur is represented (W.G. 199); and it may be that the pyramid of .Riqqah, which has carving at two angles, may have been a second monument of this king bearing the same name, *Men·asut*.

There is a variation in the spelling of the name of An, a name compounded with his being written as (An·n·y)ankh, and (An·n·a)ankh (M.M. 255; R.E. 4).

V. 7. MEN·KAU·HOR about 3589–3580 B.C.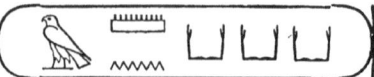

Pyramid, *Neter asut* (unknown).
Portrait block (R.S.D. vi.; L.D. iii. 291, 19).
Rock tablet, Sinai (L.D. ii. 39 e).
Statuette, alabaster, Sakkara (G. Mus.).
Scarabs.

The pyramid of this king has not yet been discovered, but many priesthoods give the name of it as *Neter asut.* The priests and prophets of the king (K) and of the pyramid (P) are as follow—

P Ptah·hotep (R.S.D. 99).
P Akhet·hotep (R.S.D. 101).
P Ra·ankh·ema (M.M. 280).
P Ptah·nefer·art (M.M. 322).
P Sneferu·nefer (M.M. 395).
P Sem·nefer (M.M. 398).
P Ked·khenes (M.M. 402).
K Ati (M.M. 418).

FIG. 46.—Slab with figure of Menkauhor, found re-used in Serapeum (P. Mus.).

An interesting slab of this king has survived (Fig. 46), having been built into a wall of the Serapeum. It represents Men·kau·hor standing, holding the baton and staff; over him flies the vulture Nekhebt; in front of him is a vase on a stand and a long bouquet of lotus; and above that is his name, " Good god, lord of the two lands, Men·kau·hor, giving life like Ra." We have already noticed the reasons for this work being as early as the fifth dynasty, in discussing the pyramid of Men·kau·ra. (For the portrait, see R.S.D. vi.; L.D. iii. 291, 19.)

In late time this king was still honoured, as on a stele

of the period of the empire Thuthu adores Duamutf, Kebhsenuf, and Men·kau·hor (P.R. ii. 28).

The rock tablet at Wady Maghara is small, and partly destroyed; but gives the *ka* name, Men·khau, as well as the cartouche (L.D. ii. 39 e). An alabaster statue of this king was in the group of royal figures found at Sakkara (G. Mus.). Of small objects, there are said to be three scarabs (W.G. 200).

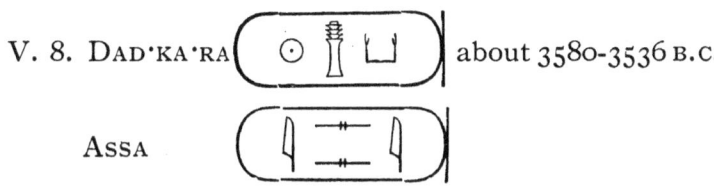

V. 8. DAD·KA·RA   about 3580-3536 B.C.

ASSA

Of these two names the equivalence is fixed by an inscription, "Suten bati (Ra·dad·ka) sa Ra (Assa)" (R.S.D. 100); and by many notices of the pyramid *Nefer*, with each cartouche.

Pyramid, *Nefer* (place unknown).
Rock tablets, Wady Maghara (L.D. ii. 39 d).
,, at mines ,,   ,,   (A.Z. vii. 26).
,, (E.G. 536).
,, Hammamat (L.D. ii. 115 l).
Papyrus of accounts, Sakkara (G. Mus.).
Alabaster vase (P. Mus.). Flint paint-slab (F.P. Coll.).
Cylinder (E. Coll.) and scarabs.

FIG. 47.—Scarab (F.P. Coll.).

The pyramid is frequently named on monuments, both as the *Nefer* pyramid of Dad·ka·ra, and the same of Assa. The prophets of it are—

Ma·nefer (L.D. ii. 65–70).
Snefru·nefer (R.E. ix. 3, 4).
Ra·ka·pu (M.M. 272).
Akhet·hotep (M.M. 421).
Sem·nefer (M.M. 398).
Hesat (R.E. ix. 3).
(Unknown) (L.D. ii. 78 d).
Atush, *uab* (M.M. 296).

The name of Assa is frequently found in farm names, as might be expected from his long reign (L.D. ii. 71, 76; M.M. 351, 383).

There seems to have been a greater activity in the eastern deserts than under previous kings. Three tablets are found in the Wady Maghara, and the long series of inscriptions in the Wady Hammamat begins in this reign. A portion of a stele at Wady Maghara gives the *ka* name and cartouche Dad·ka·ra; with *sa Ra*, the new title which began to come in general use at this period, written after the *ka* name (L.D. ii. 39 d). Another tablet was found in the same place at the mines by Major Macdonald, which mentions the reckoning of cattle, etc. (Birch in A.Z. vii. 26). Ebers found the remains of another rock tablet in very bad condition (E.G. 536); and Brugsch reports two other tablets, which may well be the same copied twice (B.T. 1494, 19, 21). At Hammamat there is an inscription of an official Ptah· hotep, naming Assa (L.D. ii. 115 l).

Of small objects, some have been attributed to this king, which, from their style, evidently belong to his namesake of the XXVth dynasty, Dad·ka·ra, Shabataka, the Ethiopian. But several are clearly of the early period. An alabaster vase (P. Mus.) is dedicated on "the first festival of the *sed* feast by the king Ra·dad·ka, beloved of the spirits of Heliopolis, giving life, stability, power, expansion of heart for ever and ever." An exquisite polished ink-slab in fawn-coloured chert, bearing his cartouche, is said to have been found in a pottery jar at Dahshur (F.P. Coll.) (Fig. 48). A

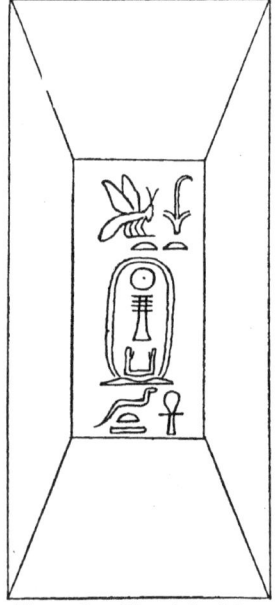

FIG. 48.—Flint ink-slab. (F. P. Coll.).

cylinder of black steatite names a prophet of Hathor and of Net, with the *ka* name of the king twice repeated (E. Coll.). Two scarabs are also of this early king, one plain, and one (figured above) with scrolls.

The oldest dated papyrus was found in 1893 at Sakkara, near the step pyramid, by fellahin digging there. It contains accounts of the reign of Assa; and this, or another found with it, has the name of Kakaa and of the Set·ab·ra obelisk. Unhappily, having been found by natives, it was separated and sold in fragments, which have reached the Ghizeh Museum, Prof. Naville, and M. Bouriant.

This reign is also signalised by the earliest well-dated papyrus composition, the Proverbs of Ptah·hetep. Although the actual copy that we possess (Bibliotheque Nationale, Paris) is probably of the XIIth dynasty, it appears to have been copied from a more cursive original (S.B.A. xiii. 65), which might be of the date of the actual composition; and there seems no reason to question the statement that Ptah·hetep, in the reign of Assa, wrote this work. He seems to have been an aged tutor of the king, who received royal encouragement to place his wisdom and courtesy before the world. The position of Ptah·hetep was of the highest; he was "son of the king, of his body," and therefore probably uncle to king Assa, his pupil. These proverbs are so well known in various translations, literal and metrical, that, as they belong more to literature than to history, we need not quote them here.

V. 9. UNAS (𓋴 𓇑 𓂝) about 3536–3503 B.C.

Pyramid, *Nefer asut*, Sakkara.

Mastabat el Faråun, Sakkara.

Rock tablet, Elephantine (P.S. xii.).

Alabaster vases (B.M.; F.M.).

Scarabs.

FIG. 49.—Stele at Elephantine. Scale $\frac{1}{40}$.

No second name has been found which can be referred to Unas; and it seems as if he had retained his personal name throughout life, and never adopted a throne name compounded with *ra*.

The pyramid of Unas was found at Sakkara in 1881 (Fig. 50). The entrance is by means of a sloping passage from the north. This reaches a small horizontal chamber, and a passage, which is built of granite shortly before reaching three portcullises, and for some way beyond them. It ends at a square chamber covered with inscriptions. From the west end of this chamber a short passage leads to another chamber, more than half inscribed, containing the basalt sarcophagus. And from the east end another short passage leads to a cross-passage with three small chambers. In a corner of the latter was a heap of small wooden instruments, handles of knives, axes, etc.; these had probably served for the ceremonies of interment, and were left here on the same principle that the long texts of the funeral service were carved on the walls (Rec. iii. 177; iv. 41). Beside the pyramid, which was undoubtedly for this king, the Mastabat el Faråun (M.M. 361), at the south end of the pyramid field of Sakkara, has his name in the quarry marks on the backs of the blocks. This building is a rectangular mass, like the usual mastabas, but larger; it was evidently cased with fine masonry, which has now all disappeared, leaving rough steps. The entrance is from the north, as in the pyramids. A sloping passage turns horizontal at the bottom, passes three slides for portcullises, and lastly opens into a chamber running east and west, with a ridge roof. From the west end opens another chamber with barrel roof. And from the east end of the south side is a short horizontal passage, with four recesses and

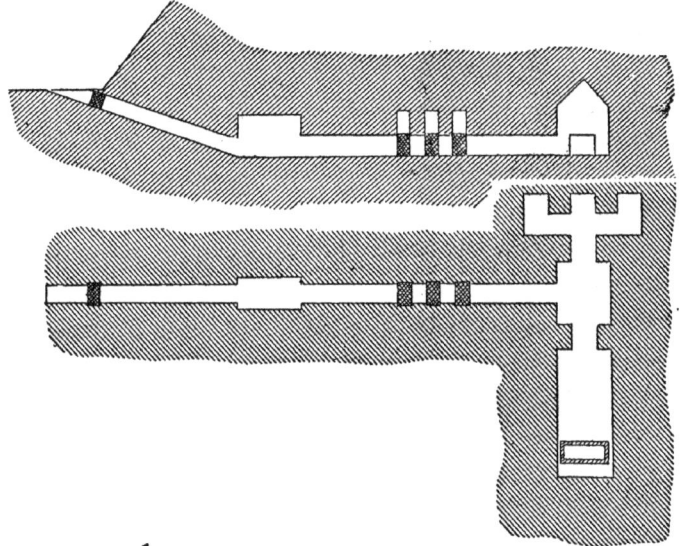

FIG. 50.—Section and plan of passages of the pyramid of Unas. Scale $\frac{1}{500}$.

a small chamber. The arrangement is closely like that of a pyramid; and every part is equalled in that of Unas at Sakkara, though rather differently arranged. Possibly this structure may have been the tomb of a successor of Unas, who used some old blocks marked with his name. The pyramid of Teta, who followed him, is known; but no tomb of User·ka·ra, the next but one, has yet been found, so that the Mastabat el Faråun may perhaps have been built for him.

On referring to the priests of Unas, there is, however, a curious discrepancy. One of them, Akhet·hotep, has two steles in his tomb; on one stele he is called "prophet of the Unas pyramid *Nefer asut*"; but on the other he is "prophet of the Unas pyramid *Asut asuti*" (?), written with five *as* signs. If this is not a mere error, it may be that Unas had two pyramids (as we have seen to be probably the case with Sneferu and Menkaura); and so the inscribed pyramid and the Mastabat el Faráun may both belong to him. The prophets of the pyramid are—

> Dep·em·ankh (M.M. 195).
> Ra·hent (princess) (M.M. 360).
> Sabu (M.M. 375).
> Ptah·shepses (M.M. 377).
> Akhet·hotep (M.M. 422–424).

It appears that he built a temple to Hathor at Memphis, as Dep·em·ankh was "prophet of the house of Hathor, who loves Unas" (R.S.D. 105; M.M. 195).

The tablet of Elephantine (P.S. xii.) is finely cut on a large rounded mass of granite, in the path to the village, near the ferry place. It is interesting for giving a remarkable spelling of Khnumu with three rams; and it served as a nucleus for four inscriptions of later kings. It is the earliest dated inscription at the Cataracts.

An inscription at Hammamat mentions a man named Unas·ankh; but it is therefore probably later than Unas (L.D. ii. 115 m; G.H. 7).

The Turin papyrus is in good condition at the end of this dynasty, and gives the last three kings and their years of reigning. The numbers do not coincide with those of Manetho: for Men·kau·hor the difference between eight and nine years may easily be owing to omitting the months; for Dad·ka·ra the forty-four years instead of twenty-eight is a difference too large to be accounted for by any co-regency; but for Unas the difference of thirty-three and thirty years may be easily due to three years' co-regency with his predecessor. In the tomb of Snezem·ab his relations to

Assa and Unas suggest that their reigns may have been contemporary (R.S.D. 102). At the end of this dynasty, after Unas, the Turin papyrus gives a summary of kings; but the entry only shows that the reckoning was given from Mena to this point, both the numbers and the years being lost.

Of small remains there are two fine alabaster vases (B.M., from Abydos; and F.M.). The scarabs are commoner than those of any king before this; but there is no variety or interest in them.

The fifth dynasty is marked by its priestly character from the first. Its origin appears to have been a re-assertion of the Heliopolitan element, which may have had a Mesopotamian origin, and which took the form of a usurpation by the priests of Ra in the Delta, who then established the claim to divine descent from Ra, which was maintained by all the later kings of the land. And this priestly tendency is shown by the great attention to religious foundations, there being a dozen or more priests known of each of the earlier kings of the dynasty. The same character is seen in the absence of foreign wars and of great monuments; the kings retained their hold of the Sinaitic peninsula, but the main attention of the age was given to fine tombs and religious foundations.

The productions of the time show much falling off from the splendid style of previous reigns. The masonry is less careful, the forms and colouring are becoming formal; and vivacious as some of the work is,—as in the tomb of Thy,—it is yet miserably flat and coarse when compared with the brilliant and vital representations in the sculptures of the previous dynasty. Declension is evident on all sides, and the work, large and small, is done more for the sake of its effect than for the consciousness of its reality.

CHAPTER V

THE SIXTH DYNASTY

	MANETHO.	LISTS.	MONUMENTS.	YEARS.	B.C. about
				M. T.P.	3503
1	Othoës	Teta	Teta	30 ...	
2	..	User·ka·ra	Aty	... 6	3473
3	Fios	{ Mery·ra. A. { Pepy. S.	{ Mery·ra { Pepy (I.)	53 20	3467 3447
4	Methusūfis	{ Mer·en·ra { Mehti·em·sa·f	{ Mer·en·ra { Mehti·em·sa·f	7 4	3443
5	Fiōps	Nefer·ka·ra	{ Nefer·ka·ra { Pepy (II.)	95 9-	3348
6	Menthesūfis	{ Mer·en·ra { Mehti·em·sa·f	{ Mer·en·ra { Mehti·em·sa·f	1 1	3347
7	...	Neter·ka·rà	...	... ...	
8	Nitōkris	{ Men·ka·ra { Net·aqerti	...	12 ...	
					3335
		Total stated 203, actually		198	

IN this dynasty a new and more vigorous line of kings comes forward. The greater number of monuments, and the wide extent of country over which they are found, show this plainly. There is some uncertainty as to the end of the dynasty, but the greater part is well assured.

VI. 1. TETA  about 3503-3473 B.C.

Pyramid, *Dad·asut*, Sakkara (Rec. v. 1).
Rock graffito, Hat-nub (F.H. iv. xv.).
Alabaster vase, Abydos (G.M.; M.A. 1464).
Alabaster lid (B.M.; P.Sc. 57).

Fig. 51.—Alabaster jar lid. Scale ¼.

It appears that Teta never adopted a throne name, but, like Unas, only used his personal name throughout his reign; even in his pyramid no other name is found but Teta. His *ka* name, *se·hetep·taui*, is only found in a graffito at Hat-nub (F.H. xv.).

The pyramid is arranged in exactly the same manner as that of Unas, excepting that the three small chambers have been thrown into one. But it has suffered far more from the spoilers, who, in search of treasure, have largely destroyed the walls of the chamber at the end of the long passage. Probably this was one of the first pyramids opened by such plunderers; as they have burnt and broken their way through the granite portcullises, instead of cutting a way over them as elsewhere, and they have here smashed the walls, and so gained the experience which showed them that it was useless to search thus in other pyramids. The texts which cover the walls show a decrease in the size of writing, from those of Unas; a change which was carried further in the small hieroglyphs of Pepy. The subjects are more religious, and less of a direct ritual, than those of Unas, though many passages remain identical (Rec. v. 1).

The priests of the pyramid are—

Sabu (M.M. 375).
Ptah·shepses (M.M. 377).
Hapa (R.E. ix. 3).
Asa (P.R. ii. 76).
Mera (tomb at Sakkara).
(Unknown) (L.D. ii. 116 c).

while

Ra·hent (M.M. 360) is prophetess of the *Mert* of Teta.

The name of Teta occurs on a part of the coffin of Apa·ankh (Berlin, L.D. ii. 98; see M.G. 98). As apparently a private name, it is written in a square, with a seated man determinative, twice over in the alabaster quarry of the XIIth dynasty at Hat-nub (P.A. xlii.). And it again occurs as a private name at Zauyet el Maiyitin (L.D. ii. 110 o, r). As it is, however, a common name in early times, these are probably independent of the king's name. Written in a cartouche in a compound name, Teta·ankh, it is among the graffiti of El Kab (L.D. ii. 117; A.Z. xiii. 70). Manetho preserves a tale that this king was killed by his guards, and as a weak reign succeeds him, this is not unlikely.

Of small remains there are very few. An alabaster vase found at Abydos (M.A. 1464) gives the name of "Teta beloved by Dadet," with a figure of Osiris Ba·neb·dadet with the ram's head. This, and the other vase of Unas found at Abydos, suggests that all this class of vases with royal names have come from there. A lid with his name, figured above, is in B. Mus. No scarabs or cylinders are known of him.

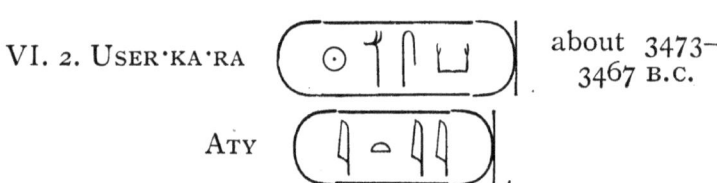

VI. 2. USER·KA·RA about 3473–3467 B.C.

ATY

The name of User·ka·ra occurs in the list of Abydos, without any equivalent in the list of Sakkara, and the Turin papyrus is here defective. No other trace of his name has been found. But a king Aty, who apparently reigned for a short time, is recorded in an inscription of his first year at Hammamat, where he sent for stone to build his pyramid. As he appears to belong to this

USER·KA·RA

age, it is conjectured that he is the same as User·ka·ra. There being very few throne names in these dynasties left unfixed to a personal name, this conjecture is not improbable (R.S.D. 149).

The inscription at Hammamat mentions the visit of an official, Ptah·en·kau, with bands of archers and workmen, to bring stone for building the pyramid *Bau* of king Aty. And adjoining this is the name of the noble Aty·ankh (?), the last part of the name having been destroyed (L.D. ii. 115 f; G.H. vii.).

VI. 3. MERY·RA   about 3467–3447 B.C.

PEPY (I.)

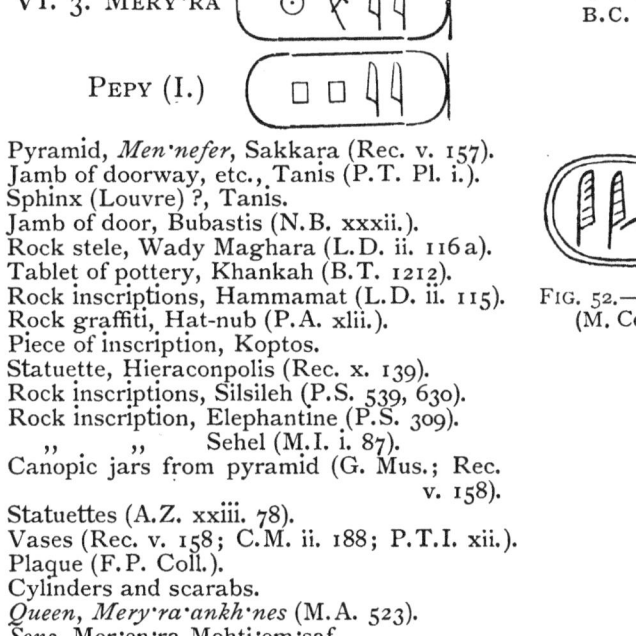

FIG. 52.—Scarab (M. Coll.).

Pyramid, *Men·nefer*, Sakkara (Rec. v. 157).
Jamb of doorway, etc., Tanis (P.T. Pl. i.).
Sphinx (Louvre) ?, Tanis.
Jamb of door, Bubastis (N.B. xxxii.).
Rock stele, Wady Maghara (L.D. ii. 116 a).
Tablet of pottery, Khankah (B.T. 1212).
Rock inscriptions, Hammamat (L.D. ii. 115).
Rock graffiti, Hat-nub (P.A. xlii.).
Piece of inscription, Koptos.
Statuette, Hieraconpolis (Rec. x. 139).
Rock inscriptions, Silsileh (P.S. 539, 630).
Rock inscription, Elephantine (P.S. 309).
„   „   Sehel (M.I. i. 87).
Canopic jars from pyramid (G. Mus.; Rec. v. 158).
Statuettes (A.Z. xxiii. 78).
Vases (Rec. v. 158; C.M. ii. 188; P.T.I. xii.).
Plaque (F.P. Coll.).
Cylinders and scarabs.
Queen, *Mery·ra·ankh·nes* (M.A. 523).
Sons, Mer·en·ra Mehti·em·saf.
        Nefer·ka·ra Pepy II.

This king has left more monuments, large and small, than any other ruler before the XIIth dynasty; and he appears to have been one of the most active and vigorous of all the early monarchs.

His pyramid was known as Men·nefer, and was opened at Sakkara in 1880. It is of the same type as those of Unas and Teta, except that the eastern chamber is all one, and is not divided into a cross passage and three small chambers. The walls have been greatly destroyed, and the fragments half filled the chambers; many of these pieces covered with inscriptions have been brought to Europe, from the heaps which lay about at the pyramid. An entrance had been forced by mining downward in the middle of the pyramid, and breaking up the deep beams of stone which form the roof of the sepulchral chamber; and this is now a clear section of a pyramid, showing the methods of construction. Not only were there sloping roof beams, of about five or six feet in depth, meeting above in a ridge; but these beams were so long, and went so far into the wall, that their centre of gravity was well within the wall-face, and hence they acted as cantilevers, resting on the wall without any need of touching each other at the top. Not content with one such roof, three roofs of this construction were built thus, one over the other, in contact; in this manner there was an ample surplus of strength. The spiteful destruction of this pyramid is far beyond what would be done by treasure-seekers. Every cartouche in the entrance passage is chopped out; and the black basalt sarcophagus has been elaborately wrecked, rows of grooves have been cut in it, and it has been banged to pieces, breaking through even a foot thickness of tough basalt.

Sunk in the floor is a granite box, in which were placed the alabaster canopic jars and vases (Rec. v. 158). The lid of the box had no fastening, but was merely a slab, a double cubit square.

The inscriptions that remain in this pyramid are of the same type as those of Teta (Rec. v. 157, vii. 145, viii. 87). The body of the masonry, instead of being of hewn stone, is merely built of walls of flakes, filled in with loose chips; showing the feeble work in these later pyramids (Fig. 53).

The prophets of Pepy are numerous. They belong to the pyramid *Men·nefer* (P), to the *Het·ka*, or

Fig. 53.—Rubble walls and chips forming the mass of the pyramid. At the right is the top of the chamber masonry.

dwelling of the *ka* (K), and to the place called *Mert* (M). In one case a *mer* or keeper is named instead of a prophet, and this is noted here.

P	Mera	Sakkara	Tomb.
P	Adu	Khenoboskion	(L.D. ii. 113 g).
P	Zauta	,,	(L.D. ii. 114 g).
P	Una	Abydos	(M.A. No. 529).
P	Shesha	,,	(M.A. 532).
P	Mery·ra·ptah·se·ankh	,,	(M.A. 532).
P	Pepy·na	,,	(M.A. 528).
M,P	Sesa	Sakkara	(M.M. 420).
P	(unknown)	Silsileh	(P.S. 630).
mer P,M	Assa·kha . . .	Sakkara	(M.M. 456).
K	Ata	Zauyet el Maiyitin	(L.D. ii. 110 e- g).

K	Kaka	Zauyet el Maiyitin	(L.D. ii. 110 n).
K	(unknown)	,,	(L.D. ii. 111 k).
?	Uha	Posno coll.	(W.G. 210).
?	(unknown)	Sharona near Minia	(Acad. 1885, 135).

And an overseer (*mer*) of the sculptors of the pyramid, named Theta, is recorded at Hammamat (L.D. 115 c).

Of buildings of Pepy there remain a door jamb of red granite with deeply cut hieroglyphs, and a block of granite, at Tanis (P.T. i.); another door jamb at Bubastis (N.B. xxxii.); and a fragment in limestone from Koptos. He is stated to have erected an obelisk at Heliopolis (Pliny), and the foundation of the temple of Denderah is also referred to him in a Ptolemaic inscription there. It seems, therefore, that he was a great builder, as we might gather from the number of quarry inscriptions of his reign. A grand stele was carved by him on the rocks of the Wady Maghara, recording an expedition there in his eighteenth year (L.D. ii. 116 a).

One of the most important monuments of his reign appears to be the great sphinx in red granite from Tanis, now in the Louvre, and companion to a broken one still *in situ*. The original king's name is in a cartouche on the base, at the right side of the sphinx; and, though carefully erased, yet traces of three hieroglyphs remain, as reed *a*, an upright sign (column *an*?) and a drill cap *t*. These show the scale of the signs, and indicate that the whole cartouche held between twenty and thirty signs. Few such long compound cartouches are known except of Pepy I., who often employed such; and the signs would agree well to "*Heru mery taui*, beloved of such and such gods, Pepy, living like the sun." Though the attribution is not proved, it is at least a very probable one; and if accepted, we have here the earliest sphinx known, and a fine portrait of Pepy. Unhappily, no photographs of the Louvre antiquities are available.

At Elephantine he added a line of his name and titles above the stele of Unas (P.S. 309); the cartouche appears to have been altered, and shows traces of a name, Ra .... nefer, which cannot be well referred to any king earlier than Pepy, unless to Nefer·f·ra, which is hardly likely. At Sehel occurs an inscription of a man named Pepy ankh (M.I. i. 87). At Silsileh there is a single cartouche, Pepy, not far above the river, on the rocks in the narrow strait (P.S. 539); also an inscription of a prophet of his pyramid, whose name is lost (P.S. 630).

In the quarry of Hat·nub, in the desert behind Tell el Amarna, ten miles from the Nile, are many inscriptions of Pepy. One is dated in the twenty-fifth year, another is at the entrance to the quarry, and a third was carved by a noble named Tehuti·nekht, who was governor of the Oryx nome. Of the same region is Beba, at Shekh Said, who was "*heq hat Pepy.*"

At Hammamat are many inscriptions, carved by the workmen who were sent to quarry stone. The largest (L.D. ii. 115 g) is of special value as naming a Sed festival in his eighteenth year; and this festival recurred at intervals of thirty years, or one week's shift of the heliacal rising of Sirius. It has been supposed that kings held a Sed festival on the completion of thirty years of rule; yet this Sed festival in the eighteenth year points to its being purely astronomical in that age. There is another inscription of the workmen, recording the names of the chiefs of the parties (115 b, c); another of Mery·ra on the throne as king of Upper Egypt, and Pepy on the throne as king of Lower Egypt, back to back, naming the Sed festival (115 a); another with Pepy adoring Min (115, e); another with only the names of the king (115, i); and lastly, a tablet of the chief of the works, Mery·ra·ptah·mery·ankh (115 k).

The graffiti inscriptions at El Kab are entirely of private persons, many of whom are named after Pepy; as Pepy·ankh (L.D. ii. 117 g, h, i, k, l); Mery·ra·senb (117 r); and Mery·ra·ankh (117 p, q, s, u, v). See also A.Z. xiii. 70.

In this reign we meet for the first time with a continuous historical document, which is of great interest as showing what the activities of the Egyptians were in travel and conquest in this age. The biographical inscription of Una was found in his tomb at Abydos (now in G.M.), and it describes the various labours of his life (R.S.D. vii. viii.; A.Z. xx. 2). He begins by mentioning that first landmark of an Egyptian boy's life, the being girded, or wearing a waist-cloth; equivalent to being "put into trousers" to an English boy. This was under king Teta; and the short reign of User·ka·ra was passed over in his youth. As he grew up, various offices, supervision of the pyramid priests, and a judgeship were conferred upon him, and he came into great favour with Mery·ra. The first honour done to him was the supplying of the fine stonework from the royal quarries of Turrah, near Cairo, for his tomb at Abydos; he specifies the white stone sarcophagus, its cover, the great stele or false door for the shrine, its settings, two foundation blocks, and altar of offering (S.B.A. xi. 316). He took the evidence alone at the trial of the queen Amtes, and wrote the report with one other judge. The royal favour, which gave him facilities of transport for his tomb work, was next extended by setting him over a great raid on the Amu Bedawin to the east of Egypt. Tens of thousands of soldiers were levied from South and North Egypt, and—like the Sudani regiments of the present day—from the negroes of Aarthet, Maza, Aam, Wawat, Kaau, and men of the land of Thamehu. Maspero (R.C. 1892, 364) identifies Aarthet as the region from Derr to Dongola, or Upper Nubia on the west. Aam is between Aarthet and Aswan, or Lower Nubia on the west side; and Wawat opposite to that on the east. The Thamehu are identified with the people of the oases. The whole management of the expedition, and of the officials employed, seems to have been in the hands of Una, and his success in it was the great event of his life. After that, he went on five lesser expeditions, to keep the land in subjection; and he was made governor of the south country, from Aswan northward, by king Meren·ra. He then was employed to bring the special stone for the pyramid of Meren·ra. From

Abhat he brought the sarcophagus of black granite, and a top stone for the pyramid; from Elephantine he brought the granite false door and its sill, and the granite portcullises and their settings, for the interior of the pyramid; also the granite doorway and sills for the exterior temple. And then he was sent to Hat·nub to cut out and bring the great alabaster table of offerings. We now know the exact quarry at which he worked, where the names of Meren·ra still remain, which were probably cut on this occasion. Time ran short before the subsidence of the inundation, and he built a boat during the seventeen days of the month Epiphi, in which he was extracting the stone; he brought it down, but the dry ground was already appearing when he reached Memphis, and he could not safely bring the boat over the inundated ground. This fact shows the season of the month Epiphi in that age, from which—by the shifting of the calendar round the seasons in each Sothis period of 1460 years—it is possible to get an approximate date for the reign of Meren·ra at about 3350 B.C. (P.S. 20). After having thus provided the great stonework for the interior, Una went shortly afterwards to excavate five canals in the south, and build vessels in the land of Wawat to bring down still more granite, for which he was supplied with acacia-wood by the chiefs of the Nubian lands Aarthet, Aam, and Maza, and did the whole work in a year.

This long inscription of fifty lines gives our first clear view of the active, self-satisfied Egyptian officials who did such great and lasting works for their country.

The family relations of Pepy are given in a tablet found at Abydos (M.A. 523). From this we learn that the queen was named Mery·ra·ankh·nes (or Pepy·ankh·nes in another tablet, M.A. 524); and that Meren·ra was the eldest son, and Nefer·ka·ra Pepy II. the second son. Meren·ra died young, and was thus succeeded by his brother. The queen's father and mother were named Khua and Nebt, and her brother Za·u. She also appears as wife of Mery·ra and mother of Nefer·ka·ra in a tablet at Wady Maghara (L.D. ii. 116 a).

Of small remains there is a statuette of black granite found at Hieraconpolis (now in G. Mus., Rec. x. 139); and portions of two statuettes of Mery·ra, one in hardstone, and one in green glaze (A.Z. xxiii. 78). Some vases of alabaster are in the Louvre, one of them naming the Sed festival (C.M. ii. 188, 6); and a lid in England (P.T. xii. 5). Also a monkey vase in Vienna (W.G. 213). A pottery tablet with Pepy's name and

FIG. 54.—Cylinder (Tylor Coll.).

titles was found at Khankah (B.T. 1212); and a green glazed pottery tablet bears the name, "Ra·mery beloved of Min" (F.P. Coll.). Several cylinders of copper and of stone are known (Paris, Posno, B. Mus., Kennard and Tylor Collections); and several scarabs.

· The granite altar in Turin with the name of Pepy is certainly of late date (S.B.A. Trans. iii., 110–112).

VI. 4. MER·EN·RA 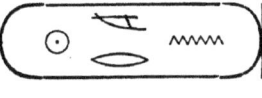 about 3447-3443 B.C.

MEHTI·EM·SA·F

Pyramid, *Kha·nefer*, Sakkara (Rec. ix. 177).

Steles, Aswan (P.S. 81, 338; Rec. xv. 147).

Stele, Hammamat (L.D. ii. 115 d).

Vases, alabaster (B. F. and G. Muss.).

Box, ivory, Louvre (C.M. ii. 188, 7).

Scarab (F.P. Coll.).

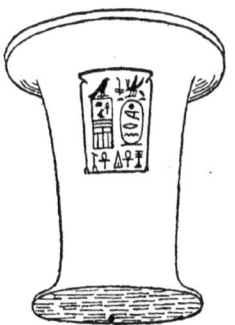

FIG. 55.—Vase (Flor. Mus.).

The pyramid of this king was found at Sakkara in 1880. It is constructed like that of his father Mery·ra. We have already noticed the preparation of the materials in the preceding section, when stating the work of Una. The spoilers have violently ruined the pyramid, and destroyed some of the walls of the chambers; but the black granite sarcophagus is yet in good condition. The inscriptions are mainly the same as those in the other pyramids (A.Z. xix. 1; Rec. ix. 177, x. 1, xi. 1).

The body of Merenra was found in the chamber, despoiled of all its wrappings, but in good preservation; it is now in the Ghizeh Museum. From the body we learn that he died young; even the youthful lock of hair is said to be still on the head (W.G. supp. 22). This agrees with Merenra's short reign of 4 years (T.P.); the 7 years of Manetho is unlikely, as his brother was only six when he succeeded him (Manetho). Considering that the two sons of Meryra were born about 10 years and 2 years before his death, it is very unlikely that he reigned 53 years as Manetho says; the 20 years of the Turin papyrus is far more likely. We may then, from all considerations of reigns and ages, lay out the family chronology in this approximate order, assuming that the eldest son was usually born when a king was about twenty years of age.

B.C. about
3499 0 Aty born.
3479 20 son born = 0 Meryra born.
3473 26 succeeded.
3467 32 died.   12 succeeded.
3459   20 son born = 0 Merenra born.
3449   30 son born   = $\begin{cases} 0 \text{ Neferkara} \\ \text{born.} \end{cases}$
3447   32 died   12 succeeded.
3443   16 died   6 succeeded.
3349   100 died.

As Una records that he was girded under Teta, say at 10 years old, his age during these reigns might be about 12–18 under Aty, 18–38 under Meryra, when he made his great expedition, 38–42 under Merenra, during which time he finished the sculpture of his tomb, having already built it before his expedition. Then after forty-two he probably settled down in private nobility, while others took the lead during the minority of Neferkara, as he does not allude to that at all.

Several prophets of the pyramid of Merenra are known. Una himself held this office, as we learn by a stele from Abydos. The excavation there having been left to natives, we do not know the original places of the steles and inscriptions, and all such records are lost for ever; but the high titles of the stele (M.A. 529) make it practically certain that it belongs to the same person as the long inscription.

Ahy	Sakkara	(M.A.F. i. 204).
Una	Abydos	(M.A. 529).
Una (another)	,,	(M.A. 533).
Una (uncertain)	,,	(M.A. 541).
Pepi·na	,,	(M.A. 528).
Adu	Khenoboskion	(L.D. ii. 113 g).
Za uta	,,	(L.D. ii. 114 g).

A stele on the rock at Aswan records the visit of the king there to receive the submission of the chiefs of Arthet and Wawat in the fifth year (Rec. xv. 147); and another stele (L.D. ii. 116 b; more in P.S. 338) shows an official adoring the king with the two royal names. A third stele is dated in the fourth year (P.S. 81). And at Hammamat is a stele with the royal names (L.D. ii. 115 d).

In the last reign we considered the inscription of Una which relates to his raids on the Amu under Mery·ra, and his bringing of granite for the pyramid of Merenra. We now turn to another invaluable biographical inscription, which relates mainly to this reign, but partly to the next. It is on the front of a tomb in the cliffs of Aswan (S.T.; R.C. 1892, 358), and records the deeds of a governor of the South named Herkhuf. His father, Ara, seems to have been the immediate successor of Una in the Nubian affairs; as he begins by recording that Merenra sent him with his father on an expedition to Aam (or Lower Nubia, on the west) to explore ("find roads") for seven months; they returned with large quantities of tribute, or plunder. Then Merenra sent Herkhuf a second time alone; he pushed through to Arthet, or Upper Nubia, making an unheard-of circuit of the western countries, during eight months, returning with great tribute. A third time he was sent, starting from Asyut, across the desert, and found the king of Aam (Lower Nubia) on an expedition against the Themhu, "at the west point of heaven," *i.e.* in the western oases: the Egyptians followed the Aam in their raid, and acted so vigorously with them that they thanked all the gods for the king. Having then appeased the chief of Aam, the Egyptians went through Aam to Arthet (or Western Upper Nubia), and returned through Sethu and Wawat on the eastern bank, finding the people all in peace. From these countries they brought 300 asses laden with incense, ebony, leopards' skins, elephants' teeth, etc. For when the tribes saw the soldiers of Aam with the Egyptians, they gave tribute of oxen, goats, and all kinds of produce. On the return of Herkhuf in triumph, the king sent an official up the river to meet him, with a boat laden with delicacies, as a refreshment after the arduous campaign. In the identification of the lands mentioned, Maspero's view has been followed (R.C. 1892, 358); but Schiaparelli places these countries even farther south. Another curious document is also placed on this tomb, apparently resulting from another expedition in the beginning of the reign of Nefer·ka·ra. It is dated in the second year of that king, and was a royal rescript addressed to Herkhuf in reply to despatches sent from him while he was in the South, probably at Aswan. It begins by saying that Herkhuf having returned as far as Aam in peace, with his soldiers, and brought all good tribute, and this Deng, who is a dancer of god (performing some remarkable religious dance?) from the Land of Spirits, like the Deng that was brought by Ba·ur·dedu from Punt in the time of Assa, and all his work being very excellent; —therefore his majesty orders that when the Deng goes with Herkhuf, attendants shall watch him that he fall not in the water, and shall sleep with him that he run not away; for his majesty (who was then eight years old) loves to see this Deng more than all other tribute. And if Herkhuf keeps him safe and sound, he shall be more honoured than Ba·ur·dedu was by Assa; and all provisions and necessaries are to be furnished for him on the journey to the court (see also A.Z. xxx. 78; A.R. 1894).

We learn from this that even in the time of Assa expeditions had been sent to Punt, and distant products had been brought back. We gather also that the Egyptians established a considerable hold on Upper Nubia, and drafted soldiers from there and received tribute; while from time to time exploratory parties were sent out to examine fresh districts, and to collect by force or favour all that they could.

Of minor remains of Merenra there are some alabaster vases, from Elephantine (M.D. 54 g) and Abydos (M.A. 1465) (both in G.M.), and others in

Florence (C.M. iv. 424, 24) and London. An ivory box with his name is in the Louvre (C.M. ii. 188, 7). And one scarab of his, in blue glazed pottery (Fig. 56), is known (F.P. Coll.).

There is some doubt as to the reading of the second cartouche; the first sign in it has been variously read, Hor, Sokar, or Mehti; and as the Greek version of it is Methusūphis, it seems indicated that we should read it as Mehti·em·sa·f.

FIG. 56
(F.P. Coll.)

VI. 5. NEFER·KA·RA about 3443–3348 B.C.

PEPY (II.)

Pyramid, *Men·ankh*, Sakkara (Rec. xii. 53, 136).
Stele, Wady Maghara (L.D. ii. 116 a).
Graffiti, Hat-nub (F.H. iii. iv.).
Sculptures, Koptos.
Stele, Elephantine (P.S. 311).
Base of alabaster figure (W.G. 215).
Granite mortar (G. Mus.).
Limestone jar (G. M.) (B.R. i. 10, 5).
Vase lid, Elephantine (M.D. 54 g).
Vase lid (F.P. Coll.).
Cylinder (M.D. 54 f.). Scarabs.

FIG. 57.—Rosette (G. Coll.).

The pyramid of this king, named *Men·ankh*, was found at Sakkara in 1881. Its construction is the same as that of the previous pyramids; but the inscriptions are in smaller writing, and are longer. The texts are mainly already known in the other pyramids, and are partly religious, partly of ritual. The walls have been considerably destroyed by treasure-seekers. The granite sarcophagus remains in good condition; and the lid has not been overthrown, but is only pushed aside on to the bench of brickwork which existed in all these pyramids, between the sarcophagus and the wall, to support the lid until the closing of the sarcophagus.

Some prophets of this pyramid are known—

Adu	Khenoboskion	(L.D. ii. 113 g)
Zauta	,,	(L.D. ii. 114 g)
Aba	Deir el Gebrawi	(A.R. 1893, 14; Rec. xiii. 67)
Zau	,,	(A.R. 1893, 14; Rec. xiii. 66)

At Wady Maghara is a very fine stele, which was carved in his second year; and as he began his reign at the age of six, it was done during his minority. His mother is prominently placed upon it, in name, in her royal connection, and in figure; and from the form of her titles it appears as if she were formally regent at the time (L.D. ii. 116 a).

At Elephantine is a fine stele adjoining that of king Unas (P.S. 311); this mentions the second *Sed* festival of the king, agreeing with his long reign, in which he had three or four such festivals.

In the alabaster quarry of Hat-nub, opened by Khufu, are many inscriptions of this king; three tablets with his names have writing of several lines, one dated in the sixth year; and a deeply-cut group of the royal names is near the entrance. It is these inscriptions which name the place as Hat-nub (F.H. iii. iv.).

At Koptos two slabs of sculpture of this king indicate that he built in the temple (Fig. 58).

Of private tombs mentioning this king there are several. Mery at Kauamat acted under the orders of Neferkara (L.D. ii. 113 f). At Aswan Herkhuf gives the royal letter about the Deng dancer, and as the boy-king was then only eight years old, the subject was likely to captivate his fancy (S.T. 19). Saben was an official connected with the pyramid (Rec. x. 184); and Nekhu, also at Aswan, has the name of the king in his tomb (S.B.A. x. 37). At Sakkara Saui·khu is priest of the pyramid of the king (M.A.F. i, 199). At Girgeh Sesa was represented in his tomb adoring Nefer·ka·ra

(A.Z. xx. 124). And at El Kab a piece of limestone stele names the king (A.Z. xx. 124).

FIG. 58.—Slab from Koptos.

A high lady at the court, Nebt, named also Beba, held offices under this king (M.A. 527); and Khua had a son named Nefer·ka·ra·ankh (M.A. 525).

Of small remains of this king there are a base of a seated figure in alabaster, found at Sakkara (W.G. 215); a large black granite mortar with his name belonged to a king's brother, Amenisenb (G. Mus.); a vase lid from Elephantine (M.D. 54 g); a limestone jar (in G.M.; B.R. i. 10, 5); and many scarabs, which are commoner than those of any other king of the old kingdom (Fig. 59). Several others, however, attributed to Pepy II., certainly belong to Shabaka of the XXVth

FIG. 59.—Types of scarabs of Pepy and following dynasties.

dynasty, and to other kings with the common name Neferkara. In many museums are alabaster vases with the cartouche Nefer·ka·ra; probably one or two may be genuine, though I have not noticed such as yet; but most of them have forged names on genuine vases, the very shapes of which show that they were made in the XIXth dynasty rather than in the VIth dynasty.

VI. 6. MER·EN·RA }
     MEHTI·EM·SAF }
about 3348–3347 B.C.

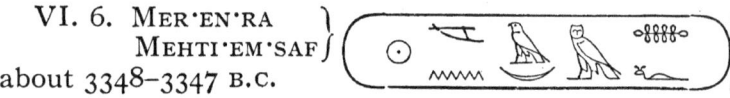

That these two names belong to the same king is certain, as the combined cartouche given above is found in the list of Abydos. In Manetho likewise a Menthesufis succeeds the second Pepy. The Turin papyrus has lost the names of this part, but a fragment with the numerals can be identified by the unique reign of Nefer·ka·ra, for over ninety years. The following reign is but one year, and probably refers to this king. No monuments or contemporary remains of him are known.

VI. 7. NETER·KA·RA

This name occurs next to the above in the Abydos list; but there is no trace of it elsewhere.

VI. 8. MEN·KA·RA   about 3347–
                    3335 B.C.

NET·AQER·TI

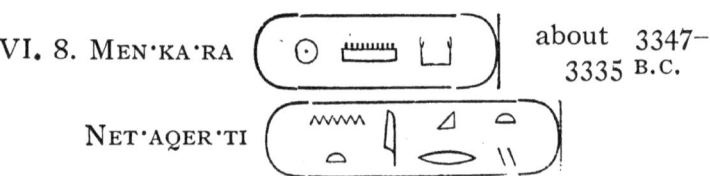

This last reign of the dynasty (according to Manetho) is one of the most questionable. Men·ka·ra succeeds

Neterkara in the list of Abydos, and no other trace of the name is known. On the other hand, the dynasty closes with Nitokris in Manetho, next after Menthesufis. And the reality of this name is confirmed by the Turin papyrus entry of Netaqerti, on a fragment which may reasonably belong to this period.

The only connection between Menkara and Netaqerti is provided by a curious error of late times. The third pyramid of Gizeh is stated by Manetho to have been built by Nitokris.; and Herodotos attributes the same to the beautiful Rhodopis (ii. 134), evidently another version of Nitokris, whom Manetho describes as fair and ruddy. But though the third pyramid has been enlarged, it is certain, from the excellent masonry of the core, from the granite casing of the outside, and from the absence of all inscription inside, that it belongs entirely to the fourth dynasty, and has no connection with the rubble pyramids of the sixth dynasty at Sakkara. There is only one possible origin before us for this tale. The real builder of the pyramid being Men·kau·ra, he has been confounded with the queen Men·ka·ra of the end of the sixth dynasty; and these tales thus lead us to associate the name Men·ka·ra with that of Netaqerti or Nitokris, to whom the pyramid is otherwise attributed.

The close of the dynasty appears to have been troublous. According to Herodotos (ii. 100), the brother of Nitokris was slain, and she in turn treacherously avenged him on his murderers. Whether this brother was Mer·en·ra or Neter·ka·ra, there is no evidence. But the former only reigned a single year. It seems that the long reign and great age of Pepy II. had allowed disorder to arise; owing to his feebleness, and probably the number of rival claims in various generations of his descendants, the kingdom had become disorganised; and, after a few brief reigns, the dynasty failed, and a long era of confusion followed. Even the close of the dynasty is uncertain, as we shall see in considering the next era.

Two kings that may be referred to the IVth-VIth dynasties should be stated here, although their exact place is unknown, as they are only found on isolated objects.

Neb·kha·ra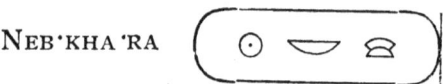

Fig. 60.—Scarab (H. Coll.).

occurs on a scarab of this age (H. Coll.).

Hor·nefer·hen

Fig. 61.—Alabaster. ½ scale (F.P. Coll.).

This name is in a cartouche on a piece of an alabaster lid (F.P. Coll.), apparently of the IVth dynasty. It may well be the same as a name read by Deveria 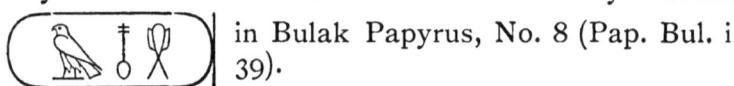 in Bulak Papyrus, No. 8 (Pap. Bul. i. 39).

This dynasty differs from either of those which preceded it. It has neither the simplicity of the IVth nor the priestly character of the Vth dynasty. The ideal of the time was active foreign conquest and exploration. Monuments sprang up in all parts of the country, and a general development of national life appears which was unknown before.

The art of the time, though becoming more general, is lower in character. The pyramids, instead of being solid masses of stone which rival the hills, are merely heaps of chips and rubble retained by rude walls, and covered with a smooth casing. The tombs of private persons have not the solidity of those of their ancestors. But the execution of small objects is very fine and sumptuous, as in the ivory box and head-rest in the Louvre. We see in this age the regular effects of the diffusion and cheapening of works which were formerly a rare luxury. Yet there is by no means the depraved showiness which marks the works of the later times of the XVIIIth–XIXth dynasties.

CHAPTER VI

Seventh to Tenth Dynasties

The lack of any prominent landmarks among the names preserved to us in these dynasties makes it needful to treat them together as a whole.

The actual documents concerning them are here arranged, according to what seems to be their most probable relations, the details of which are discussed later on.

Turin Papyrus.	Abydos List.	Manetho and Eratosthenes.	Monu
9 Neferka			
10 Nefer·s			
11 Ab			
12 ....y			
Sum dynasty 181 years. Years from Mena 1755.		By sum stated at end of XIth dynasty ∴ years from Mena 1756 about 3322 B.C.	
1 (Lost)	. . .		
2 Nefer·ka·ra	Nefer·ka·ra		
3 Kheti	. . .		
4 ......y	Nefer·ka·ra Neby	. . .	Neby
5 (Lost)	Dad·ka·shema·ra	Thuosimarēs	
6 Nefer·ka·ra	Nefer·ka·ra		
7 Khety	Hor·meren		
8 S......	Snefer·ka		
9 (Lost)	Ra·en·ka	. . .	Ra·en·
10 (Lost)	Nefer·ka·ra Tererel	Thirillos	
11 Hor?.....	Hor·nefer·ka		
12 H.......	. . .		

SEVENTH TO TENTH DYNASTIES

Turin Papyrus.	Abydos List.	Manetho and Eratosthenes.	Monuments.
13 (Lost)	Nefer·kaˊra		
	Pepy·senb		
14 S?	Snefer·ka·Annu	Semphrukrates	
15 (Lost)	. . ukau·ra		
16 (Lost)	Nefer·kau·ra	(VIIth dynasty	
17 (Lost)	Hor·kau·ra	5 kings, 70 years	
18 (Lost)	Nefer·ar·ka·ra	VIIIth dynasty	
Sum dynasty		27 kings, 146 years)	
18 kings			
		about 3106 B.C.	
		1 { Akhthoēs, Man.	{ Ab·mery·ra
		{ Khūthēr, Erat.	{ Khety
		2 . . .	Ka·mery·ra
		3 Meures, Erat.	Maā·ab·ra
			4 Skha·n·ra
		(IXth dynasty	5 Kha·user·ra
		4 kings, 100 years)	6 Aa·hotep·ra
			7 Aa
		about 3006 B.C.	
		(Xth dynasty	Khyan
		19 kings, 185 years)	Uazed
			Yapeqher
		about 2821 B.C.	
		about 2985 B.C.	
. . .	. . .		Antef I.
. . .	. . .		Mentu·hotep I.
. . .	. . .		Antef II.
(Lost)	. . .		Antef III.
(Lost)	. . .		Mentu·hotep I
(Lost)	. . .		Antef IV.
(Lost)	. . .	(XIth dynasty	Antef V.
Neb·kher·ra	Neb·kher·ra	16 (? 6) kings,	Mentu·hotep II
Sankh·ka·ra	Sankh·ka·ra	43 years)	Sankh·ka·ra
		about 2778 B.C.	

The first entries of the Turin papyrus after Netaqerti have been usually set down to the VIIth dynasty, only because Manetho does not state any ruler after that queen in the previous dynasty. But there are good reasons for supposing that the VIth dynasty really lasted on for four reigns longer. (1) The Turin papyrus makes no break after Netaqerti, but goes on with four kings more, and then makes a long summary both of the dynasty and of all the kings from Mena. Such a summary is due at the end of the VIth dynasty, but is not to be expected in, or after, the VIIth, which was closely allied to the VIIIth. (2) The total of 181 years is stated at this summary; though only the number remains, yet it cannot be of kings, as not half of that number had reigned since Mena. Now we have seen good reason for taking the Turin numbers rather than those of Manetho; and, adopting them, the dynasty from Teta to Netaqerti occupied 168 years, leaving it thus 13 years short of the Turin total, which would well agree with there being four short reigns more. (3) There is another evidence, which seems at first but very uncertain, yet it agrees so well internally, that it is worth notice. Manetho states the total years from Mena to the end of the XIth dynasty as 2300; and his most probable readings for the length of the VIIth to XIth dynasties are $70 + 146 + 100 + 185 + 43$ years $= 544$ years. Deducting this from 2300 years, we reach 1756 years for the close of Manetho's VIth dynasty, agreeing to the 1755 years for the same epoch in the Turin papyrus. It is true that this entry is actually ..... 755; but the number is too great to be anything but years, and either 755 or 2755 would be equally impossible for the period since Mena; hence there can be no doubt as to the reading 1755 years, which so remarkably accords with Manetho.

We see, then, good reason to assign these four kings, between Netaqerti and the summation in the Turin papyrus, to the close of the VIth dynasty, thus allowing three or four years each for their reigns.

After a disastrous break, there are two fragments (known as Nos. 47 and 48) of the Turin papyrus. Wilkinson arranged them side by side, and supposed that a number of kings must have double cartouches here, an arrangement quite unknown in all the rest of the document. Brugsch omits No. 48 altogether, as considering that it does not belong to Wilkinson's position. But there seems no reason why frag.

48 may not precede 47, which latter reaches the base of the column; the total length thus entailed is only in accord with the length of other columns of the papyrus, and a fair coincidence is thus obtained with the total number of kings stated at the end of the dynasty, and with the list of Abydos. Accordingly I have here placed a bracket against each of these fragments of this list; and it should be remembered that the first piece is not quite certain in position.

The sum at the end of the dynasty gives eighteen kings, and this number is exactly made up in this arrangement of the fragments. On turning to the list of Abydos, we find only fifteen kings; hence certainly three in the Turin list are not in Abydos. In attempting to adjust the two lists together, then three blanks must be inserted in Abydos, and we cannot expect to find the personal name Khety which occurs at Turin, as the Abydos list is only of throne names. Remembering these points, there is not a single case of contradiction between the lists, and there are some good connections, Nefer·ka·ra, ... y for Neby, Nefer-kara, S .... for Snefer·ka, Hor? ..... (certainly a bird) for Hor·nefer·ka, and S? for Snefer·ka·annu. This last name was miscopied by Duemichen as Ra·nefer·ka, and his error is followed by Brugsch, Wiedemann, Bouriant, and Budge. Three small errors beside this in Duemichen's copy also serve to ear-mark this source of the published copies.

Taking this adjustment as provisional, the question is, what dynasties these kings represent. Manetho gives, according to the most probable text, five kings for the VIIth, and twenty-seven kings for the VIIIth; so these lists could be only a selection out of the thirty-two kings of these dynasties. That these names do not belong to the IXth or Xth is indicated by two points. (1) It is probable that the kings Ab·mery·ra and Ka·mery·ra, found at Asyut, belong to the Herakleopolite IXth and Xth dynasties; but no names of this type occur in these Abydos names. (2) The list of Eratosthenes, though corrupt as to spelling, is remarkably free from misplacement of names. He gives only a selection of kings; and beginning at his fifteenth, where we reach history, his list and the actual names are as follow—

Saofis	Khufu.
Saofis II.	Khafra.
Moskheres	Men·kau·ra.
Mousthis	Im·hotep?
Pammes	Pepy I.
Apappous (of 100 years)	Pepy II. (100 years).
Ekheskosokaras	?
Nitokris	Netaqerti.
Myrtaios	?
Thuosimares	Dad·ka·shema·ra.
Thirillos (or Thinillos)	Tererel (or Tereru).
Semphrūkrates	Seneferka.
Khūthēr (Akhthoes, Man.)	Khety.
Meures	Maā·ab·ra.

Now it seems pretty certain that "Khuther Taurus, the tyrant" of Eratosthenes, is the "Akhthoes who was more dreadful than all who went before him, who did evil throughout Egypt, and, being seized with madness, was destroyed by a crocodile," as recorded by Manetho. Hence, as this king begins the Herakleopolite dynasties (IXth–Xth), those before him in Eratosthenes belong to the VIIth–VIIIth dynasties; and thus we can assign the period of the list at Abydos, and see that it contains nothing between the VIIIth and XIth dynasties. Further, the next name in Eratosthenes is Meures, probably pronounced Mevres; and this agrees with the king Maā·ab·ra or Maāavra, known on scarabs. From the internal evidence of the reigns, it seems that the XIth dynasty was about contemporary with the Xth; but no kings earlier than Mentuhotep III. were reckoned in the series, and he was adored as a founder in later times.

Having now dealt with the connection of the dynasties, and the nature of the lists, we will turn to consider the few remains that we have of this age.

VII.–VIII. 4.
NEFER·KA·RA
NEBY
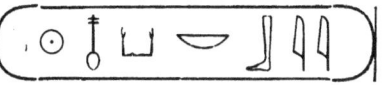
about
3290–
3280
B.C.

Three scarabs are known of this king, one in G. Coll. (Fig. 62), and two others blundered. The style of them is closely like some of Pepy, and they certainly belong to this period.

FIG. 62.—Scarab (G. Coll.).

VII.–VIII. 6. NEFER·KA·RA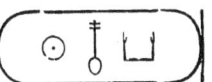

Some of the many scarabs bearing this common name apparently by their style belong to this age. They show the first introduction of the symmetrical designs.

FIG. 63.—Earliest symmetrical scarabs.
(B. Mus.).   (F.P. Coll.).

VII.–VIII. 9. RA·EN·KA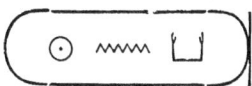
about
3230–
3220
B.C.

A few scarabs are known of this king.

Fig. 64.—Scarab (P. Mus.).

I.—8

IX.–X. 1. AB·MERY·RA

KHETY

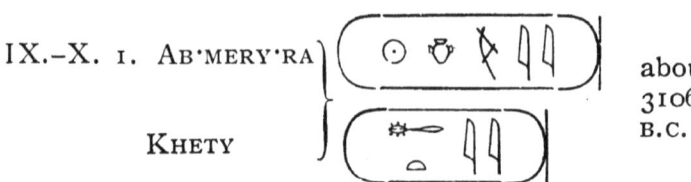

about 3106 B.C.

FIG. 65.—Scarab (P. Mus.).

These two names are known to belong to one king by the fragments of some copper open-work, which may have been parts of a brazier or some round object (Fig. 66). They are now in the Louvre (S.B.A. xiii. 429). There is also a scarab of this king (P.M.), closely like those above

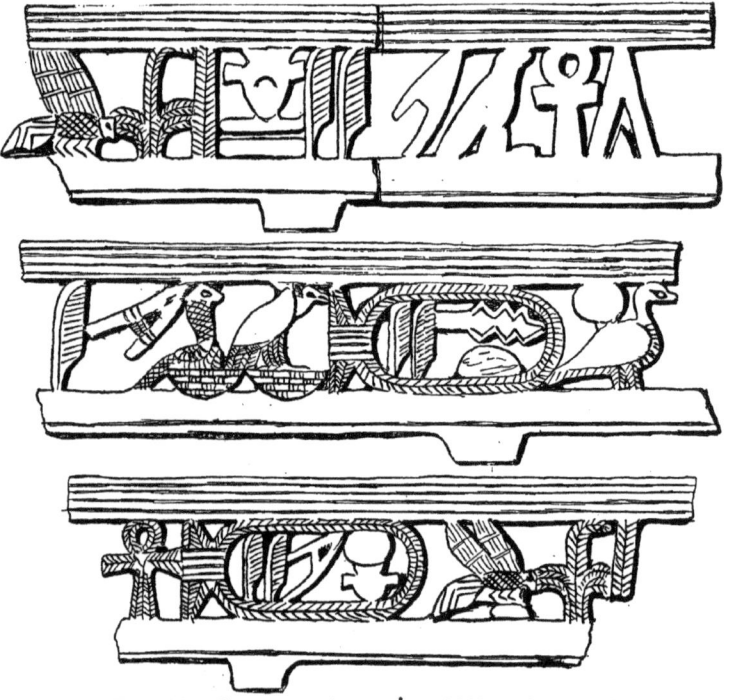

FIG. 66.—Copper-work, brazier of Khety (P. Mus.).

attributed to Ra·en·ka and Nefer·ka·ra of the preceding dynasty (see above). And his name occurs on the rocks at the First Cataract (Acad., 1892, 333). The name Khety is so common as a private name (there being thirty-six in Lieblein's dictionary), that it is of little value for identification; but as this king has left some tangible remains, he may well be the Khety = Akhthoes, the first of the IXth dynasty, who has left the strongest impression behind him, in Manetho. The Khuther of Eratosthenes may easily be a corruption of Khuthes, as final *rho* and final *sigma* are readily confounded in cursive Greek.

IX.–X. 2. KA·MERY·RA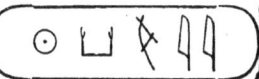

This king is known on a palette in the Louvre (Fig. 67), which was found with the fragments of copper of Ab·mery·ra, probably in a tomb near Asyut. And his name also occurs in a tomb at Asyut (G.S. xiii.). As these tombs throw light on the time, we will briefly notice them. There are three tombs of the princes of Asyut in the IXth and Xth dynasties, Khety I., Tefaba, and Khety II. The first two (according to Maspero, R.C., 1889, 421) were actively engaged in wars against the Theban princes. Khety I. recounts that he cut a canal at Asyut, and so obtained, during the dry season, a full supply of water, by which he irrigated his own nome and enriched the country; he organised the administration, and his justice procured the friendship of the king. Tefaba—probably his son—tranquillised the country, and abolished robbery. The South rebelled from Elephantine to Qau, and he had naval conflicts with the Thebans on

FIG. 67.—Wooden palette (P. Mus.) (lower end omitted).

the Nile. The next prince, Khety II., lived under Ka·mery·ra, and built a temple and prepared a tomb for himself; he also chastised the southerners, the king joining in the campaign; after which the people of the capital, Herakleopolis, came out to meet the king in triumph. We see here how the Thebans were almost independent, constant wars going on between them and the IXth and Xth dynasties. The earlier part of the XIth dynasty is therefore probably contemporary with this Xth dynasty, to which Ka·mery·ra appears to belong; and this agrees with Manetho only stating 43 years for the XIth out of the 160 years or so of those kings, leaving 120 years to overlap the Xth dynasty.

IX.–X. 3. MAĀ·AB·RA

This king appears to be the same as the Meures of Eratosthenes, and therefore belongs to the IXth or Xth dynasty. His scarabs are common, and are all of the same style of work.

FIG. 68.—Scarab (G. Mus.).

Four other kings of this same period are only known to us by their scarabs, viz.—

IX.–X. 4. S·KHA·N·RA,  whose scarabs are as common as those of Maā·ab·ra.

FIG. 69.—Scarab (F.P. Coll.).

IX.–X. 5. KHA·USER·RA,  of whom two scarabs are known (both G. Coll.).

FIG. 70.—Scarab G. Coll.).

IX.–X. 6. ĀA·HOTEP·RA,  of whom also two scarabs are known (F.P. and Berlin).

FIG. 71.—Scarab (F.P. Coll.).

IX.–X. 7. ĀA,  of whom four scarabs are known (G.M. and Evans' Coll.).

FIG. 72.—Scarab (G. Mus.).

Another king of this age, Nefer·hepu·ra, is reported to be found named at the First Cataract (Acad. 1892, 333).

We have now seen how the Memphite dynasties of the VIIth and VIIIth dynasties fell through decay. The seat of government retreated southward to Herakleopolis, above the Fayum, where it was in constant feud with the neighbouring power of Thebes, which was gradually rising into importance. What was then the cause of this retreat southward? Some catastrophe must have happened to drive them from the ancient seat of power to a comparatively obscure town; and such can hardly be aught else than the intrusion of some foreign power into the Delta. Within the last two or three years we have obtained a glimpse of this power

118   KHYAN   [DYN. IX.-X.

in the person of one king who became Egyptianised, and who has left monuments behind him which imply that he obtained a suzerainty over all the country, like the Hyksos in later times.

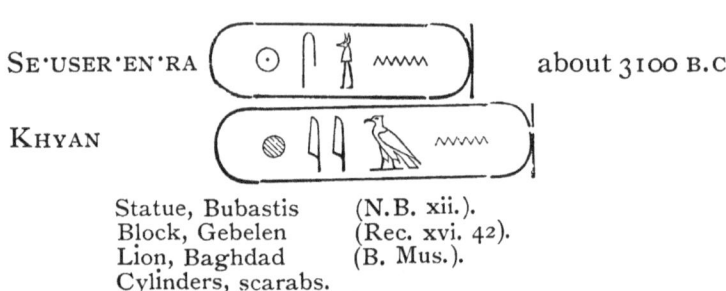

SE·USER·EN·RA   about 3100 B.C

KHYAN

Statue, Bubastis   (N.B. xii.).
Block, Gebelen   (Rec. xvi. 42).
Lion, Baghdad   (B. Mus.).
Cylinders, scarabs.

FIG. 73.—Base of statue of Khyan, Bubastis (G. Mus.).

The lower part of the statue of this king in black granite was found in the temple of Bubastis. It is of

Egyptian style, but has unusual titles. Another block of black granite, found at Gebelen, bears the same cartouches; and a lion found at Baghdad, or near there, has an effaced cartouche, which, after much dispute, is now seen clearly to belong to this king. There are also two cylinders and five scarabs which have only risen into importance since the discovery of the statue.

We will now consider the results shown by these remains. In the first place, the scarabs are of two types—(1) with scroll-work down the sides, but not connected across top or bottom, *i.e.* a discontinuous scroll; and (2) usually with a vertical line down each side of the name, and debased hieroglyphs at the edges.

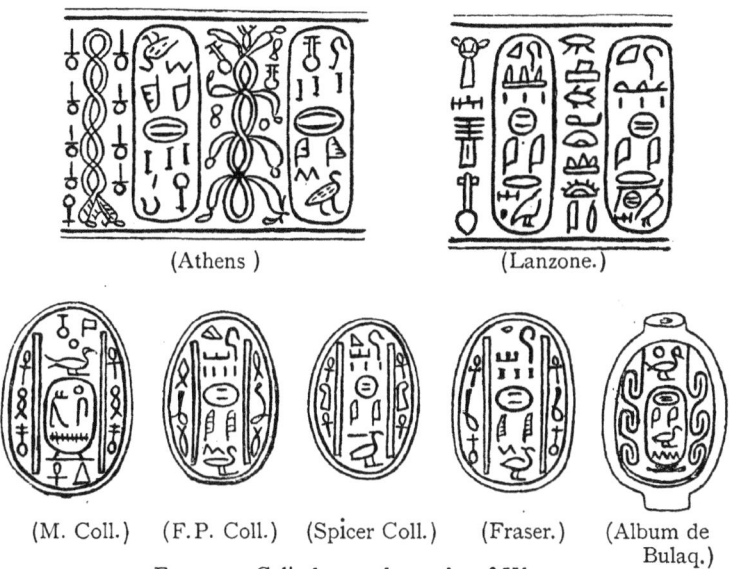

(Athens) (Lanzone.)

(M. Coll.) (F.P. Coll.) (Spicer Coll.) (Fraser.) (Album de Bulaq.)

FIG. 74.—Cylinders and scarabs of Khyan.

Now, both of these types are common on the scarabs of Pepy, and also in those of Māa·ab·ra of the IXth dynasty. But, on the other hand, not a single scarab of the XIIth, or later dynasties, is known with such designs. It is therefore impossible to assign this king to the Hyksos period, as was supposed at first. Also, it should be noted that the name is Khyan, and not Rayan, as it has been read. On the statue and the block from Gebelen the *Ra* is always carefully differenced from the *Kh*, either by the added uraeus, or by an unusually large central boss. On the four scarabs and two cylinders, which give the personal name, the *Kh* is always uniformly differenced from *Ra* by two transverse lines. It is therefore impossible to read it otherwise than Khyan. Now, on both the cylinder and scarabs he is named *Heq Setu*, "prince of the hills" or desert. This same title belongs to the immigrant chief Absha at Beni Hasan. It refers to a rule over the deserts east of Egypt, and Bubastis is the most likely of all the cities for an eastern invader to seize, lying as it does at the mouth of the Wady Tumilat. That Khyan was powerful is evident by his conquering most of Egypt, and apparently ejecting the native kings from their old capital, Memphis. That he ruled over a civilised part of Egypt, appears by the excellent work of his great statue, and the number of his scarabs. He must therefore have been a powerful ruler before he subdued a part of the land. How far his rule extended we cannot be certain; but that a lion of his should be found at Baghdad (B.M.)—too large to be carried in the pocket, too small to have been a trophy of a later conqueror—suggests that he was king, or great shekh, of all the north of Arabia, and ruled from the Euphrates to the Nile.

The Egyptian titles he assumed are peculiar. His *ka* name is *anq adebu*, "embracing territories," a name suggestive of a wide rule. His title after the cartouche is *ka·f mery*, "beloved of his *ka*." To an Egyptian such a title would be absurd, as the *ka* was the man's own double; but to a Semite, whose great belief is in guardian angels and genii attached to individuals or places, the *ka*, or invisible double, would be naturally used as a term for the angelic double. Hence *ka·f mery* would be a likely rendering of "beloved of his guardian angel."

Both of the cylinders are of a rude and ignorant

style. That of Athens has only the plural three lines of *setu*, the three hills of the sign having been confounded with them, and dropped out. The Lanzone cylinder could not be read without other examples to explain it; but, having got the title *heq setu* and *Khy* of the name, we can hardly deny its identity with the other instances of Khyan. It may be that it reads *Khy, aȧ* the island sign, *ȧ* the eagle, *n, Khyaȧȧn*. That the eagle was written thus—much like the goose —is already proved by the scarabs of a seal-bearer, Har.

It is possible that this king has even been entered in the royal list of Tahutmes III. at Karnak. Among the kings on the left side of the chamber, which are all before the XIIIth and later dynasties, there is User·en· ra·; and this can hardly be the king of the Vth dynasty, as he already figures in this list as An. Moreover, the position of Userenra is between Mentuhotep III. and an unknown king, and in the same line are kings of the XIth and XIIth dynasties. The position, therefore, would well agree to a contemporary of the beginning of the XIth dynasty; and the only difficulty is in such a foreign prince being included among Egyptian kings. If, however, the so-called Hyksos statues are really of these foreign invaders,—and Amenemhat III. appears to show a resemblance to that type,—it is possible that the foreigners were included in the ancestry of the Egyptian kings.

Two other kings appear to belong to this same period, by the style of their scarabs.

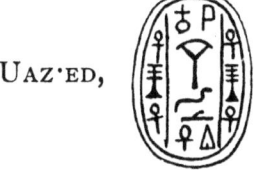

UAZ·ED, of whom three scarabs are known, the one figured, one with the addition Ra·uazed (F.P. Coll.), and one with discontinuous scroll (G.M.).

FIG. 75.—Scarab (G. Coll.).

YAPEQHER,  of whom two scarabs are known, one with continuous scroll (P.M.).

FIG. 76.—Scarab (M. Coll.).

As these three kings all bear un-Egyptian names, they appear to belong to a series of foreigners; and their remains all point to their being contemporaries of the IXth-Xth dynasties of the Egyptians.

CHAPTER VII

Eleventh Dynasty

For this period we have no good list, and need to combine various broken fragments of information. It has been often supposed that the Antef kings and the Mentuhotep kings were of different periods. But there are solid grounds for believing them to be closely interrelated as one family. The tablets of Shut er Regal show us an Antef adoring a Mentuhotep, accompanied by Mentuhotep's vizier (P.S. 443, 489). Then among private names of that age we find Antefs and Mentuhoteps entirely mingled together, as if the names were equally fashionable and usual at the same time. And in the list of Karnak a Mentuhotep comes between two Antefs.

The total number of these kings is also uncertain; so far as monuments go, there is no reason to accept more than nine, including Sankh·ka·ra at the end of the dynasty. The Turin papyrus does not allow of more than six, apparently omitting the first three as being usurping princes, contemporary with other rulers. Such is Maspero's view (R.C. 1889, 421). Manetho states that sixteen kings reigned for forty-three years; and after them Ammenemes for sixteen years. It seems not impossible that Manetho originally wrote six kings, in accord with the Turin papyrus, and that the sixteen has crept in as a corruption copied from the sixteen years of Ammenemes.

From the Karnak list and the monuments the following seems to be more likely than any other arrangement—

KARNAK.		MONUMENTS.	B.C. about
	Erpa·ha Antefa		3005
1 An(tef I.)	Ra·seshes·her· her·maāt	Antefāa (I.)	2985
2 Men(tuhotep I.)	Neb·hotep	Mentuhotep (I.)	2965
3 An(tef II.)		Antefāa (II.)	2945
4 Antef (III.)	Ra·seshes·up· maāt	Antefāa (III.)	2940
5 (Mentuhotep II.)?	Neb·taui·ra	Mentuhotep (II.)	2922
6 Antef (IV.)	Hor Uah·ankh	Antef·āa (IV.)	2902
7 Nub·kheper·ra	Nub·kheperu·ra	Antef (V.)	2852
8 Neb·kher·ra	Neb·kher·ra	Mentuhotep (III.)	2832
9 Sankh·ka·ra	Sankh·ka·ra	(Antef VI.)?	2786
			2778

There are some absolute data for this list, and some merely presumptive. The number of the kings is fixed by the list of Karnak in this order; but one name is lost, which is here filled in presumably as a Mentuhotep.

Of the last three kings there is no question, as they are always distinguished by their Ra names. The real crux is to unravel the first four Antefs; and our first clue to them is in the style of their coffins. In the British Museum is a gilded coffin of fine work (Fig. 81); and in the Louvre is a coffin, rather simpler (omitting the ear) but otherwise so closely like the other that they probably came from the same hands (Fig. 79). Now, on the Louvre coffin it is stated that it was made by a king Antef for his brother, and this just accounts for these two Antef coffins being so very closely alike; the British Museum coffin was for the younger brother, who ordered the gilt coffin in the Louvre to be made through his fraternal piety. In the list we see two Antefs coming next to each other, the IInd and IIIrd, and we can hardly do otherwise, therefore, than attribute the gilt coffin of the Louvre to Antef II., and that of the British Museum to Antef III.

There is also another Antef coffin in the Louvre, that of Ra·seshes·her·her·maāt, as he is inscribed on the breast. This is quite different from the others; in place of finely carved features, and richly gilded and worked stucco from head to foot, it is coarsely carved and hideously painted (Fig. 78). In a rising dynasty it would be impossible to attribute such work to a later date than the finely-wrought and gilded coffins; hence it can only be of Antef I.

The next most important monument is that of An·āa or Antef·āa, whose Horus name was Uah·ankh. His tomb stele with his four hounds is well known, and there is also a rock stele at Elephantine. This cannot be Antef III. or V., as their Horus names are different; nor Antef II., as Uah·ankh was succeeded by his son. From the good execution of the carving, it is unlikely to be Antef I., and hence we are limited to placing him as Antef IV., with whose successor—Antef V.—the style of work has an evident connection.

Although there might have been another Antef or another Mentuhotep, we have no monumental warrant for inserting any but those already in the Karnak series. It has been supposed—on the strength of the title being Hor, and not any greater—that the first three Antefs of the Karnak list were not the same as the kings of whom we have actual remains. But it is very improbable that obscure princes would be picked out for insertion on such a monument, to the exclusion of the more important kings of their same family. The Antefs of Karnak must be the greatest rulers who owned that name.

Of the Mentuhoteps there is far less to debate. There are only three distinct ones known; the last of these is fixed by his Ra name; and of the two others,

Neb·taui·ra is so much more important than Neb·hotep, that he is almost certainly later.

Prince Antefa  about 3005?–2985? B.C.

The stele of this prince was found near the Antef pyramids at Thebes, and a portion of it is here copied. It shows him to have been a ruler of the South under some king not named. He is entitled "The hereditary noble, ruler of the Thebaid, satisfying the desire of the king, keeper of the gates of the frontier, pillar of the South, the administrator, making to live his two lands, chief of the prophets, devoted to the great god, Antefa." It is important that he is said to "make to live his two lands" (*sankh taui f*), for, as he speaks of his king, it is clear that he did not rule over Upper and Lower Egypt, and hence his two lands must refer to the two banks of the Nile; this seems to settle the real meaning of *taui*. We see then that he ruled the Thebaid and the South, and provided for the country, probably by irrigation (see photo Ms. G. 34, and M.D. 50 b). This chief was therefore ruling under the Herakleopolitan kings of the tenth dynasty. The style of his work is rough and formless, but retains somewhat of the largeness of the Old kingdom, and of the character of scenes of that time.

FIG. 77.—Prince Antef (part of stele, G. Mus.).

XI. 1. Ra·seshes·
her·her·maāt

Antef·āa I.

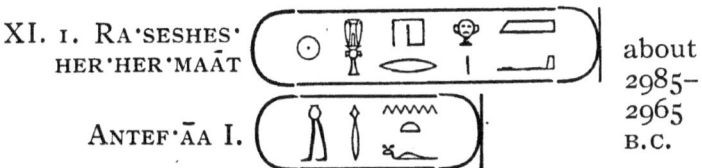

about
2985–
2965
B.C.

This king is only known from his coffin, which is now in the Louvre (P.R. 185; A.Z. vii. 52) (Fig. 78); it is coarsely carved in wood, and painted with a pattern

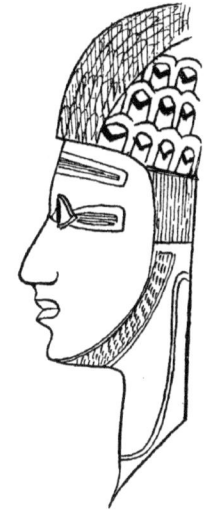

Fig. 78.—Coffin of Antef I. (P. Mus.).

representing wings covering the whole body. The adorning is in blue, red, and dull yellow, and is but rudely applied.

XI. 2. Neb·hotep
Mentu·hotep I.
about 2965–2945 B.C.

Temple, Gebelen, G. Mus. (Rec. xiv. 26; xvi. 42).
Rock tablet, Konosso (L.D. ii. 150 b).
Stele (private), Louvre, 676 (A.Z. 1869, 52).

The remains of a temple of this king at Gebelen were re-used by Ptolemy VII. The king is shown slaying the Nehesi, Sati, and Tehenu, or the races bordering on Egypt, on the south, east, and west.

A rock tablet at the First Cataract on the island of Konosso is headed by the king's names, but without any figure of him, only portraying three divinities, Khnum, Min, and Sati. The king is promised to have "all lands under his feet." Another tablet at Konosso (L.D. ii. 150 c) and one at Hammamat (L.D. ii. 150 d) may probably belong to this king, as *se ra* is included in the cartouches, which is not usual under later Mentuhoteps. A private stele in the Louvre (676) shows an official adoring Mentuhotep, who is seated holding a long *heq* staff.

XI. 3. ANTEF·ĀA (II.) about 2945–2940 B.C.

This king is only known from his coffin in the Louvre, which was found at Thebes (A.Z. vii. 52;

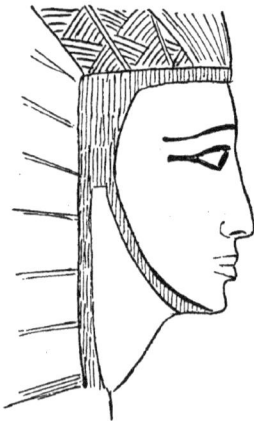

FIG. 79.—Coffin of Antef II. (P. Mus.).

P.R. i. 86). Having been plundered by natives, the site of it is not fixed, but it was almost certainly near the Antef tombs. He appears to have died suddenly and early, for he was succeeded by his younger brother, another Antef, who made this coffin for him, as he records upon it. The coffin is on the same pattern as the rude coffin of Antef I., but it is well carved and gilt all over.

XI. 4.
RA·SESHES·UP·MAĀT

ANTEF·ĀA III.

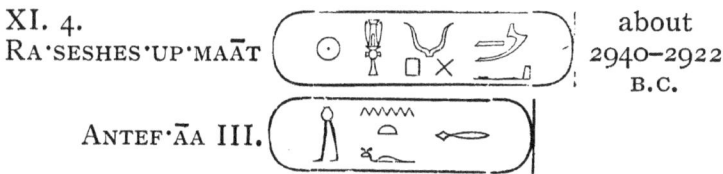

about 2940-2922 B.C.

Pyramidion (B.M. 578).
Coffin (B.M. 6652; A.Z. 1869, 53).
Funeral box (P. Mus. 614).

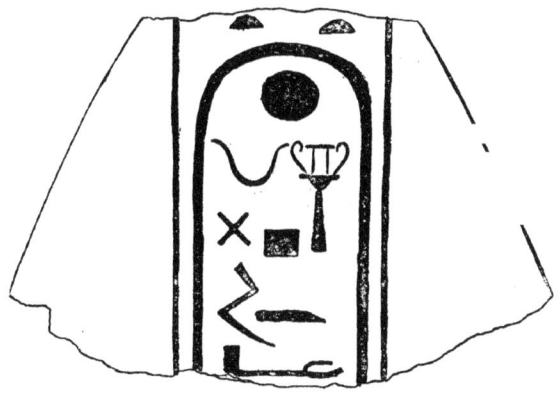

FIG. 80.—Pyramidion of Antef III. (B. Mus.).

The identity of this king with Antef III. rests on a presumption from associated objects. The gilt coffin (Fig. 81) in the British Museum, we have already shewn, belongs to Antef III.; also in the British Museum is a small pyramid of Antef Ra·seshes·up· maāt. Then in the Louvre is his brother's coffin, probably from the same or an adjacent tomb; and also a funeral box for canopic jars from the tomb of Ra·seshes·up·maāt.

The tomb is mentioned in the Abbott papyrus concerning the inspection of royal tombs. "The monument of king Ra·seshes·em·upu·ma, son of the sun, Antuf·āa. It was found to have been pierced by the

FIG. 81.—Coffin of Antef III. (B. Mus.).

hands of the thieves at the spot where the tablet of the monument is fixed. Examined on that day, it was found entire, the thieves not having been able to penetrate into it." So, as late as the end of the XXth dynasty, some sixteen centuries after the burial, the king yet remained undisturbed.

The style of these coffins sufficiently rebuts Mariette's

abuse of the work of the Antef kings, without further argument. The style is as good as that of Aahmes, and fully comparable with any remains of the Mentuhoteps.

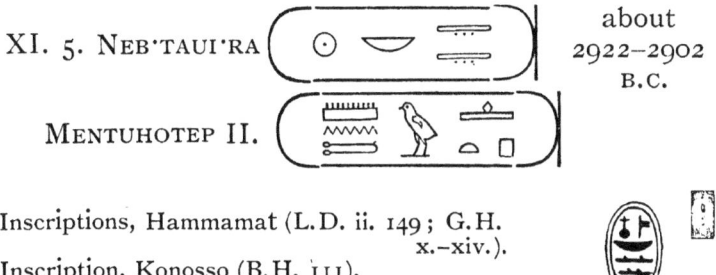

XI. 5. NEB·TAUI·RA

about 2922–2902 B.C.

MENTUHOTEP II.

Inscriptions, Hammamat (L.D. ii. 149; G.H. x.–xiv.).
Inscription, Konosso (B.H. 111).
Scarabs.
Mother, Queen Aam (L.D. ii. 149 f).

FIG. 82.—Scarab (P. Mus.)

Most of what we know of this king is from the inscriptions cut by the working parties in the quarries of Hammamat. We find that in his second year a *Sed* festival of Sirius' rising took place; another instance which shows that these festivals were then at fixed astronomical dates, and not dependent on the years of the reign. Most of these inscriptions relate to the party who prepared the royal sarcophagus, under the direction of the noble, the vizier Amenemhat, in the second year of the king's reign. They are all dated in the month Paophi, in the second year. The first tablet records a marvel of how a gazelle ran up toward the army, to the rock near where they were, and brought forth her young there, whereat they caught and sacrificed her. This is placed by the side of a tablet of Neb·taui·ra offering to Min, dated on the third day. On the fifteenth day is dated a great tablet set up for the king, who says that he caused Amenemhat to go out with 10,000 soldiers from the nomes of the south, from the south country, from the interior, and from the

Uabu nome, to bring the pure hard stone which is in the rock, to make a sarcophagus as a remembrance for eternity, and for monuments in the temples of the south. On the same day is dated a private tablet of Amenemhat, recounting all his offices and titles, and saying that he was sent with quarrymen and artisans and sculptors, and many other kinds of workmen, and that he brought a great sarcophagus. The soldiers returned without loss, even of one ass. On the twenty-third day an inscription records that they had cut out the sarcophagus, and that they had made a pool of water ten cubits square at a well that they found in the middle of the valley. It was guarded pure from the animals, and carefully hidden from the Troglodytes. And though soldiers and kings of old had passed there, they had never before found this well. Lastly, on the twenty-eighth day, is a postscript added to the royal tablet, stating that they had extracted the lid of the sarcophagus as a block 4 cubits wide, 8 cubits long, and 2 cubits thick; and that then they slaughtered oxen and gazelles, and incense was offered upon the censer. And 3000 sailors from the nomes of the north were following with the expedition. We notice that in one inscription the king is called the son of the royal mother Aam; this not only gives her name, but it suggests that she was queen-regnant during a minority, like the mention of the mother of Pepy II. during his minority.

At Konosso a tablet records the conquests of this king over thirteen tribes (B.H. III).

Several scarabs are known with the name Neb·taui·ra; and as half of them have the royal titles *neter nefer*, or *suten*, they evidently belong to this king. This is the first appearance of scarabs in this dynasty; and they are very small and poor.

XI. 6. HOR UAH·ANKH

ANTEF·ĀA IV.

about 2902–2852 B.C.

Pyramid, Thebes.
Stele (G. Mus.; M.D. 49).
Rock stele, Elephantine (P.S. 310).

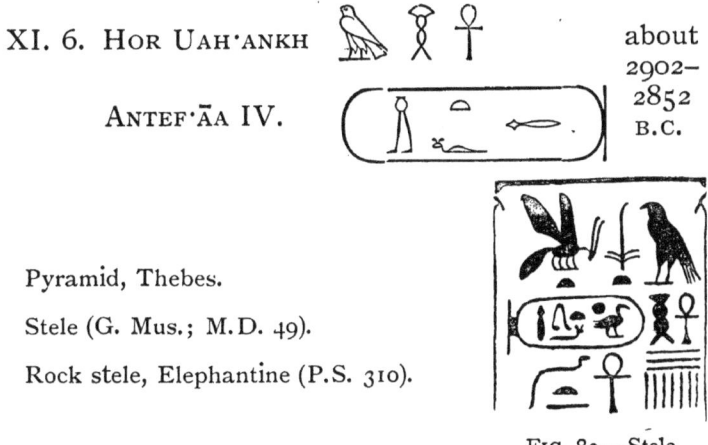

FIG. 83.—Stele, Elephantine.

The brick pyramid of this king contained a stele (now in G. Mus.) representing the king standing with four dogs. The stele was broken away at the upper part when found by Mariette, and since then it was broken up by the natives, but partly recovered by Maspero. Hence the full name and titles of the king are lost, along with the top, and we do not know the Ra name of this king. The stele was made for the "*Hor Uah·ankh*, the king (An āa) living anew." And, further, before the king is a line naming the usual offerings for the "*Hor Uah·ankh*, the king (Antef·āa)." It has been supposed that these two names must refer to different kings, but the construction does not seem to imply that; and as in no dynasty did two kings take the same *ka* name (or Horus name), it is very unlikely that the name *Uah ankh* can belong to different persons; rather the An of the first cartouche is an abbreviation of Antef.

The Abbott papyrus mentions this tomb the first of all in the inquest on the condition of the royal tombs under Ramessu X. It records "The monument of king Sa ra An·āa, which is at the north of the temple of Amenhotep of the terrace. This tomb is injured on the surface opposite the spot where the tablet is placed; on the tablet is the image of the king, standing, having between his feet his dog named Behukaa. Examined on that day, it was found in good condition."

The subject of the stele is the king standing with four hounds, which bear Libyan names with Egyptian interpretations — "the gazelle," "the greyhound," "the black," and "the fire-pot." A servant, bearing also a Berber name, Tekenru, stands behind the king. Unhappily all the top of the slab is lost, and with it half of the inscription. We glean, however, that Antef had provided libations, built and endowed the temples, and established offerings and services; he had cut a canal; he had captured the nome of Abydos and opened its prisons; he had glorified and benefited his city, and had left the succession to his son; and in the fiftieth year this tablet was established for the Hor *Uah·ankh*, the king, son of the sun, *Anāa*. A fine rock-tablet of his adjoins those of earlier kings at Elephantine (P.S. 310) (see above).

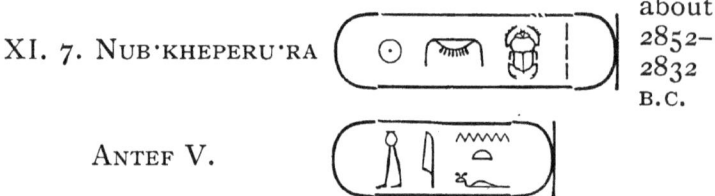

XI. 7. NUB·KHEPERU·RA

ANTEF V.

about
2852–
2832
B.C.

Tomb and obelisks, Thebes (M.D. 50 a).
Temple, Koptos.
Decree, Koptos.
Statuette (Lee Coll.).
Scarabs.

FIG. 84.—Scarab (F.P. Coll.).

We find at this point a greater fulness of royal titles appearing; the *ka* name and vulture and uraeus name being different; besides the personal and throne names. The two small obelisks, 11½ ft. high, bear all the names and titles; they stood in front of the tomb, but are now lying wrecked somewhere in the Nile near Qamuleh, and no attempt has been made to recover them.

The tomb was visited by the Ramesside inspectors, who record "The monument of king Nub·kheper·ra, son of the sun, Antuf, was found to have been pierced by the hands of the thieves, who had made a hole of

FIG. 85.—Slab with head of Antef V., Koptos.

two and a half cubits in its surrounding wall, and a hole of one cubit in the great outer chamber of the sepulchre of the chief of the transport of offering, Auri of Pa-amen, which is in ruins. The royal tomb was in good condition, the thieves not having been able to penetrate into it."

At Koptos, Antef appears to have rebuilt the temple after the disasters of the previous age. About forty slabs of his work were found turned face down to form the pavement of a later rebuilder. These slabs were mostly small, and all of them thin; they were not blocks thick enough to build a wall, and this shows that the temple was only of brick faced with stone. The subjects were of Antef offering to Min, Horus, and a goddess; and the work was some in relief, some intaglio.

A long decree, dated in the third year of Antef, is inscribed on the side of a great doorway of Usertesen I. at Koptos (now in G. Mus.); by the position it seems to have been recopied there, but the style of the cutting is like that of the Antef IV. stele. In any case, it is doubtless an exact copy of the royal decree, placed here where every person must see it, as being the title-deed of the prince of Koptos. It throws so much light on the administration of the Antefs, and the organisation of the country, that we may well read it here. "The third year, month Phamenoth, 25th day, of his majesty the king (Ra·nubu·kheper, sa·ra·, Antef) giving life like the sun for ever. Decree of the king to the chancellor, prince of Koptos Min·em·hat, the king's son administrator of Koptos Qa·nen, the chancellor Menkh·Min, the scribe of the temple Nefer·hotep·ur, all the garrison of Koptos, and all the officials of the temple,—

"Behold ye this decree has been brought to you that ye may know that my majesty has sent the scribe and divine chancellor of Amen Amen·se, and the *semsu hayt* Amen·user, to make inquisition in the temple of Min :—

"Whereas the officials of the temple of my father Min came to my majesty to say that an evil thing is come to pass in this temple, even a harbouring of enemies by (blasted be his name) Teta, son of Minhotep :—

"Therefore let him be cast out upon the ground from the temple of my father Min, let him be driven from his office of the temple, to the son of his son, and the heir of his heir; may they be cast abroad upon the earth, let his bread and his sacred meat be seized, let his name not be remembered in this temple, as is done to one like him who has transgressed in the matter of an enemy of his god; let his writings in the temple of Min be destroyed, and in the government office on every roll likewise:—

"And every king and every puissant ruler who shall forgive him, may he not receive the white crown, or support the red crown, or sit upon the throne of Horus the living; let not the two diadems grant him favours as beloved of him; and every administrator or prince who shall approach the Lord to forgive him, let his people, his possessions, and his lands be given to the endowment of my father Min of Koptos; also let not any man of his circle, of the relations of his father or of his mother, be raised to this office:—

"Also that this office shall be given to the chancellor, overseer in the palace, Min·em·hat, and let there be given to him its bread and its sacred meat, established unto him in writings in the temple of my father Min of Koptos, to the son of his son and the heir of his heir."

Here we have the complete formula of a royal commission for one of the greatest acts of administration, the degradation of one of the feudal princes on account of treason, and the establishment of a new ruling family in his place.

Some blocks previously removed from this temple were seen here by Harris long ago built into the bridge, but they have now disappeared.

A statuette shows the king as triumphing over Asiatics and Negroes (Lee Coll.).

The scarabs are rather common in collections, nine being known. All of them are of a symmetrical type, mostly with two uraei, and the name between them. This symmetrical type belongs to the scarabs of the VIIth and VIIIth dynasty, which are probably Memphite in origin. A panther's head in soft blue paste bears the name of this king (B. Mus., glass).

XI. 8. NEB·KHER·RA   about 2832–2786 B.C.

MENTUHOTEP III.

Pyramid, *Akhet·asut*, Thebes (M.A. 605).
Temple, Thebes (S. Cat. F. i. 192).
Tablets, Shut er regal (P.S. 489, 394, 443).
Tablets, Aswan (P.S. 213, 243; L.D. ii. 149 b).
Altar (C.O.E. ii. 78).
Scarab (B. Mus.).   Gold heart (P. Mus.).
Menat (XXVI. dyn.). (S.B.A. ix. 181).
Queens—Tumem (M.A.F. i. 134). Aah (P.S. 489).

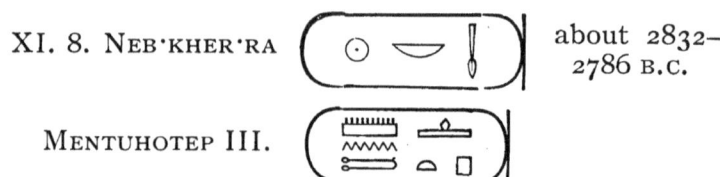

FIG. 86.—Scarab (B. Mus.).

This king was the greatest of his dynasty, judging by the number of his monuments; but his unusually long reign may have led to his being thus well represented.

His pyramid is unknown except from a mention of it on a stele at Abydos (M.A. 605) of Tetu, who was chief reciter at the pyramid *Akhet·asut* of Neb·kher·ra, and prophet of *Hor sam taui*, the ka name of the same king. But it was officially examined under Ramessu X., and recorded to be then intact. Schiaparelli states that Maspero found at Thebes an architrave with the cartouches of this king, which had been part of his temple (S. Cat. F. i. 192).

The largest existing monument of his is the tablet (Fig. 87) carved on the sandstone rocks of a valley about four miles below Silsileh, known as Shut er regal, or Soba Rigaleh. This shows a colossal figure of Neb·kher·ra standing, with a smaller figure of *sa ra* Antef facing him. This lesser personage is probably a son of his, associated in the kingdom with him, and using a cartouche, but not a Ra name like the father. As the successor of Neb·kher·ra was S·ankh·ka·ra, it is probable that Antef was the personal name of that king, which is as yet unknown. That the king's son is here shown is the more likely, as a queen behind Neb·kher·ra is entitled "The royal mother, his beloved,

Aāh." Behind the king's son Antef is the vizier Khety (P.S. 489). The same Khety is shown on another tablet (P.S. 443) adoring Neb·kher·ra deceased; and he appears on a third tablet, at Aswan (P.S. 213), dated in the forty-first year of Neb·kher·ra. He therefore lived at the end of the reign, and this agrees with his appearing in attendance on the co-regent son Antef. The tablet of the forty-first year records some business with the boats of Wawat, or Lower Nubia. Another tablet of the forty-first year of Neb·kher·ra is carved at

FIG. 87.—Figures at Shut er Regal.

Aswan by an official Mererty (P.S. 243), commissioner in the Heliopolitan nome, and royal friend in the east desert. A short inscription at Aswan gives only the royal names (L.D. ii. 149 b). A block of sculpture (G.M.) shows Neb·kher·ra associated with Uazyt of Buto, and points to this king having worked in the Delta (W.G. 227).

An altar of this reign shows two figures of the Nile offering, and the names and titles of the king repeated: it is described by Chabas from a paper impression by Prisse (C.O.E. ii. 78). Contemporary private works also record this king. In Turin is a large family tablet of Meru, dated in the forty-sixth year of the king, which is the highest recorded year of his reign. Another tablet of his time (in P.M.) is of Mertisen (L.A. ix.; Pr. M. vii.; S.B.A.T. v. 555), who was a chief artist, and describes his skill. He "knew the mystery of the divine word, an artist skilled in his art. I know what belongs to it, the sinking waters, the weighings done for the reckoning of accounts, how to produce the forms of going forth and returning, so that the limb may go to its place. I know the walking of the image of man, the carriage of a woman, the two arms of Horus, the twelve circles of the injurious (the hours of the nightly passage of the sun), the contemplating the eye without an equal which affrights the wicked" (a play on his name, which is "the two eyes which are equal"), "the poising of the arm to bring the hippopotamus low, the going of the runner. I know the making of amulets which enable us to go without the fire giving its flame on us, or without the flood washing us away. No one succeeds in it but I alone, and the eldest son of my body. God has decreed him to excel in it, and I have seen the perfections of his hands in the work of chief artist in every kind of precious stones, of gold and silver, of ivory and ebony." This curious description of the various branches of his art throws some light on the different subjects usually set to students for practice. First, the figures in slow action, then the differences of the male and female figure, then mythological subjects, then figures in rapid action, and, lastly, the trade secrets of the potency of amulets.

A stele of Anmerts names Amen·ra and Neb·kher·ra as the gods (Rec. xiv. 21). Later references to Neb·kher·ra prove how much honoured he was as a restorer of the kingdom. On the statue of Amenemhat (F. Mus.; S. Cat. F. i. 192) there is the usual formula addressed to the royal *ka* of Neb·kher·ra, as to a deity. In tombs of the XVIIIth dynasty at Thebes, Khabekht adores him with the kings of that age (L.D. iii. 2 a), and Khaui does the same (L.D. iii. 2 d). In the XIXth dynasty the libation table at Marseille bears his name with those of later kings. And in the Ramesseum he is honoured with Mena and Ahmes I. as one of the great kings in the procession of figures.

Of small remains there are remarkably few. Only a gold heart (in the Louvre) and one beautifully-carved scarab (B.M.) can be attributed to his time. Of later work there is, however, a green glazed *menat* with written inscription of this king, probably made in the XXVIth dynasty (S.B.A. ix. 181). His queen is said (M.A.F. i. 134) to be Tumem, who is otherwise said to be an unclassed queen (A.Z. xxi. 77).

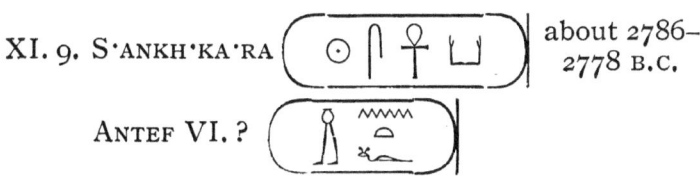

XI. 9. S·ANKH·KA·RA   about 2786–2778 B.C.

ANTEF VI. ?

Inscription, Hammamat (L.D. ii. 150 a).
Inscriptions, Shut er regal (P.S. 359, 466).
Statue, Sakkara (W.G. 221).
Alabaster block, Erment (B.T. 1455).
Alabaster plaque (G. Mus.). Gold ring with stone
   (G. Mus., see W.G. 221). Scarab (F.P. Coll.).
Prayer to S·ankh·ka·ra (P.T. II. xlii.).

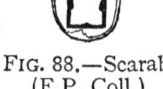
FIG. 88.—Scarab (F.P. Coll.).

The inscription of Hammamat is the only important document of this reign. It records an expedition to the sacred land of Punt, which was the south end of the Red Sea, both on the Somali coast and in Yemen. The regular road to this region was across the desert from Koptos, through the valley of Hammamat to the Red Sea. The general in command was Henu, who had three thousand soldiers with him, drawn from the country south of Thebes, in order to better bear the heat. To cross the desert he provided yokes and skins for the water, and gave a measure of water and twenty biscuits for each man daily. Large reservoirs were dug at four different points. On reaching the coast, vessels were built to transport the men. The proceeds of the expedition were all kinds of products found in the ports of the Divine Land; and on his return road, through Wady Hammamat, he brought stone for statues of the temples (L.D. ii. 150 a; B.H. 114; Masp. Rev. Hist. ix. 8). This inscription is dated in the eighth year, which shows that this reign was not very short.

In the valley of Shut er Regal the great stele of Neb·kher·ra shows us that he is honoured by an associated son named Antef; and as he was succeeded by Sankhkara, according to the Karnak list, and we do not know the personal name of Sankhkara, we cannot do better at present than identify him with Antef VI. (P.S. 489). Besides this, at the farther end of the rocks is a tablet showing Sankhkara seated on his throne, wearing the crown of Upper Egypt. A dog is seated below the throne. Before the king is a table of offerings, and two attendants with gazelles; behind him kneel, with folded arms, two nobles, the Erpa Tehuti, and another (P.S. 359). Lower down, in the same valley, is the *ka* name of the king (P.S. 466).

A block of alabaster, with the names of this king, from some temple decoration was found at Erment (B.T. 1455).

A statue of Sankhkara was found at Sakkara, but seems to have been lost sight of since. Deveria took an impression of it, now in the Louvre (W.G. 221).

A double statuette of a man and wife was found at Khataaneh, near Faqus, with a prayer to Sankhkara as a deity (E. Coll.; P.T. ii. xlii.).

Of small objects there is an alabaster plaque from Draa-abul-Nega, naming "King Sankhkara beloved of Mentu, lord of the Thebaid" (G. Mus.), a gold ring with a stone (G. Mus.; W.G. 221), and one scarab (F.P. Coll.) of delicate work.

Having now reconstructed the dynasty thus, we may look back and see how far our results are harmonious. We have a steady growth of the royal style: first *Erpa*, then a Ra name where the line of kings succeeds to the

IXth dynasty, then the *sa ra* taken out of the cartouche, and made a regular prefix. We see that no scarabs can be fixed to the earlier kings; they first appear, but poor and small, under Mentuhotep II.; under Antef V. they improve; under Mentuhotep III. the example we have is fine; and under his successor Sankhkara the work is beautifully delicate. In the spread of power we see same growth. Limited first to his nome, prince Antef is a humble servant of the suzerain in Herakleopolis; next, the king Mentuhotep I. asserts his royalty on the southern frontier; next, Antefs II. and III. appear with a fine royal tomb at Thebes, and well-executed gilt mummy-cases; then Mentuhotep II. brings stone from Hammamat, and boasts of conquering thirteen tribes in the south; Antef V. builds at Koptos, puts up obelisks at Thebes, and boasts of conquering both Asiatics and negroes; Mentuhotep III. builds a temple at Thebes, puts up many monuments, encourages art, and is reverenced to late ages; while, lastly, Sankhkara sends out a foreign expedition, having apparently little to distract him at home. The march of development of this dynasty shows hardly a break; of Antef IV. the deficiency of monuments prevents our noting an advance; but there is no evidence of retrogression. The only points where any change is likely to be made by fresh discoveries is in the number of Antefs before Mentuhotep I., and in the position of the remains we have attributed to Antef IV.

As to the duration of this dynasty, we have but little information. Sankh·ka·ra reigned over 8 years; Neb·kher·ra reigned over 46 years; Nub·kheperu·ra appears to have had a longish reign; Antef IV. reigned over 50 years, and therefore Antef V. might have been his grandson; but that is balanced by the fact of Antef II. being brother of Antef III. On the whole, we seem to count here nine generations; and if we allow not the thirty years of an average European generation, but twenty years each for a succession of Oriental eldest sons, we may set it down as at least 180 years for the whole duration of this list of kings, or 120 years for the six independent kings recognised in the Turin papyrus; but the statement of 43 years in Manetho points to most of this dynasty having been contemporary with the Xth dynasty.

We should now note some remains whose position is uncertain, but which belong to an earlier date than the XIIth dynasty. Of uncertain remains of the Antef period is a false door at Abydos, which mentions the king (sa·ra·Antef·āa) as living then (M.A. 544); a stele of Aui, who names Amenāaa as the great *hen ka* in the house of Antef (W.G. 225); and the song in the palace of Antef by the harper, on the vanity of life, a well-known literary work, of which many copies have come to us more or less mutilated (R.P. iv. 117, vi. 129; Jour. Asiat. vii. xv. 398). A queen Mentuhotep is known to us from her coffin and toilet box (A.Z. xxx. 46, xxxi. 23). The coffin is now destroyed; but a copy of its inscriptions shows that it was for the "great royal wife Mentuhotep, begotten of the vizier, the keeper of the palace, Senb·hena·f, and born of the heiress Sebekhotep" (S.B.A. xiv. 41). A prince of this line is also known, "Heru·nefer, son of king Mentuhotep and the great royal wife Shert·sat" (S.B.A. xiv. 41). In the Vatican is a head of a statue of rough work with the name of "the good god Mentuhotep."

A scarab has the name An·n·n·t·u·f, a spelling which is unexpected at this period (G. Coll.).

At Khataaneh, a queen's name, Sent, is found; she was heiress, royal wife, and royal mother, and is attributed to this period (N.G. ix.).

CHAPTER VIII

Twelfth Dynasty

Manetho.	Lists.	Monuments.	Years.		B.C. about
			M.	T.P.	Mon.
1 Ammenemēs	S·hetep·ab·ra	Amenemhat I. 16	[1]9		20 2778
		Coregency			10 2758
2 Sesonkhōsis	Kheper·ka·ra	·Usertesen I. 46	45··		32 2748
		Coregency			2 2716
3 Ammanemēs	Nub·kau·ra	Amenemhat II. 38	...		30 2714
		Coregency			3 2684
4 Sesōstris	Kha·kheper·ra	Usertesen II. 48	[2]9		10 2681
5 Lakharēs	Kha·kau·ra	Usertesen III. 8	3–		26 2660
6 Ammerēs	Maāt·en·ra	Amenemhat III. 8	4–	44	2622
				m.d.	
7 Ammenemēs	Maā·kheru·ra	Amenemhat IV. 8	9· 3·27	6	2578
8 Skemiofris	Sebek·neferu·ra	Sebek·neferu·ra 4	3·10·24	...	2569
					2565

Totals stated { 160   213·1·17?
       245

THE twelfth dynasty is perhaps the best known chronologically of any before the Greek times; yet here in

I—10

some reigns uncertainties beset us. The first four kings are well fixed, by monuments with double datings, which prove exactly when each king took his successor into coregency. Thus only the total lengths of their reigns remains unsettled.

Of Amenemhat I. we have the double date of his 30th year = 10th of Usertesen II. (M.A. 558). Manetho omitted him from the XIIth, and put him as an addendum of 16 years at the end of the XIth. But the far earlier Turin papyrus puts him down as the first of the XIIth dynasty, and makes the summaries count from him.

Usertesen I. had 10 years or more with his father, and 32 years alone, associating Amenemhat II. in the 42nd year; as there is a double date of his 44th = 2nd of Amenemhat II (L.A. x. 3).

Amenemhat II. had two or three years with his father, about 30 years alone, and three or more with his successor; as there is a double date of his 35th year = 3rd year of Usertesen II. (L.A. x. 4).

Usertesen II.'s reign is very unsettled. Manetho gives 48 years for it, but this seems quite unsupported. No higher date has been found than year 10. But we shall see from the totals of the dynasty that there is some reason to assign 29 years to Usertesen II. until the coregency of his successor; and he appears to have lived about ten years more, as (except a war-record of Usertesen III. in his eighth year) there is no dated record of Usertesen III. until the tenth year.

The Turin papyrus shows—9 years; suggesting 29 years for this reign before the coregency.

Of Usertesen III. we may glean somewhat from the lists. His monuments go to the 26th year, the Turin papyrus shows over 30 years, and the 8 of Manetho suggests that it was 38.

Amenemhat III. had apparently no coregency, as monuments are dated in his first and second years. We can hardly do better than accept the highest datum known of his, 44 years. And there is no evidence that the short 9 years of Amenemhat IV. or

TWELFTH DYNASTY

the 4 years of Sebekneferu were shared with any other ruler.

We have then the following data :—

	YEARS BEFORE SON'S COREGENCY.	TOTAL YEARS.	B.C. about
			2778
Amenemhat I.	20	30	
			2758
Usertesen I.	42	45	
			2716
Amenemhat II.	32	35	
			2684
Usertesen II.	29?	39?	
			2660
Usertesen III.	38	38	
			2627
Amenemhat III.	44	44	
			2578
Amenemhat IV.	9	9	
			2569
Sebekneferu	4	4	
			2565
Totals here	218	244	
Total in T.P.	213,	in Man. 245	

Here we see that the only datum we have partly assumed—the reign of Usertesen II.—serves to bring the total of the dynasty near that of the Turin papyrus, and the total of the reigns to agree with Manetho in Eusebius, as the difference of some few years is easily made up by whole years being counted instead of years and odd months and days. We have, however, adopted the total of the T.P., and thrown the whole difference on Usertesen II. in the dates B.C., as that is the least certain point. The other total given in Manetho by Africanus is a copyist's correction after the corruption of the years of reigns, as 160 is just the total of the figures as they stand in Manetho now.

XII. 1. SE·HOTEP·AB·RA

about 2778–2748 B.C.

AMENEMHAT I.

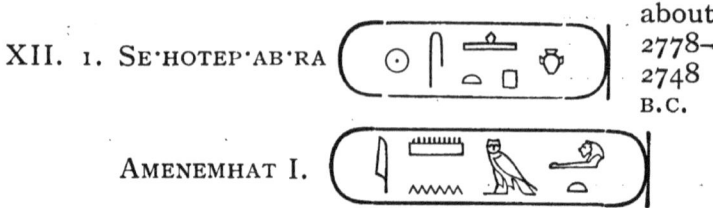

Pyramid	*Ka nefer* (site unknown)	(P.R. ii. 108).
Tanis	Statue	(P.T.I. i. 3; xiii. 1).
Khataanah	Lintel	(A.Z. xxv. 12; N.G. 9 a).
Bubastis	Jamb	(N.B. xxxiii. A).
Memphis	Altar	(M.D. 34 f).
Krokodilopolis	Statue	(L.D. ii. 118 e, f).
Abydos	Altar	(M.A. 1338).
Hammamat	Inscriptions	(G.H. ii. 4, iii. 3, viii.).
Koptos	Sculpture	
Karnak	Altar and statue	(M.K. 8 d, e).
Elephantine	Inscription	(P.S. 308).
Aswan	Inscriptions	(P.S. 67, 179).
Korosko	Inscription	(A.Z. xxii. 30).
(In Berlin)	Altar	(L.D. ii. 118 i).
Cylinders and Scarabs.		
Papyri	Instructions of Amenemhat I.	(S.S.A.).
	Sa·nehat's Adventures	(Ms. C. 95; S.B.A. xiv. 452).

Fig. 89.—Scarab (E. Coll.).

Although the latter part of the XIth dynasty seems to emerge from the confusion into a tolerably stable and important condition, yet it was the glory of the twelfth dynasty to promote far more organisation and justice than had been reached before. We see this reflected in the *ka* names of the kings, which form a sort of summary in mottoes of the aim of each monarch. Antef III. is "opening or beginning justice"; Mentuhotep II. is "lord of the two lands," a matter merely of possession and might; Mentuhotep III. is "uniting the two lands"; Sankhkara is "making his two lands to live"; and Amenemhat I., having entered into full possession of the country, needs not refer to its division, but takes the motto "renewing births" as reinstituting the living organisation of everything in the country; while Usertesen I. carries on the idea in the phrase "life of the births," or the national life as renewed and born again. Thus in this series we see expressed the royal motto of each king, that name which he took for his *ka* on his accession, apparently as his claim to the favour of the gods, when his *ka* should appear before them, and join Ra after his death. These mottoes generally refer to the care of the king for his royal duties to the country over which he ruled; and in this case of an emerging civilisation, the sentences give a beautiful sketch of the progress of the country under a line of strong rulers, granting justice, subduing the land, uniting it, making it live, renewing its birth of social life, and cultivating the renewed life thus regained.

The document which gives most direct light on the state of the country is the biography of the grandfather of Khnum·hotep at Beni Hasan. The king Amenemhat I. placed the grandfather (who appears to have been a previous Khnum·hotep) "as hereditary prince, administrator of the eastern desert in the town of Menat·khufu; establishing for him the south landmark, and making firm the northern one like heaven, and dividing for him the great river down its middle, setting its eastern half to the nome of the 'Rock of Horus,' reaching to the east desert. Whereas his majesty came that he might abolish wrong, gloriously appearing even as the god Tum himself; that he might set right that which he found ruined, and that which one city had taken from its sister city; that he might cause one city to know its boundary with another city; establishing their landmarks as heaven; reckoning their waters according to that which was in the writings, apportioning according to that which was in antiquity, of the greatness of his love of right. He arose and placed him (Khnum·hotep) as hereditary prince, favoured by the royal hand, great chief of the Oryx nome. He set up the landmarks; the southern one as his boundary to the Hare nome, his northern one to the Jackal nome; he divided the great river valley down its middle, its water, its fields, its wood, its sand, as far as the western desert." We see here the personal care of a vigorous administrator in renewing the birth of all the social organisation of the country (G. Bh. 58).

In every part of Egypt we find alike this remarkable vigour of the new administration. Amenemhat must have been one of the most active and capable monarchs in the whole history of Egypt. From the edge of the Delta at Tanis to the wilds of Upper Nubia at Korosko we alike find the remains of his works. Instead of one or two monuments, as of the previous kings, we see a number which shows that he built and offered in most of the great towns of the country.

Beginning at the north, it appears that he must have decorated the temple of Tanis, an excellent statue of his, still remaining there (Fig. 90), brutally usurped in after times by Merenptah (P.T. I. i. 3; xiii. 1). And from the quality of the red granite resembling that of the granite columns there, and from the brilliant finish of these columns, we can hardly doubt that they are a part of a rich temple built there by this king.

FIG. 90.—Head of Amenemhat I., red granite, Tanis.

At Khataanah, near Tanis, is a fine lintel of a doorway erected by Amenemhat I. in red granite; and the later additions there by his successors point to a noble building having stood there (A.Z. xxv. 12; N.G. 9 a).

At Bubastis a block of this king records his making monuments to his mother Bast (N.B. xxxiii. A).

At Memphis, in the Kom el Qalah, was a red granite altar dedicated by the king to Ptah (M.D. 34 f.).

At Krokodilopolis is the lower part of a red granite seated group of Amenemhat and Bast, side by side (L.D. ii. 118 e, f. ; but see P.H. 57).

At Abydos was found a red granite altar, dedicated by the king to Osiris (M.A. 1338).

In the Wady Hammamat is a long inscription of an official, a priest of Min, named Antef, who was sent to Rehenu to bring noble hard stone. For eight days he sought for it in the mountain, and could find none suitable. In despair, he threw himself on his face and prayed to Min, Mut, Urt·hekau, and all the gods of the desert, and offered incense. The next day he searched in four rocks more, and at last found the stone. This touching record of his troubles is irregularly squeezed in at the bottom of the fine, pompous inscription, which he evidently set his masons to cut when beginning this weary eight days' search, and before he anticipated his difficulties (L.D. ii. 118 d ; G.H. viii.). Two other inscriptions of the same reign record the work of one Ada in bringing stones for Zautaker, a divine father and priest of Min ; probably for decorating the temple of Min of Koptos. He brought two stones of 10 cubits long (G.H. ii. 4), and one of 12 cubits, for which he had a party of two hundred men, two oxen, and fifty asses (G.H. iii. 3).

At Koptos, a beautifully-sculptured slab in relief (Fig. 91) shows that this king rebuilt or decorated the temple there.

At Karnak is a group of two figures with the names of Amenemhat (M.K. 8 d), and, as at so many other places, an altar of granite with his dedication, in this case to Amen·ra (M.K. 8 e). These show us the beginning of the decoration of the temple, founded by Mentuhotep, which afterwards became so great by successive additions.

At Elephantine, Amenemhat added his tablet on the rock of kings, which already bore the names of four monarchs (P.S. 308). And a little farther we find, just above the cataract, a high pile of rock by the river bearing his name on the very top of it, and referring apparently to the obtaining of stone for his pyramid (P.S. 67); while another rude inscription by the cataract is dated in his reign (P.S. 179).

Nubia also was subject to this king. In the "Instructions of Amenemhat to his son," he declares that he had fought the Wawat (Nubians), the Mezau (S. Nubians),

FIG. 91.—Slab of Amenemhat I. Koptos.

and the Sati (Asiatics). That this Nubian conquest was more than a boast is proved by the pithy record on a rock at Korosko: "In the 29th year of S·hotep·ab·ra, ever living, they came to overthrow the Wawat." This campaign was doubtless carried on by Usertesen I., like the campaign against the Libyans in the following year, during which the old king died in Memphis.

Of his pyramid, called *Ka nefer*, we do not yet know the place; and the name of it is only recorded on a stele of Hor, who was a priest of the pyramid in the ninth year of Usertesen I. This, dating by the young king a year before the old king's death, shows how completely the reins had fallen from the hands of that great man, whose abilities had again raised Egypt to the front rank of the world. He died early in his thirtieth year of reign, on the 7th of Paophi. (See Sanehat.)

Several private monuments are dated in this reign; but when such do not refer to historical events, we shall not notice them in this account, except where the name of a king is so rare that the smallest detail is of value.

Several scarabs and a cylinder of Amenemhat are known. Some rude scarabs, inscribed Ra·s·hotep·ab, may, however, rather belong to the kings of that name in the XIIIth dynasty. Some of the work of the scarabs is most exquisite in detail.

We shall now turn to a vivid picture of the life and connections of Egypt at this age, in the Adventures of Sa·nehat, or the "Son of the Sycamore." As the tale will soon be printed in full, we will only epitomise it to point out its interest. The story is in the form of an autobiography, and Sanehat begins by stating his titles, which were of high rank,—hereditary prince, royal seal-bearer, confidential friend, judge, keeper of the gate of the foreigners, true and beloved royal acquaintance, follower of the king, of the household of the queen. He was in the army commanded by the coregent Usertesen I. on an expedition against the Temehu, or Libyans. As they were returning, laden with spoil, messengers came to the coregent to inform him secretly that his father had died. Sanehat was standing by, and overheard the news. At once he was seized with panic fear, and fled away to Syria. The cause of his terror has always been a question to translators; but we may guess, from the familiar manner in which he is received by the royal family on his return in his old age,—with a stipulation that none of his children should come with him,—that he may have been a son of Usertesen I. During his father's life he would be safe, but so soon as the old king died, he dreaded being cut off by the heir, who might see in him a possible rival. Thus the difficulties and unexplained points of the tale receive a consistent solution: the many high offices held by one who was quite young; the frantic terror of his flight, the familiar reception on his return, and the leaving of all his family and goods behind him on re-entering Egypt.

After fleeing from the army, when he heard of the king's death on the road from the Natron lakes, he went south, slept one night in the open field, got to about Gizeh the next afternoon, ferried himself over the river on a raft, passed Gebel Ahmar, and came to a frontier wall. After a rest there, he went on by night to escape the guards, and reached the Wady Tumilat next day, where he almost perished from thirst. Some Bedawin found him and rescued him, and he passed on from tribe to tribe till he reached Edom. There, after a time, he found favour with the prince of the hill country of Judea, who was probably in the region of Hebron, judging by the allusions to a goodly land, with figs and grapes, honey, olives, and fruits, barley and wheat without end, and much cattle. There he married the eldest daughter of the prince, and his children each became shekh of a tribe. He generalled the fighting men of his father-in-law, and had a grand single combat with a champion of a neighbouring tribe, in the manner of Goliah. In his old age he longed to see again his native land, and sent a petition to Usertesen, in which he recites his present condition, and asks, "Let this flight obtain thy forgiveness, that I may be appointed in the palace, that I may see the place where my heart dwells. How great a thing is it that my body may be embalmed in the land where I was born! To return there is happiness." The king replied to him, with presents, and the royal family sent him greetings. The royal message was gracious, accepting his assurances, informing him that the queen and family were well, and telling him, "Leave all the riches that thou hast, and that are with thee, altogether. When thou shalt come into Egypt, behold the palace; and when thou shalt enter the palace, bow thy face to the ground before the Great House; thou shalt be chief among the companions. And day by day behold thou growest old; thy vigour is lost; and thou thinkest on the day of burial. Thou shalt see thyself come to the blessed state; they shall give thee the bandages from the hand of Tait, the night of applying the oil of embalming. They shall follow thy funeral, and visit the tomb on the day of burial, which shall be in a gilded case, the head painted with blue, a canopy of cypress wood above thee, and oxen shall draw thee, the singers going before thee, and they shall dance the funeral dance. The weepers crouching at the door of thy tomb shall cry aloud the prayers for offerings; they shall slay victims for thee at the door of thy pit; and thy pyramid shall be carved in white stone, in the company of the royal children. Thus thou shalt not die in a strange land, nor be buried by the Amu; thou shalt not be laid in a sheepskin when thou art buried; all people shall beat the earth and lament on thy body when thou goest to the tomb."

Sanehat was delighted at this reply, and sent a long letter of adoration to the king, in which he says, "I who speak to thee shall leave my goods to the generations to follow in this land." He then made a feast, and bade farewell to all, giving his goods and estates to his eldest son. And, setting forth, he was received by the frontier officers, and passed on to the palace, meeting royal provision sent for him by the way. From this he gave presents to his followers who had come so far with him, and sent them back, committing himself entirely to the four messengers sent to conduct him. The king received him graciously, and then called in the queen and family, who could not recognise him at first. When assured of the wanderer's return, the royal daughters performed a dance and chorus of praise to the king. Then Sanehat was accompanied out of the palace, hand in hand with the royal children, and given an establishment. He cast away his foreign dress, and had his long hair shaved off; he dressed in fine linen, anointed himself with the finest oil, and slept on a bedstead, no longer lying on the sand. A grand tomb was built for him by the king, and he ends by a wish that he may continue in the king's favour. From the absence of any account of his burial, it seems that this was a real autobiography, composed by the old man before he died. It gives a very curious view of the relation of Egypt to Syria at the beginning of the twelfth dynasty. A fugitive Egyptian was superior to the Syrians, and by his education and ability might rise to high power, much like some English adventurer in Central Africa at the present time.

XII. 2. KHEPER·KA·RA about 2758–2714 B.C.

USERTESEN I.

Wady Maghara	Stele	Brugsch, Hist. 139.
Sarbut el Khadem	Stele	
Tanis	Statues	(P.T. i. 4, ii. 5, 8, xiii. 2, 3, 4) (and Berlin).
Faqus	Sphinx	(A.Z. xxiii. 11).
Heliopolis	Obelisk	(L.D. ii. 118 h).
Begig	Obelisk	(L.D. ii. 119).
Hat-nub	Graffito	(F.H. x.).
Abydos	Statue	(M.A. 345).
Hammamat	Inscription	(My. E. 326).
Koptos	Sculptures	
Karnak	Inscription	(M.K. 8 a–c).
Taud	Altar	(A.Z. xx. 123). (F.P. Coll.).
Hieraconpolis	Columns	(My. E. 508).
Aswan	Inscriptions	(L.D. ii. 118 a–c; P.S. 91, 113, 271, 273).
Wady Halfa	Brick temple	
Wady Halfa (Florence)	Stele	(S. Cat. F. 1542).
Wady Halfa	Stele	(Ashmolean Museum).

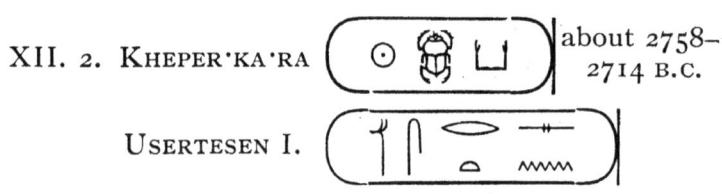

FIG. 92.—Scarab

Statue	(B. Mus.).
Statuette, carnelian	(Formerly in Louvre).
Glazed vase from Abydos	(M.A. 1466).
Marble vase	(Piece in B. Mus.).
Shells	(B. Mus., etc.).
Weight of Hor·mera	(Vienna Rec. xii. 10).
Scarabs and Cylinders.	

As we have seen, under the last reign, Usertesen was associated for ten years with his father; and during at least the latter part of that time he carried on the external affairs of the kingdom, by expeditions both to the south and the west. So feeble does the old king appear to have become, that the internal administration also devolved upon the son very soon after his accession.

A leather roll, written under Amenhotep IV., professes to give a copy of the account concerning the building of the temple of Heliopolis in the third year of Usertesen, that is, seven years before his father's death; and he is stated to have been crowned with the double crown, and surrounded by his courtiers. Little, however, can be learned from this composition, which is poetical in arrangement, and appears to be entirely a piece of "fine writing." But as the ceremonial reciter (*Kher·heb*) is stated to have stretched the cord and laid the foundation in the ground, it must speak of an original building, and not of a mere restoration (A.Z. xii. 85, R.P. xii. 53). Of the work of this temple nothing now remains but the one celebrated obelisk of Heliopolis (L.D. ii. 118 h), which records that it was made in the beginning of the *Sed* festival of thirty years. The fellow obelisk to this was not overthrown till 1258 A.D. according to Makrizi; and in 1200 A.D. the obelisks still retained their ancient caps of copper, according to Abd el Latif (cap. iv.).

From a tablet of the first year at Aswan (P.S. 271), and this above record of the third year, there is a series of dated inscriptions, mostly private, which extend throughout the reign to the forty-fourth year. This custom of dating monuments is but little known before the XIIth dynasty, and is not so usual after this period ; but a special fashion of precise dating seems to have prevailed during this age. As there is apparently little to be learned from these private monuments that are dated, we shall continue to notice the remains in geographical order, as that yields a view of the regions of activity in the various reigns.

In the Sinaitic peninsula Usertesen again asserted the Egyptian power, and at Wady Maghara (Br. Hist. 139) and Sarbut el Khadem are memorials of his time.

FIG. 93.—Bust of Usertesen I., black granite, Tanis.

At Tanis he placed at least three statues. The bust of one of these still remains (Fig. 93), in black granite, of glass-like polish (P.T. I. phot. xiii. 2). Another, also in black granite, is perhaps unique among Egyptian sculptures for having no back pedestal or pier, the whole body being admirably carved on all sides (P.T. I. phot. xiii. 3, 4) ; this was more complete in Burton's time, and is shown by his copy to belong to this king. Yet a third statue of grey granite is in evidence, by a piece of the base (P.T. I. ii. 8). All of these were barbarously ruined by Merenptah, who battered his name in upon the exquisitely finished surfaces. Near Tanis, at Faqus, a red granite sphinx has been found, which is probably of Usertesen (A.Z. xxiii. 11).

Passing Heliopolis, above noted, and the temple of Memphis, which seems to have been completed before

Usertesen, a remarkable red granite obelisk is found in the Fayum, at Begig. This differs from all other monoliths in Egypt, being rounded at the top with a cylindrical curvature parallel with the wide face (L.D. ii. 119). The steles of Medum are rounded with a spherical curve, which shows of course most prominently on the broad face; whereas this is rectangular in front view, and only curved in side view. The subject of decoration is also peculiar. The upper part of the face is occupied by five courses of scenes, and 13 lines of hieroglyphs below them. Each course re-

FIG. 94.—Road up to tomb of Ameny, Beni Hasan.

presents Usertesen adoring four divinities, twenty in all. The block was 41 feet high and 7 and 4 feet at the base; but it is now overthrown and broken in two. This shows that the Fayum continued to attract attention, Amenemhat I. having begun to occupy it, and Amenemhat III. having specially developed it, as we shall notice further on.

Next, at Beni Hasan (Fig. 94), is one of the fullest records of this time, in the tomb of Ameny. He was the hereditary noble of the Oryx nome, and succeeded to the

princedom in the eighteenth year of Usertesen I., as his tomb is dated in the twenty-fifth year of his rule and the forty-third of the reign of the king. He records:
"I followed my lord when he sailed up the river to overthrow his enemies in the four foreign lands (probably Upper and Lower Nubia, east and west). I sailed up as the son of the prince (*i.e.* before the eighteenth year of the king), royal seal-bearer, commander of the soldiers of the Oryx nome, as a man replaces an aged father, according to the favours of the king's house and his love in the palace. I passed through Ethiopia in sailing southward, I removed the boundary of the land. I brought the tribute of my lord, my praise reached unto heaven. His majesty arose, and went in peace. He overthrew his enemies in Kush. Following his majesty, I returned, sharp of face, and without loss of my soldiers.

"I sailed up the river to bring treasures of gold to the majesty of Usertesen I. I sailed up with the hereditary prince, the eldest son of the king, of his body, Ameni (afterwards Amenemhat II.). I sailed up with 400 men of every chosen man of my soldiers. Returning in peace, they had not diminished. I brought the gold appointed to me, and I was praised for it in the palace, and the king's son thanked God for me.

"I arose and sailed up the river to bring treasures to the city of Koptos with the hereditary prince, the vizier Usertesen, I sailed up with 600 men of every valiant man of the Oryx nome, I returned in peace, and my army safely, I had done all that was ordered to me.

"I was in favour and much beloved, a ruler who loved his city. Moreover, I passed years as ruler in the Oryx nome. All the works of the king's house came into my hands. Behold he set me over the gangers of the lands of the herdsmen in the Oryx nome, and 3000 bulls of their draught stock. . . . . . Not a daughter of a poor man did I wrong, not a widow did I oppress, not a farmer did I oppose, not a herdsman did I hinder. There was not a foreman of five from whom

I took his men for the works. There was not a pauper around me, there was not a hungry man in my time. When there came years of famine, I arose. I ploughed all the fields of the Oryx nome, to its southern and its northern boundaries. I made its inhabitants live, making provision for them; there was not a hungry man in it, and I gave to the widow as to her that had

FIG. 95.—Usertesen I., Abydos.

a husband: nor did I favour the elder above the younger in all that I gave. Afterward the great rises of the Nile came, producing wheat and barley, and producing all things, and I did not exact the arrears of the farm" (G.B.H. 25).

Here we have a picture of the occupations of the old feudal families of the various districts, tamed down and kept under restraint by the power of the Theban kings; and employed in various public missions and wars, or else ruling their districts with care and justice.

At Abydos Usertesen was engaged on the temple of Osiris. Mentuhotep, the chief architect, was also governor of the east desert or red country, and a man of almost royal importance; among other works he built the temple of Osiris, and sunk a well (M.A. 617). These are probably the same as works mentioned by an inferior official, Mery (P.R. ii. 104), who prepared a noble place of eternity for Osiris, with a wall that pierced heaven, a well that reached down to the river, and gates that hid the sky. And this same well appears to be mentioned by Strabo, who describes a well at Abydos, with a descent roofed by admirable blocks of stone. A statue of Usertesen has also been found there (Fig. 95) (M.A. 345; M.A. ii. 21; R.A. phot. 111, 112). This building is referred to in the XIIIth dynasty, when the colours and ornaments of Usertesen I. were restored; and in the XXth dynasty, when "the house of Amen dated from Usertesen I. and needed to be renewed" (B.H. 142, 133).

FIG. 96.—Usertesen I., Koptos.

The deserts were visited as under the previous kings, and an inscription at Hammamat (My. E. 326) shows the royal power. At Koptos a portion of a noble gateway and blocks of sculpture indicate that Usertesen much adorned, if he did not rebuild, the temple. He is shown adoring Min, Bast, and Nekhebt in different parts (Fig. 96).

At Karnak the works begun by Amenemhat were carried on by his son. A block bears his name, and others, apparently of the same work, are dated in the twentieth year (M.K. 8 a–c).

Farther south, at Shekh Taud, the Greek Tuphion, opposite to Erment, was found a red granite table of offerings (now in G. Mus.; A.Z. xx. 123). Beyond that, at Hieraconpolis, in the mounds of the town were found polygonal columns of this king (My. E. 508).

At the cataract are some rock inscriptions, dated in the first year (P.S. 271), thirty-third year (L.D. ii. 118 c), forty-first year (P.S. 91), and two undated (P.S. 113, 273).

But the important memorial in the south is the tablet from Wady Halfa (now in Florence), which records the conquest of several negro tribes, Kas, Shemyk, Khesaa, Shat, Akherkin, etc. (S. Cat. F. 1542). Unfortunately the front edge of the inscription is broken; but a fragment with the date of this expedition in the eighteenth year has been lately recovered by Captain Lyons, who has also found another tablet (now in Oxford, S.B.A. xvi. 16), and has examined the brick temple of this king at Wady Halfa.

Several private monuments are dated in the king's reign; and the following persons are more or less of interest—

Khnem·nekht was born in first year of Amenemhat, and dated his stele in seventh year of Usertesen, when he was therefore 27 years old, at Abydos (A.Z. xix. 116).

Hor, priest of the pyramid Ka·nefer of Amenemhat I., dated his stele in ninth year of Usertesen (P.R. ii. 108).

Heru·em·hat, an unusual name (Leyden, Lb. D. 102).

Mery, builder of temple of Abydos, ninth year (P.R. ii. 104).

Up·uat·aa, stele double dated in the forty-fourth year, and second year of Amenemhat II. (Leyden, L.A., x.).

Mentuhetep, builder of the temple at Abydos (M.A. 617).

Hepzefa, of the great tomb at Asyut (G.S. iv.).

Of small objects, there are some shells inscribed with the royal names (B. Mus.); a carnelian statuette was in the Louvre, but was stolen in the Revolution of 1830; a glazed vase was found at Abydos (M.A. 1466); a piece of a vase of the blue-white marble, characteristic of this age, bears the name (B. Mus.); there are also many scarabs, some plain, others of the symmetrical style of ornament, and with scroll-work; also a few cylinders of glazed stone.

An interesting weight, bearing the name of the king, belonged to a goldsmith, Hormera (Vienna, Rec. xii. 10); it weighs 853 grains, or four of the gold standard of 213 grains. Probably the plaque with the same name (formerly in the Palin Coll.), is another weight of this person.

XII. 3.
NUB·KAU·RA

about
2716–
2681 B.C.

AMENEMHAT II.

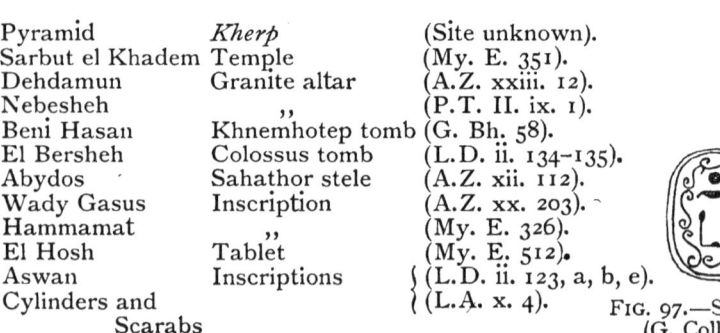

Pyramid	*Kherp*	(Site unknown).
Sarbut el Khadem	Temple	(My. E. 351).
Dehdamun	Granite altar	(A.Z. xxiii. 12).
Nebesheh	,,	(P.T. II. ix. 1).
Beni Hasan	Khnemhotep tomb	(G. Bh. 58).
El Bersheh	Colossus tomb	(L.D. ii. 134–135).
Abydos	Sahathor stele	(A.Z. xii. 112).
Wady Gasus	Inscription	(A.Z. xx. 203).
Hammamat	,,	(My. E. 326).
El Hosh	Tablet	(My. E. 512).
Aswan	Inscriptions	{ (L.D. ii. 123, a, b, e).
Cylinders and Scarabs		{ (L.A. x. 4).

FIG. 97.—Scarab (G. Coll.).

As we have already seen, the new king began his reign at least two years before the death of Usertesen I. He appears to have kept up the traditions of the dynasty, but no great events marked this time.

The pyramid of this king was named Kherp, as shown by a stele of a priest of the pyramid (B. Mus.; A.Z. xii. 112). And as no two pyramids are known to have the same name, this serves to identify the king with an abbreviated form of his name, where Sa·hathor says that he was beloved of Nub·kau·ra, and was sent to do the work for the temple of Amenu at the *Kherp* pyramid (S.B.A. xiv. 39). Thus Amenu (and probably Ameny) was a recognised familiar name for the longer Amenemhat, for royal persons, as it was also in private life at Beni Hasan.

Nub·kau·ra appears to have formally established the mining works at Sarbut el Khadem (Fig. 98), and to have founded the temple there (My. E. 351). But in Eastern Egypt his work is not found at the great centres of Tanis or Bubastis, but only at the lesser sites, which perhaps he was the first to adorn. At Dehdamun, near Faqus, a granite altar of his was found by an Arab of the district, and sold to the Ghizeh Museum; it is of veined red granite, and very finely worked (A.Z. xxiii. 12). And in the same region, at Nebesheh, were the remains of an altar of black granite, which bore a remarkable added inscription of later date by a royal seal-bearer (P.T. II. ix. 1).

But at Beni Hasan is the principal inscription of this reign in the tomb of Khnem·hotep (Tomb 3). He states that Nub·kau·ra raised him to the place of his father as prince in the nineteenth year, in the town of Menat-Khufu. He then describes all the religious and funerary foundations that he established, both for his father and for the various festivals. He also arose to favour and power at the court. His son was advanced to be ruler of the Jackal nome, and the boundaries and details were settled by the king. His other son was also advanced. And lastly, he describes a grand mortuary chapel for his father, which he had constructed (G. Bh. 61). All of this is quite different from the labours of the earlier reigns. No great settlement of the country, no foreign warlike expeditions, break in on the prosperous tranquillity of either sovereign or subject.

The tombs of El Bersheh are now of importance at this period; and the tomb of Tahuti·hotep bears

FIG. 98.—Sarbut el͜Khadem.

the celebrated scene of the dragging of a colossus on a sledge by gangs of labourers (L.D. ii. 134, 135).

Abydos continued to be of the greatest importance for burials. The tomb of Sa-hathor there records that he was beloved by the king Nub·kau·ra, and was sent on many missions. Among others he went to the town of the *kherp* pyramid of Amenu to do work on fifteen statues of hard stone, which he finished in two months. In his youth he worked the mines in Nubia, and made the chiefs have gold washed for him (A.Z. xii. 112). The other tablets of the tombs record nothing of importance in this uneventful reign.

The desert, however, was worked as before. At Wady Gasus a small temple existed, from which two steles have come, one of this reign, one of the next. The first records how it was put up by a noble named Khenti·kheti·ur, seal-bearer, keeper of the storehouse, who came in peace from Punt with his boats in the twenty-fourth year (A.Z. xx. 203).

In Hammamat there is said to be an inscription also of this king (My. E. 326). And one has been seen at El Hosh, near Silsileh, dated in the seventeenth year (My. E. 512).

At Aswan there are a few inscriptions of this time, but none of historical import (L.D. ii. 123, a, b, e).

Among the private tablets, one of Mentu·sa (B. Mus., Sharpe, i. 83) records that he was born in the first year of Amenemhat I., and erects his tablet in the third year of Amenemhat II., when he must therefore have been 52 years old.

The end of this king, according to Manetho, was that he was slain by his chamberlains: an inglorious end to a tranquil life of easy prosperity.

There are many small amulets, cylinders, and scarabs; but the workmanship shows a great falling off from that of the previous reigns, and the old high level of delicate and regular work was never reached again in this dynasty.

The scarabs of Sankh·ka·ra, Amenemhat I., and Usertesen I. are perhaps unrivalled in any other period for their finish.

XII. 4. KHA·KHEPER·RA 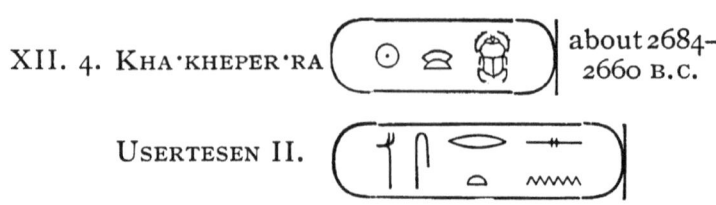 about 2684–2660 B.C.

USERTESEN II.

Pyramid	*Hotep*	Illahun.
Tanis	Queen Nefert	(P.T. II. xi. 171).
Memphis	Inscription	(M.D. 27 a).
Illahun	Pyramid and Temple	(P.I. ii. xiv.).
Ahnas	Blocks	(N.A. i.).
Beni Hasan	Khnem hotep	(N.Bh. xxxviii.).
Qosēr	Stele	(A.Z. xx. 204).
Hieraconpolis	Statue	(Rec. x. 139).
Aswan	Stele	(L.D. ii. 123 d).
Statues	Berlin and Louvre.	

Scarabs, cylinders, etc.
Queen—Nefert (P.T. II. xi. 171).
Daughters—Atmu neferu (?) (P.I. xii. 6, 7, 8).
Sat·hathor (Dahshur).
Sent·s·senb (Dahshur).

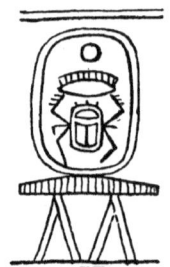

FIG. 99.—Cylinder (B. Mus.).

Of this king we have fortunately found the pyramid and pyramid-town, which gives a more complete idea of the civilisation of this reign than we have yet obtained of most other periods. The pyramid of Illahun is at the mouth of the channel in the desert which leads into the Fayum; and we have already noticed how the kings of this dynasty have left their remains in the Fayum, and organised that province. Usertesen II. placed his pyramid where it was still in the Nile valley; but from the top of it the Fayum is visible on looking up the channel between the desert slopes.

The pyramid is peculiar (Fig. 100); the lower part of it is of unmoved rock, which has been isolated from the hill by a deep and wide cutting. Upon that rock walls of large blocks arise, both diagonal and square with the faces, and between these walls is filled in a brick pyramid. The outside was cased with fine limestone, like the other pyramids. It seems that the pyramids of the earlier kings had fallen a prey to violence already; the signs of personal spite in the destructions are evident (P.P., 2nd edition, 66, 67). Therefore Usertesen II. determined to abandon the old system of a north entrance in the face, and to conceal the access to the interior by a new method. The chambers were all excavated in the solid rock without any upper opening, so that they could not be reached

FIG. 100.—Pyramid of Illahun from the south (excavations in chips around it).

by tracking between the rock and the building. And the entrance was by a shaft outside of the south face of the pyramid. Two shafts were made, and but for such a doubling of these weak points, for the convenience of access of the workmen, it might have remained inviolate (Fig. 101). The main shaft was so carefully concealed under a deep mass of rubbish in the plain, that it has never been found; but the small secondary shaft was only covered by the pyramid pavement, and was opened up when that was removed by Ramessu II.

The interior has a long sloping passage, rising upwards, so that water could not flood the sepulchre; this passage leads to a large chamber lined with limestone, and that opens into another lined with red granite, in which stands the sarcophagus (P.I. 1–4). There is a curious passage cut in the rock passing around the granite chamber, as if to prove to any searcher that no other way opened out of that. In the chamber stood the alabaster altar of offerings, finely inscribed to Osiris and Anubis (P.I. iii.). The red granite sarcophagus is exquisitely wrought; the

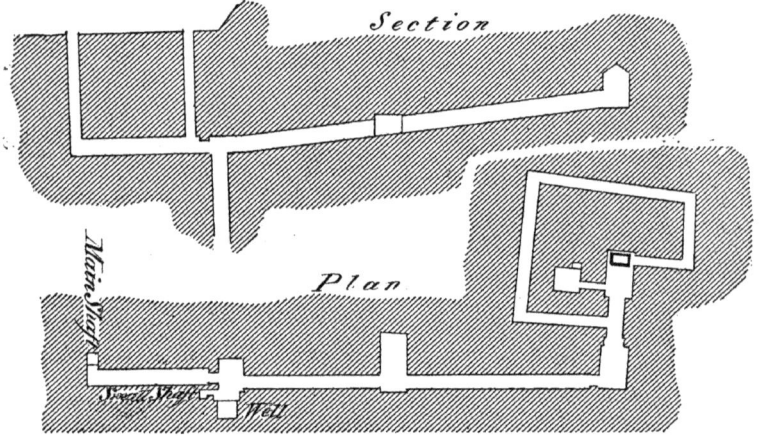

FIG. 101.—Section and plan of passages in pyramid of Illahun. Scale $\frac{1}{1000}$.

errors of flatness and straightness being matters of thousandths of an inch (P.I. 3). It has a peculiar lip around it, which has given some weight to the theory that it has been reset in a new position, and that it had been originally sunk in the floor. But any such theory of arrangement requires us to suppose a great amount of reconstruction, of which there is no evidence whatever.

Against the east face of the pyramid was a shrine for the worship of the king, richly carved and painted. The whole of this was smashed up by the masons of Ramessu II., who have left his name written on a block. And the stonework from here appears to have been removed to Ahnas, where the name of Usertesen II. occurs on a block reworked by Ramessu II.

About a mile to the east of the pyramid, opposite the middle of the face, is a temple of larger size. This stands on the edge of the desert hills, and would probably be the public temple, while the shrine by the pyramid might be only for the priests. This had all been destroyed, and only a coat of chips covered the ground, many of them showing brilliant work and colouring. A basalt statue had been here, of which only a flake of the thigh remained; also a shrine of red granite, and a smaller statue of black granite, of which chips were found. In the centre of the area was a pit in the rock with foundation deposits (P.K. 22).

Near the large pyramid stood a smaller one, the chambers of which are also cut entirely in the rock, without any opening but the entrance, which must be at some distance, as it was not found in a wide clearance around the site. A fragment of the shrine gives the name of a princess beginning with Atmu, probably Atmu-neferu (P.I. xii. 6, 7, 8).

By the site of the larger temple is the town of the workmen who built the pyramid and temples; this place was known as "Hat·hetep·Usertesen," and is now named Kahun. Part of it is entirely denuded away, but it yet occupies about 18 acres, within which are over two thousand rooms. All of these have lately been cleared, and the plans of the streets and houses completely published (P.I. xiv.). From this we learn the details of the houses of that age; both the mansions of the high officials, and the rows of little dwellings for the workmen. The objects found in this town throw much light on the civilisation; and the papyri form the majority of those known of this age. The town appears to have been half deserted after the pyramid and temple were finished; and the inhabitants who were left used the empty houses for rubbish holes. But it seems that few, if any, people remained there during the troubles of the Hyksos period. A few houses were occupied under the beginning of the XVIIIth dynasty, and then it was left to the jackals, and gradually weathered down.

At Beni Hasan is one of the most interesting records of this age. Khnem·hotep is represented as receiving a group of thirty-seven Aamu of the eastern desert, bearing a tribute of *kohl*, or eye paint. The figures of these foreigners are very important, as showing what kind of civilisation was already spread in the countries between Egypt and Mesopotamia. The royal scribe, Neferhotep, who introduces the party, bears a tablet on which is written, "Year six, under the majesty of Horus, the guide of the two lands, the king of Upper and Lower Egypt, Kha·kheper·ra, the number of Aamu brought by the son of the noble Khnem·hotep, on account of the *kohl*, Aamu of Shu, number amounting to 37" (N. Bh. xxxviii.). Khety, the overseer of the huntsmen, follows the scribe, and behind him come the foreigners. First is the chief, leading a tame ibex (Fig. 102); his title and name is before him, *heq setu Absha* (N. Bh. xxviii.). We have already seen how important a *heq setu* was, in considering Khyan in the VIIIth or IXth dynasty, who occupied part of the Delta and adopted the dignity of an Egyptian king. Here again the rich clothing of these people shows that they were not mere wandering Bedawin, clad in skins; on the contrary, their gaily patterned garments remind us of the rugs of Persia in the design. They cannot have attained the means and the taste for such ornament in a savage and wandering life; and we may safely infer that they belong to a region less sterile than the bare desert of the Red Sea. Rather may we connect them with Northern Arabia, the region which the power and monuments of Khyan lead us to regard as the home of the *heq setu*, or prince of the hill

[B.C. 2684-2660.] USERTESEN II 173

country. The chief's face is obviously Semitic, being closely like that of the Bedawin of the present day; the narrow line of beard down the jaw, rising toward the corner of the mouth and then sloping away to the chin, the long aquiline nose, and the general expression, are all familiar in the Arab face. The same Semitic origin is pointed out by the name Absha, which is equal to the Hebrew Abishai, "the father of a present"; and it is likely that this was not his real name,

FIG. 102.—Chief and women of Aamu (from Beni Hasan I.).

but rather a name given him by his people in consequence of his coming to Egypt with a present or tribute to the Egyptians; just as Arabs would now name a man who brought presents as "the father of presents."

After the chief comes a follower leading an oryx; then four armed men with bow, boomerangs, and spears; two children on an ass laden with rugs; a boy with a spear; four women gaily dressed in coloured garments, patterned with stripes, chequers, and frets; another ass laden with baggage, a spear, and a shield; a man with a water-skin on his back, playing on a lyre; and lastly, a bowman with a boomerang (N. Bh. xxxi.). Here is no sign of inferior civilisation. The clothing is quite as much as the Egyptians used, the decoration of it is more profuse than on the Egyptian dress, the arms are the same as in Egypt, the bow and boomerang, and the spear is not common so early in Egypt; the sandals are as good as the Egyptian pattern, and the women have socks. Though a different civilisation, it is no way inferior to the Egyptian in the arts of life which were needful to such a people. These were the Aamu with whom the Egyptians warred with such large armies under Pepy I.; and who appear to have invaded Egypt and held the country in the time of the IXth–Xth dynasty.

At Qosēr one of the steles is dated under Usertesen II. (A.Z. xx. 204). At Hieraconpolis a statue of this king in black granite has been found, now in the Ghizeh Museum (Rec. x. 139). And at Aswan is a fine stele of a local noble, Mentuhotep, dated in this reign (L.D. ii. 123 d). The tomb of Sarenput at Aswan, and his statue of black granite (B. Mus.), also belong to this reign, as his father was called after Amenemhat II. (Rec. x. 189).

In Berlin is a statue dedicated by an official, Ser (W.G. 250); and in the Louvre a carnelian statuette is said to exist, but is not in the catalogue. It is probably a false reference for the stolen statuette of Usertesen I. (see De Rougé, Notice des Monuments, 16).

Of scarabs and cylinders there are several of this reign; ten having been found in his pyramid-town of Kahun alone.

His queen was named Nefert, as we learn from her grey granite statue at Tanis (Fig. 103) (G. Mus.; P.T. II. xi. 171). She is represented seated on a throne, with her wig brought down in two masses to the breasts, where each ends in a spiral curl. On the bosom is a pectoral, on which is the king's name between two vultures on the *nub* sign. On the throne are the titles, "The hereditary princess, the great favourite, the greatly praised, the beloved consort of the king, the ruler of all women, the king's daughter of his body, Nefert." The title ruler, or princess, of all women is

FIG. 103.—Queen Nefert.

peculiar, and suggests that the queen had some prerogatives of government as regards the female half of the population.

The small pyramid at Illahun seems to have been for a princess named Atmu . . . ; and, as many names in this age are compounded of the names of deities and *neferu*, so this may well have been Atmu·neferu, "the beauties of Atmu" or Tum. For the other two daughters see the next reign.

XII. 5. KHA·KAU·RA

USERTESEN III.

about 2660–2622 B.C.

Pyramid, Dahshur, N. brick.

Tanis	Architrave	(P.T. I. ii. 7).	
Nebesheh	Statue	(P.N. ix. 2).	
Khataaneh	Jambs	(A.Z. xxiii. 12).	
Mókdam	Statues	(N.A. iv. xii.).	
Bubastis	Architraves	(N.B. xxxiii.).	
Abydos	Statue	(M.A. 346).	
Hammamat	Inscription	(L.D. ii. 136 a).	FIG. 104.—Scarab (P. Mus.).
Gebelen	Base of statue	(G. Mus).	
Aswan	Inscriptions	(L.D. ii. 136 c).	
Elephantine	Tablet	(A.Z. xiii. 50).	
Sehel	Inscriptions	{ (L.D. ii. 136 b). (Rec. xiii. 202).	
Bigeh	Statue	(L.L. 120).	
Semneh	Fort and temple	(L.D.I. 111–112).	
Kummeh	,,	(L.D.I. 111–112).	
Scarabs and Cylinders			
Queens—Henut·taui		Dahshur	
Merseker?		(L.D. iii. 55 a).	

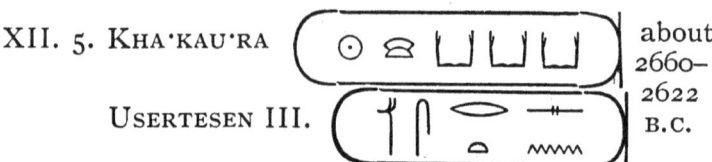

The pyramid of this king is apparently the north brick pyramid of Dahshur, from the remains discovered around it by M. de Morgan in 1894. The arrangement is unlike that hitherto known at any pyramid. In place of the well descending on the south side as at the tomb of Usertesen II., there are wells just inside the corners of the peribolus wall on the N.W. and N.E.; and probably also at the other corners. These wells are connected with long galleries parallel to the peribolus; and chambers containing sarcophagi open from these galleries. Three named interments are already known. A queen, "*khnum nefer hezt* Henut·taui," inscribed on a sandstone sarcophagus; this is probably the queen of Usertesen III., as she is queen consort at her death, and is not called royal mother. A princess, "king's daughter Sent·s·senb," inscribed on a limestone sarcophagus, probably a daughter of Usertesen II., and sister of Usertesen III., judging by the next example. And a princess, Sat·hathor, whose jewellery was found in a casket overlooked by the ancient plunderers. Her pectoral bears the name of Usertesen II., while a scarab has the name of Usertesen III.; hence she was probably daughter of the former and sister of the latter, who buried her in his pyramid mausoleum. This jewellery is a treasure only paralleled

FIG. 105.—One of the royal pectorals inlaid with stones, Dahshur pyramid mausoleum.

by that of Aah·hotep. A pectoral of gold is richly inlaid with minute work in carnelian and light and dark blue stone or paste; the design is like that of the pectoral on the breast of Nefert, her father's queen (see the Tanis statues in the Ghizeh Museum), the cartouche of Usertesen II., surmounted by *neb neteru*, and supported on either side by a hawk on *nub*, with the sun and uraeus behind. Bracelets, necklaces of gold cowries, pendants of lions and lions' claws in gold, and strings of beads in gold, amethyst, and emerald, make up this splendid equipment of a princess.

Having the north brick pyramid of Dahshur thus fixed to Usertesen III., it is possible that the two stone pyramids there belong to Amenemhat I. and Usertesen I.; as the Lahun pyramid is of Usertesen II., and the Hawara pyramid of Amenemhat III., the burials of the dynasty would be thus nearly accounted for.

The name of this king in the Greek lists, Lakheres, is quite accounted for by the corruption of X into Λ, by omission of the top; thus altering Kha·kau·ra, or Khakeres, into Lakheres.

In the Delta, Usertesen seems to have been very active as a builder. At Tanis an architrave of red granite bears his name (P.T. I. ii. 7); at Nebesheh stood statues in yellow quartzite, one of the thrones of which is preserved (B. Mus.; P.N. ix. 2); at Khataaneh are the jambs of red granite, lying by the lintel of Amenemhat I. (A.Z. xxiii. 12); at Tell Mokdam are the bases of two statues (N.A. 29, iv. xii.); at Bubastis he appears to have rebuilt the temple, there being several blocks and architraves bearing his name, and a portion of a long inscription about a war against the negroes, probably also of this time (N.B. 10, xxxiii. xxxiv.). Memphis appears to have been passed over in this reign. At Abydos is a red granite statue in the temple (M.A. 346).

At Hammamat we meet an inscription which shows that Herakleopolis, now Ahnas, was adorned by him: "In the fourteenth year, the eighteenth of Khoiak, in the reign of Kha·kau·ra, loving the god Min of Koptos, behold his majesty ordered the going to Rohanu to bring the monuments which his majesty ordered him to make for Hershef, lord of Herakleopolis (even the living chief Kha·kau·ra ever living!), in good Bekhnu stone. He sent me as overseer of works on account of my excellence, a true commander, known to his lord. He overthrew the foreigners and the Troglodytes, and brought excellent tribute of the Tehenu (Libyans); he who says what is good and reports what is desired,

Khuy, son of Hepy." The construction of this inscription is rather confused.

At Gebelen the base of a statuette of this king was found (G. Mus.). Thebes appears to have been passed by, and all the energies of the reign were concentrated on the complete subjugation of Nubia. At Aswan are inscriptions of the sixth year (a tablet of Aay, P.S. 262) and of the twelfth year (P.S. 340). At Elephantine was a tablet recording some constructions in the eighth year of this reign (B. Mus. ; A.Z. xiii. 50).

On the island of Sehel, by the cataract, is a tablet representing the goddess Anqet giving life to Usertesen, and stating that he made monuments to her, and also the canal, "most excellent of ways of Usertesen." Another tablet of great interest represents there the goddess Sati giving life to Usertesen, and states that "in the eighth year, under the majesty of Kha·kau·ra, living for ever, ordered his majesty to be made a canal anew ; the name of this canal is the 'most excellent of ways of Kha·kau·ra ever living.' Then his majesty sailed southward to crush Ethiopia the vile. Length of this canal, 150 cubits ; breadth, 20 cubits ; depth, 14 cubits." This canal was used again by Tahutmes I., and was cleared and reopened by Tahutmes III., who gave the standing order, "The fishers of Elephantine shall cut this canal every year" (Rec. xiii. 202).

No modern canal has been attempted in this place ; and instead of a canal 34 feet wide and 24 feet deep, up which any Nile boat could pass, we have resorted to a railway with a shift of cargo at each end of it.

This canal was a part of the great preparations for the conquest of Nubia, and Usertesen left his statue on the isle of Bigeh, above the cataract, in honour of the gods of the region (L.L. 120). Pressing on, he defeated the negroes in different campaigns, of which we have records of the eighth, sixteenth, and the nineteenth years. On a tablet set up at Semneh (Fig. 106), we have a characteristic inscription, showing much both of the king and the people. " In the sixteenth year, the month Phamenoth, made his majesty the southern boundary unto Heh. I (the king) made my boundary south of my father's; I did more than was committed to me by them; I the king both say and did it. It was the device of my heart, which was done by me; eager to capture, powerful to succeed, and not slothful; one in whose heart there is a word which cravens know not. Giving no satisfaction to the enemy which invades him; but invading the invader, and leaving alone the man who lets him alone. Answering a word according to its result; for a man who remains silent after an attack, encourages the heart of the enemy. Eagerness is

FIG. 106.—View of Semneh (from L.D. ii. 112).

valiant, and base is the coward who is driven back. It is truly a coward who is oppressed upon his own boundary; for the negro obeys as soon as the lips are opened; an answer makes him draw back; he turns his back to the impetuous. They are not valiant men, they are miserable, both tails and bodies (a joke at the hide girdles and tails, which always amused the Egyptians); my majesty saw it myself; it is no fable. I captured their wives, led away their peoples; I went out to their wells (in the desert valleys), and smote their cattle, and destroyed their corn, and set fire to it. By my life and my father's life, what I say is in truth.

"And every son of mine who confirms this boundary which my majesty has made, he is my son, he is born of my majesty, a son who avenges his father (like Horus), who confirms the boundary of him who begat him. But he who destroys it, even who fights not for it, he is not my son, he is not one born to me. Moreover, my majesty caused a statue of my majesty to be made upon this boundary, which my majesty made from the desire that ye should fight for it."

These conquests in Nubia were permanently secured by thus pushing back the frontier of Egypt to above the Second Cataract, and building on the hills of Semneh and Kummeh two forts commanding the river, about thirty miles above the cataract. The fort of Semneh is on the west bank, bordering on the river, and on an almost inaccessible height of platform, artificially raised, and containing a temple. That of Kummeh, on the east bank, is on a natural height, which is very strong, and also contains a temple (L.D. i. 111–112 ; Ms. A. 29, 30). A decree for the frontier guards was placed at Semneh : "This is the southern frontier ; fixed in the eighth year of the reign of his majesty Kha·kau·ra, ever living. Let it not be permitted to any negro to pass this boundary northward, either on foot or by boat ; nor any sort of cattle, oxen, goats, or sheep belonging to the negroes. Except when any negro comes to trade in the land of Aken, or on any business, let him be well treated. But without allowing any boat of the negroes to pass Heh northward for ever " (L.D. ii. 136 i).

In after ages this king was revered as the founder of Ethiopia, and the later kings of the XVIIIth dynasty specially adored him in their temples at Semneh, Kummeh, Dosheh, Shatawi, Ellesieh, and Amada.

Some private inscriptions of this reign also remain at Semneh and Kummeh (L.D. ii. 136 d–g).

A curious illustration of the worship of the kings is preserved in a long hymn to Usertesen III. on a papyrus found at Kahun. After an opening adulation of titles comes the poetical part of the hymn of praise, stanza after stanza of ten lines, the most perfect example of Egyptian poetry that we know.

I.

1 Twice joyful are the gods,
    thou hast established their offerings.
2 Twice joyful are thy princes,
    thou hast formed their boundaries.
3 Twice joyful are thy ancestors before thee,
    thou hast increased their portions.
4 Twice joyful is Egypt at thy strong arm,
    thou hast guarded the ancient order.
5 Twice joyful are the aged with thy administration,
    thou hast widened their possessions.
6 Twice joyful are the two regions with thy valour,
    thou hast caused them to flourish.
7 Twice joyful are thy young men of support,
    thou hast caused them to flourish.
8 Twice joyful are thy veterans,
    thou hast caused them to be vigorous.
9 Twice joyful are the two lands in thy might,
    thou hast guarded their walls.
10 Twice joyful be thou, O Horus! widening thy boundary,
    mayest thou renew an eternity of life.

II.

1 Twice great are the owners of his city,
    for he is a multitude and an host.
2 Twice great are the owners of his city,
    for he is a flood-gate pouring forth streams of its water-[floods.
3 Twice great are the owners of his city,
    for he is a bower, letting every man lie down in the mid-[day heat.
4 Twice great are the owners of his city,
    for he is a screen like walls built of the sharp stones of [Kesem.
5 Twice great are the owners of his city,
    for he is a refuge, shutting out the robber.
6 Twice great are the owners of his city,
    for he is an asylum, shielding the timid from his enemy.
7 Twice great are the owners of his city,
    for he is a shade in the high Nile to provide coolness in the [summer.
8 Twice great are the owners of his city,
    for he is a warm corner of shelter in the winter.
9 Twice great are the owners of his city,
    for he is a rock shielding from the blast in the stormy day.
10 Twice great are the owners of his city, [his boundary.
    for he is as the goddess Sekhet to the foes who tread on

III.

1 He has come to us, he has taken the land of the well,
   the double crown is placed on his head.
2 He has come, he has united the two lands,
   he has joined the kingdom of the upper land with the
3 He has come, he has ruled Egypt,   [lower.
   he has placed the desert in his power.
4 He has come, he has protected the two lands,
   he has given peace in the two regions.
5 He has come, he has made Egypt to live,
   he has destroyed its afflictions.
6 He has come, he has made the aged to live,
   he has opened the breath of the people.
7 He has come, he has trampled on the nations,
   he has smitten the Anu, who knew not his terror,
8 He has come, he has protected (?) his frontier,
   he has rescued the robbed.
9 He has come . . . . . .
   of what his mighty arm brings to us.
10 He has come, we bring up our children,
   we bury our aged by his good favour.

The remaining stanzas are incomplete, but we can see through this a real national fervour of delight at the repression of the negro tribes, and the establishment of security and safety in the country.

There are many scarabs and cylinders of this reign in various collections; mostly of rather rude work.

The queen in the Dahshur mausoleum is named Henut·taui, and there is a probability that a queen of Usertesen was named Merseker, as she is adored by Tahutmes III. at Semneh in the same inscription with this king (L.D. iii. 55 a); but no other trace of her has been found.

XII. 6. MAAT·EN·RA 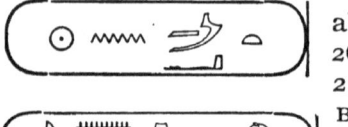 about 2622–2578 B.C.

AMEN·EM·HAT III.

Pyramid and temple, Hawara (P.K. ii.–v.).

Sarbut el Khadem	Shrine, etc.	(L.L. 301).
Wady Maghara	Inscriptions	(L.D. ii. 137).
Turrah	Stele	(L.D. ii. 143 i.).
Hawara	Pyramid	(P.K. ii.–v.).
Crocodilopolis	Pylon	(P.H. xxvii.).
Biahmu	Colossi	(P.H. xxvi.–vii.).
Hammamat	Inscriptions	(L.D. ii. 138).
Koptos	Vulture	
Hieraconpolis	Statuette	(Rec. x. 139).
El Kab	Stele	(W.G. 255).
Aswan	Inscriptions	(P.S. 84, 98, 151-3-4).
		(M.I. i. 14, 15, 27).
Kuban	Inscription	(L.D. ii. 138 g).
Kummeh	Inscriptions	(L.D. ii. 139).
Semneh	Nile levels	(L.D. ii. 139).
Statue	Berlin	(W.G. 260).
Statue	St. Petersburg	(Rec. xv. 136; i.–iv.).
Sphinx	Miramar Mus.	(Cat. xxix.).

Hawk (F.P. Coll.), scarabs, cylinders, etc.
Papyri (Kahun Papyri xiv.).
Daughters—Ptahneferu   (P.K.V.; Rec. x. 142).
    Sebekneferu, queen later on.

FIG. 107.—Scarab.

The pyramid of Amenemhat was placed by him at the entrance to the Fayum province, which he so largely organised; from the top of it almost every part of the Oasis can be seen, out to the line of hills which bound its western border. It is also within sight of the cliffs on the eastern side of the Nile; and it thus links together the valley on which all the other pyramids look down, with this western Oasis which was the special care of this king (Fig. 108).

In construction this pyramid differs from all others known, but is more like that of Usertesen II. than any other. The mass of it is entirely of brick, which was coated with fine limestone, like the other pyramids. The passages leading to the central chamber are peculiarly complex, and laboriously planned to defeat plunderers (Fig. 109). A new system was elaborated here, of dumb chambers, with gigantic sliding trap-doors in the roofs leading to further passages. The explorer who had found the entrance, in the unusual place on the south side, de-

FIG. 108.—Bust of Amenemhat III. from statue at St. Petersburg.

scended a long staircase, which ended in a dumb chamber. The roof of this, if slid aside, showed another passage, which was filled with blocks. This was a mere blind, to divert attention from the real passage, which stood ostentatiously open. A plunderer has, however, fruitlessly mined his way through all these blocks. On going down the real passage, another dumb chamber was reached; another sliding trap-door was passed; another passage led to a third dumb chamber; a third trap-door was passed; and now a passage led along past one side of the real sepulchre; and to amuse explorers, two false wells open in the passage floor, and the wrong side of the passage is filled with masonry blocks fitted in. Yet by some means the plunderers found a cross trench in the passage floor, which led to the chamber. Here another device was met. The chamber had no door, but was entered solely by one of the immense roof-blocks—weighing 45 tons—being left raised, and afterwards dropped into place on closing the pyramid. This had been mined through, and thus the royal interments were reached. They had been entirely burnt; and only fired grains of diorite and pieces of lazuli inlaying showed the splendour of the decorations of the coffins.

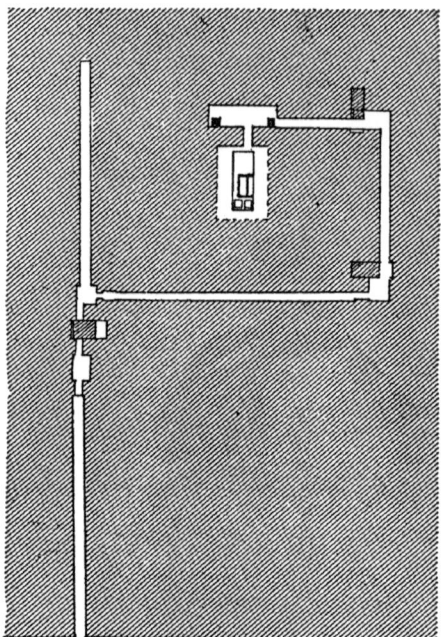

FIG. 109.—Plan of passages in Hawara pyramid. Scale $\frac{1}{1000}$.

The sepulchral chamber is one of the most remarkable works in Egypt. It is hollowed out in one block of glass-hard yellow quartzite, cut and polished with exquisite truth. It is over 22 feet long by about 8 feet wide inside, and over 2 feet thick, so that it must weigh about 110 tons. The roof of it is formed of three blocks of the same material, one of 45 tons, by which entrance was obtained, another larger, and a third smaller. All of this was built into a pit in the rock; a limestone sloping roof was placed over it, the beams of which are 7 feet thick; over that a brick arch was thrown, and the brick pyramid was built on it.

Inside the chamber is the sarcophagus of Amenemhat; flat around the sides, but with a projecting foot ornamented with panel pattern, and a curved lid. Subsequently a second coffin has been formed by building blocks between the royal coffin and the wall, and a second lid was put over the space, for covering a second burial. Behind these two coffins stood two boxes of the same design, doubtless to hold the sepulchral vases, like the square box in the floor of Pepy's chamber. All of these objects were made of quartzite, some of it white and translucent; and there is no trace of inscription on this furniture, on the chamber, nor in any part of the pyramid. Below the water, which now half fills the chamber, were found pieces of the alabaster vases with the name of the king Maāt·en·ra. And in the last of the passages was an alabaster altar and broken pieces of dishes, in the form of a half duck (all in G. Mus.), inscribed for the "king's daughter Ptahneferu," who was doubless buried in the added sarcophagus space by the side of the king. This altar is peculiar for having figures of a great number of offerings, eighty-six of which bear names (P.K. 12-17, ii.-v.) (Fig. 110).

Adjoining the pyramid on the south side stood an immense building; part of which, at least, was the temple of Amenemhat. Some of the construction was due to his daughter Sebekneferu, who afterwards came to the throne (P.H. 6, xxvii. 12). This was the building so celebrated in classical times as the Labyrinth. The site of that has been much disputed; but Strabo states that it was on the canal between the Nile and Arsinoë; and by a papyrus found at Gurob, of Ptolemaic age, we know now that boats on the canal leading to Ptolemaïs in the Fayum, passed by the Labyrinth; every part of that canal has now been examined, without finding any trace of an early building except this great site.

All of the constructions have been removed for stone, and there is no trace of the extent of the building except the concrete or *beton* beds of the foundations, and the immense masses of chips over them, which have resulted from the destruction of the building by the quarriers of Roman age. The brick houses, mistaken by Lepsius for the Labyrinth, formed the village of the Roman age, built on the top of the fragments of the temple. The whole area of the building is about 1000 feet long and 800 feet broad, or enough to include all the temples of Karnak and of Luxor. From the scanty indications of the levels of the

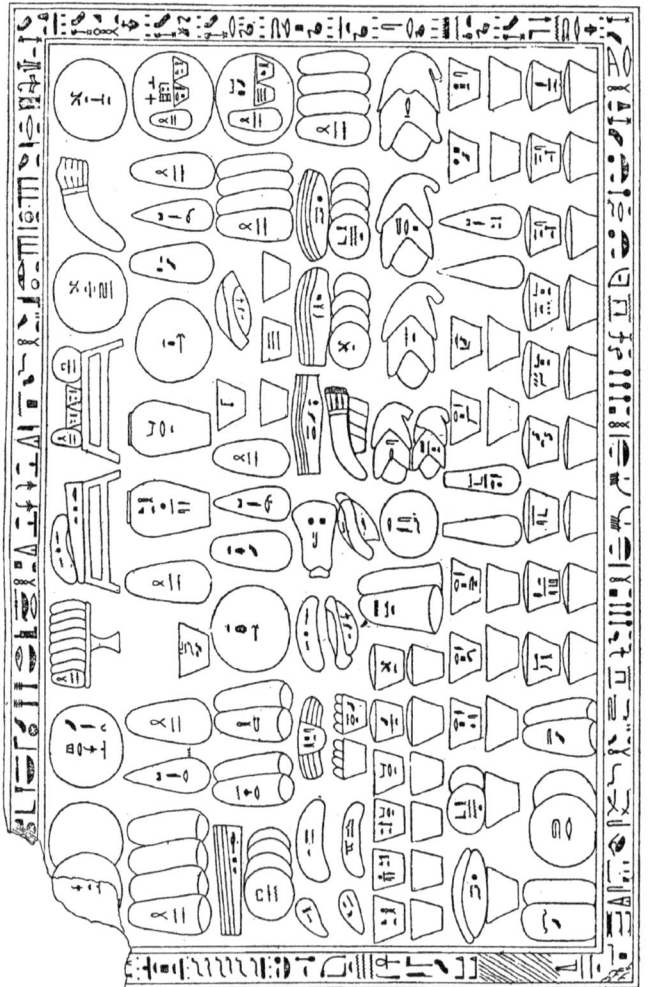

FIG. 110.—Alabaster altar of Ptahneferu, Hawara pyramid.

ground, and the fragmentary accounts of ancient authors, it appears as if the Labyrinth were a peristyle temple, with a central passage, and two great crossways: the first crossway with courts or small temples opening on each side of it; the second crossway being a hall with a long row of columns, and with courts opening on the farther side of it, much like the temple of Abydos (P.H. 4–8, xxv.). It has been supposed from the tales of Herodotos that the kings of the XXVIth dynasty had built here, either as restoring or adding to the older temples; but there seems to be no trace of works of that date to be found here. Amenemhat continued to be honoured at Hawara until Ptolemaic times, as persons were named after him (P.H. v. 4, 11).

FIG. 111.—Two tablets of Amenemhat III., Wady Maghara.

We pass now to the geographical order of the monuments. In the Sinaitic peninsula Amenemhat developed his power. At the mines of Sarbut el Khadem he excavated a small rock temple, and placed steles outside of it (L.L. 301; L.D. ii. 137; C.N. ii. 691). In the Wady Maghara are also several inscriptions, in various years from the beginning to the end of this reign; one records an expedition with 734 soldiers, to work the mines of copper and malachite (L.D. ii. 137 c–i) (Fig. 111).

The quarries of Turrah by Cairo have a fine stele of the king (L.D. ii. 143 i), showing that he obtained stone from there, probably for the Labyrinth. No such good stone could be had elsewhere in Egypt, as we learn by Una bringing from thence the best blocks for his tomb, against the Nile stream all the way up to Abydos.

The Fayum province was the great monument of Amenemhat III. The deep hollow in the desert,

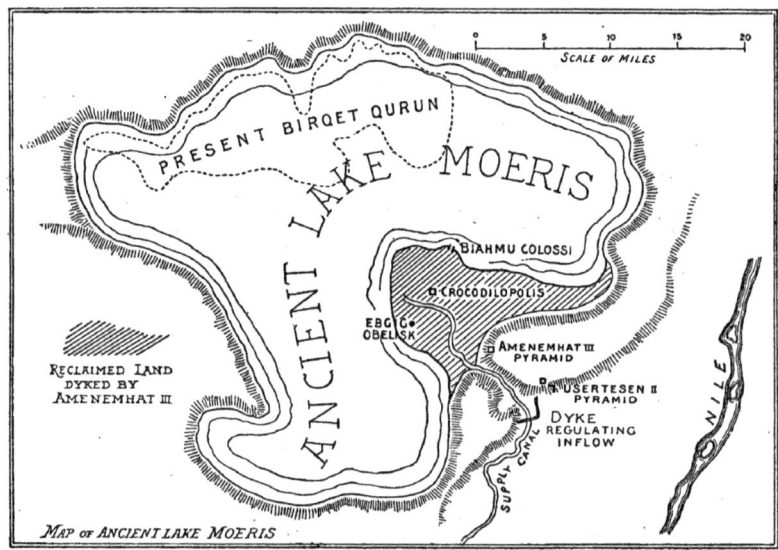

FIG. 112.—Map of the ancient Lake Moeris in the Fayum basin. The shaded part is that reclaimed from the lake by Amenemhat III.

descending over 120 feet below the sea level, was perhaps first produced by the upheavals and dislocations of the strata which caused the great fault of the Nile valley. But it is tolerably certain that from the earliest human period the Fayum was filled with water by the Nile, as there is a channel into it level with the Nile valley. This inflow of mud-bearing water had deposited beds of earth over the higher levels, where the Nile water first spread out into the lake. Of this high level period many remains are seen, pebble beaches high on the dry side of the basin, and a quay of the town of Dimey on the western side, constructed in Greek times, but now dry far above the lake. There cannot be any question, therefore, as to this condition of things having existed (Fig. 112). The keeper of the Lake of the Crocodile or *Ta·she* is mentioned from the earliest times.

The first stage of interference with nature here seems to have been under Amenemhat I., as the earlier mentions of a town or district probably refer to the shores of the lake. His statue at Crocodilopolis (Medinet) shows that he had reclaimed a considerable surface from the lake; and a fragment of a gigantic thick dyke of earth, just beyond the ancient temple, may well be a part of his first dam, enclosing the higher part of the lake bed, and so bringing it into use for cultivation, or may even belong to some still earlier reclamation. This enclosure must have extended as far as Begig, three or four miles south-west of the temple, in the time of Usertesen I., whose obelisk lies there. Then under Amenemhat III. came the great extension of this damming-out system; and by means of a vast embankment, some twenty miles in length, an almost level area of about forty square miles, or over 20,000 acres, was secured from the lake, and became one of the most fertile provinces of the country. On the prominent northern corner of this great work (now known as Biahmu) were placed two massive platforms of stone walling, filled in with earth, from which arose two seated colossi of the king. These were monoliths about thirty-nine feet high, placed upon pedestals. Carved in the glassy quartzite, and polished brilliantly, they glittered as landmarks seen across the lake (P.H. 53–56, xxvi.). These were doubtless the statues on pyramids seen by Herodotos. The fragments of the statues, etc., are now in the Ashmolean Museum at Oxford. The great work of Amenemhat was not only the reclaiming of all this land, but also the regulation of the flow of the Nile in and out of the lake. Down to the time of Herodotos this annual flow continued, and the lake served to hold part of the surplus of the high Nile, and to let that flow out again during the low Nile. Two causes, however, led to the abandonment of this system: first, the Nile always deposits more earth near its main bed than elsewhere, consequently the bed rises faster than the western side of the Nile plain, and hence there is now a difference of several feet across the Nile valley. So soon as this became considerable, it would be impracticable to get the water out of the Fayum again into the raised Nile bed. Secondly, the land was much needed for a new settlement of the Macedonian soldiers of Ptolemy Soter. Hence the inflow of the Nile was checked down to the amount actually required by the province, and the lake was gradually dried up under the earlier Ptolemies. Colonies of soldiers and their families were settled on the newly-reclaimed land, towns and temples sprang up as the lake receded, and it has been reduced to a low, though fluctuating, level ever since (P.H. 2). Amenemhat III. also rearranged the temple which his ancestor had built at Crocodilopolis; the red granite blocks of the pylon bear his name, though they have been re-used by later restorers (P.H. 57, xxvii.). The ancient name of the town, *Shed*, means the rescued or extracted, and thus refers to the extraction or saving of the land from the lake. The former theory of Linant, that the Lake Moeris was on the high plateau, was founded on a misconception of the levels, and of the physical features of the country, and needs no further consideration. As the remains within the dam—or *in* Linant's lake— are of the XIIth dynasty, and the remains outside of the dam are all Greco-Roman, it is obvious that the inside must have been dry land, while the outside was the lake, until late times.

The celebrated Lake Moeris was then the natural basin of the Fayum oasis, regulated and utilised by Amenemhat III. The extent of the basin up to Nile level was such that its circuit was equal to the coastline of Egypt, according to Herodotos, and this was approximately the case. The supposed extension of it into other desert valleys to the south-west is impossible during historical times, as the hills rise above the Nile level between the two depressions.

In the Wady Hammamat, we find that Amenemhat sent out an expedition to get stone, in his nineteenth year, for his buildings in the Fayum (L.D. ii. 138 c, e), apparently for the temple of Sebek at Crocodilopolis. The party made a causeway to draw the stones upon, and brought a statue of five cubits high. In the second year is a record of the overthrow of the negroes, and opening up of the road of the Aamu (L.D. ii. 138 a). These expeditions continued to need considerable forces, as in that of the nineteenth year "multitudes of soldiers, even two thousand," are mentioned. At Koptos a colossal vulture in hard limestone was dedicated by Amenemhat, "beloved of Sekhet" (now in G. Mus.).

The great centres of Memphis, Abydos, and Thebes seem to have been passed over by the king, only a few private dedications being found there; and we next meet with Amenemhat at Hieraconpolis, where a black granite figure of his was found (G. Mus.; Rec. x. 139). On the opposite bank, at El Kab, was a stele in the forty-fourth year, concerning the building of a wall (W.G. 255).

At Aswan are several private tablets dated in this reign, but none of historical value (P.S. 84, 98, 151, 153, 154). A stele of an official named Usertesen, at Kuban, opposite Dakkeh in Nubia, belongs also to this date (L.D. ii. 138 g).

But at Semneh and Kummeh a most interesting series of inscriptions is found, brief though they are, recording the height of the Nile. The great waterworks of Amenemhat, for the regulation of the Nile by the intake and outflow at the Fayum, required an early notice of the rise and fall of the river; and official records were kept of it on the rocks, while probably the news would be sent down by some signals from hill to hill, till it reached the lower country. These registers of the high Nile (see L.D. ii. 139) involve a difficult question, as they are about twenty-five feet above the present level of the river (L.L. 510). As the mouth sign beginning the inscription is written, bisected by the upper line in some cases, it seems as if it were the actual water level, and not a record placed at some determinate height, of ten or twenty cubits measured by a cord above the torrent of the full stream; otherwise such an explanation might seem the most feasible, as it would be easier to mark rocks, and examine old marks, on some spot well above the water. Such a possibility needs consideration on the spot. Granting, however, that these are the actual levels, the only view seems to be that the Nile has eroded its bed a depth of twenty-five feet at that point. It has often been suggested that the breaking through of barriers at Silsileh, or at Aswan, might affect it; but as those places are two or three hundred feet lower level, any change there would be as imperceptible at Semneh as a lock on the lower Thames would be at Oxford. Moreover, the early graffiti and tombs at Silsileh and Aswan are only fairly above the river at present, and show that no great change has occurred there in historical times. The Semneh levels, then, must point to a lowering of the bed in Upper Nubia, apart from Lower Nubia and Egypt; and this might occur by two causes, either by the erosion of the bed, or else by a slight elevation of the southern end of Nubia, thus making the water pour faster out of its channel, and so lie at a lower level. The gradient of the water in Nubia does not appear to exceed thirty seconds of angle, and hence a minute angular tilt of the country might flood up the upper valley, or let the water run faster out of it. Until a critical examination is thoroughly made of all the remains—especially trifling graffiti along the banks—in Upper Nubia, this vexed question must remain in abeyance (see on this L.L. 507–532).

Of other remains of Amenemhat, there is a fine statue usurped by Merenptah, possibly from Tanis, like other such usurpations, now in Berlin (W.G. 260); and also another statue at St. Petersburg (Rec. xv. 136, i.–iv.); a headless sphinx of the Miramar collection (Cat. xxix.); a small hawk inscribed on the base (F.P. Coll.); and many scarabs, cylinders, etc. One is a document of interest, giving the list of the six kings of the dynasty down to this point, in their proper order (Brocklehurst Coll.). A statue of an official of this king was in the Sabatier Coll. (Rec. xiv. 55).

Of the close of this reign the highest date is the stele at El Kab of the forty-fourth year. But a papyrus from Kahun is dated in a forty-sixth year, which can hardly be that of any king but Amenemhat III., and hence it is likely that his reign extended so far. As to whether he associated Amenemhat IV. in coregency with him we cannot be certain. Such was the principle of this dynasty, especially in long reigns like this; yet there is no certain evidence at this point. Some monuments give the two cartouches side by side as equally adored, but there is no proof that either king was alive at the time, nor that both were alive (L.D. ii. 140 m; L.A. x.). On the whole, it is not improbable that Amenemhat IV. was associated for two or three years, but no double dating of this kind is yet known.

Of the family of Amenemhat, one daughter, Ptah·neferu, appears to have died before her father, having been buried in his pyramid. Her alabaster altar and dishes remain (G. Mus.; P.K. v.); and a block of black granite with her name and titles (Rec. x. 142). The other daughter, Sebek·neferu, succeeded her brother, Amenemhat IV., on the throne.

AMENEMHAT IV

XII. 7. MAĀ·KHERU·RA 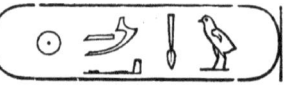 about 2578–2569 B.C.

AMENEMHAT IV.

Sarbut el Khadem	Tablets	(L.D. ii. 140 o, p).
Wady Maghara	Tablet	(L.D. ii. 140 n).
Kahun	Papyrus	(G.K. xxxiii.).
Shut er regal	Tablet	(P.S. 444).
Kummeh	Tablet	(L.D. ii. 152 f).

Paws of a sphinx, quartzite (G. Mus.).
Plaque (B. Mus.).
Scarabs (B. Mus., Louvre, F.P. Coll.).

FIG. 113.—Scarab (P. Mus.).

This reign shows the declension of the dynasty. The monuments are scanty and unimportant; they all fall, however, in the fifth and sixth year, which gives some reason to suppose a coregency in the earlier part of the nine years' reign.

At Sarbut el Khadem the *ka* name and the throne name occur in isolated fragments without longer inscription (L.D. ii. 140 o, p); while at Wady Maghara a short inscription is dated in the sixth year (140 n). The paws of a sphinx in yellow quartzite also bear his name (G. Mus.). The name does not appear at all at Hawara, which is rather strange, as that of Sebekneferu occurs sometimes in the temple. At Shut er Regal is a cartouche that may be of Amenemhat IV. (P.S. 444). At Kummeh a brief tablet of the fifth year records the rise of the Nile (L.D. ii. 152 f). One papyrus of Kahun is dated in the sixth year of the reign (G.K. xxxiii.). A plaque of green glazed schist (in the B. Mus.) bears the names of Amenemhat IV., with a cartouche Ameny; this may possibly be an associated prince, though scarcely the Ameny Ra· sankh·ab, the sixth of the next dynasty. Only four scarabs are known, one in B. Mus., one in F.P. Coll., and two in the Louvre.

XII. 8. SEBEK·NEFERU 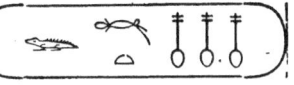 about 2569–2565 B.C.

Khataaneh   Sphinx (N.G. 9 c).
Hawara   Temple (L.D. ii. 140, F.P. Coll.).
Cylinder (B. Mus.); Scarab (G. Coll.).

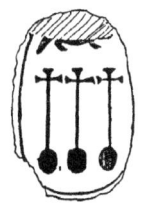

FIG. 114.—Scarab (G. Coll.).

Of this queen, stated by Manetho to have been the sister of Amenemhat IV., we have very slight remains. A sphinx of grey granular siliceous rock at Khataaneh has an effaced cartouche between the paws, which may be that of this queen; but the *ka* name is entirely gone, and the cartouche only shows traces of a Ra, a square sign (pedestal of the crocodile?), and three vertical lines. As no other cartouche agrees to this, it may be left to the credit of this queen.

At Hawara her name occurs as often as that of her father; as, beside the examples of Lepsius (L.D. ii. 140), a column (P.H. xxvii. 12) and a block (P.K. xi. 1) naming her have also been found there. How it is that she is associated with this temple, to the exclusion of her brother, is not clear; but the remains are so scanty that little can be argued about it.

FIG. 115.—Cylinder, blue on white (B. Mus.).

The finest small piece of the later part of the dynasty is, however, of this queen, a beautiful cylinder (Fig. 115) of white schist glazed blue, of unusual size, and bearing all her titles: "*Hor Ra·mert;* double diadem *Akhet kherp nebt taui; Hor nub Dad·kha; Suten bat* (Sebek·shedti·neferu) *ankh tha; Sebek shedti mery*" (B. Mus.).
A scarab of hers is also known (G. Coll.).

Before parting from the XIIth dynasty, one remarkable point should be noticed. The reigns are all long, and yet it is generally assumed that the kings were each sons of their predecessors. Though the time of life of association as coregent may have been very uncertain, yet on a series this vagueness is so subdivided that it does not much affect the question. Setting aside Amenemhat I., who fought his way to the throne probably late in life, the reigns of the other kings, from being coregent, to adopting a successor as coregent, are 42, 32, 26, 38 (?), 44 years; the average of the three certain ones at first is 33 years, or, including all of them, 36 years. Now, it is wholly unlikely that each of these kings had no son until they were so advanced in life. Either, then, their successors were not eldest sons, but only sons who were selected by the king as being most able, or sons of heiress-princesses; or else there have been several generations passed over, and grandsons were more usual as successors than direct sons. To reduce the average of 36 to the more likely average of 20 years, there must have been four grandsons adopted as coregents, passing over the direct sons. One clue to this peculiarity may lie in the female succession. There is some ground for supposing that the throne, like any other property, descended in the female line; and that the custom of brother and sister marriages arose from the desire that sons should inherit. If so, it is quite possible that the sons had no claim to the throne legally; but that the king had it in his choice to select the most suitable son or grandson, and by marrying him to a particular princess in the line, he thus created him the heir to the throne.

This great period of the XIIth dynasty is marked by somewhat the same characteristics as the first age of Egyptian development. It begins with a firm organisation of the country, and a solidity and brilliancy of work that shows great and able guidance; that is succeeded by a time of tranquil internal prosperity, under the second Amenemhat and Usertesen, as before under the Vth dynasty; and then comes the tide of foreign conquest under Usertesen III. as under Pepy I. A long and splendid reign of Amenemhat III. leads to a brief time of decay; much as the long reign of Pepy II. led to the disorganisation of the VIth dynasty. And in each case an age of short reigns, confusion, and weakness succeeds this outburst of ability. It is singular how parallel the two cycles of development run, one with another; but such seems to be much the course of government in its growth and fall in all ages; and growth, prosperity, foreign wars, glory, and decay succeed each other as the seasons of the great year of human organisation.

The work of this dynasty is among the finest. It could never profess the vitality of the early times, yet it showed a technical perfection and care which is perhaps unsurpassed. The sculptures of Amenemhat I. and Usertesen I. from Koptos, the sarcophagus of Usertesen II., and the tomb chamber of Amenemhat III., are as perfect in workmanship as anything wrought by man. It is much to be hoped that further exploration may reveal to us more of this brilliant age, and that the pyramids of other kings of this dynasty may be discovered.

The private works of this time are fine and substantial; though less spontaneous, they are yet superior to the sculptures of any time since the IVth dynasty, and mark the high level of technical and formal skill which was reached in this age.

CHAPTER IX

THIRTEENTH AND FOURTEENTH DYNASTIES

WE now reach the second of the two great periods of obscurity in Egyptian history. The dark age of the VIIth–XIth dynasties we have filled up to some extent, thanks to Eratosthenes and the scarabs, besides having the well-known list of a portion of it in the table of Abydos, and the fragmentary but useful statements in the Turin papyrus. For the period from the XIIIth to the XVIIth dynasty the materials are even less satisfactory. There is the Turin papyrus beginning in good condition, but becoming more and more broken, until dozens of names may be placed in almost any position. There is the wildly irregular list of Thothmes III. at Karnak. And there are various excerpts and summaries of Manetho by Josephus, Africanus, Eusebius, etc. Of monuments there are only scattered remains, and no contemporary evidence as to succession.

Two views have been held regarding the only series of names that is of use—the Turin papyrus. Brugsch adopts it as a continuous list of successive names, but Lieblein considers that it is compiled from six alternating sections of the kings of the XIIIth and XIVth dynasties. For this latter hypothesis there does not seem to be any sufficient ground. There could have been no reason for alternating the portions of the dynasties unless they were contemporary; if contemporary, they would be rival lines; and in the case of the IXth and Xth dynasties we see that rival lines are not reckoned in the Turin papyrus. We shall therefore treat the Turin papyrus as a consecutive record, so far as the terribly broken state of it permits ; and no arrangement of the pieces will be here adopted for which there is not good reason in the character of the writing (which varies in different parts), the spacing of the lines, the nature of the fibres, and the style and position of the lines of later accounts scribbled on the back of it. Where all these clues fail to show the order of the fragments, we shall state that the various pieces may be arranged in almost any order.

Before entering on the details of the names and reigns, it will be well to review the whole period from the XIIIth to the XVIIth dynasties, and so to see what is the general scheme of the evidence that we have.

For this the remains of Manetho are our only guide for the duration of the period. And we will first review them briefly in their most reliable forms, the text of Josephus, and the tables of Africanus and Eusebius.

AFRICANUS.			EUSEBIUS.			JOSEPHUS.
Dynasty.	Kings.	Years.	Dynasty.	Kings.	Years.	on Hyksos.
XIII.	60	453 or 153	XIII.	60	453	
XIV.	76	184	XIV.	76		484 (after confusion, at length they made a king).
XV. (Hyksos)	6	284	XV. (Theban)	*x*		250 Hyksos, 6 kings, 260 years.
XVI. (Shepherds)	32	518	XVI. (Theban)	5		190 (this people and their descendants in all 511 years).
XVII.	43	151	XVII. (Hyksos)	4	103	

Setting aside for the present the details of the reigns of the separate Hyksos kings, such are the materials for unravelling this period.

The Turin papyrus gives in many cases the length of the reigns, and the average of eleven reigns remaining is 6½ years each in the period of the first sixty kings, which is presumably the XIIIth dynasty. This points to about 390 years for the whole sixty kings, and agrees therefore with the 453 years far better than with the reading 153 years. In fact, deducting the 71 years of eleven kings from 153 years, there would only be left 82 years for forty-nine kings, which would be certainly unlikely. We may then adopt the reading 453 years as far the more probable.

The next question is, were the Hyksos contemporary with the XIIIth and XIVth dynasties? So far as the XIIIth, the distribution of the monuments of the first sixty kings of the Turin papyrus seems to show that they held all Egypt. The fifteenth king is found at Semneh and at Bubastis, the twenty-third at Tanis and in Ethiopia, and the fifty-third is Ra·nehesi, who is believed to be related to the king's son Nehesi found at Tanis, and the king Nehesi found at Tell Mokdam. We cannot then suppose the Hyksos to have been contemporary with the 453 years of the XIIIth dynasty. Probably the limit of the XIIIth dynasty is at the mark of a new section beginning at No. 56 in T.P., as two or three kings may have been omitted in this numbering.

The whole Hyksos period is stated at 511 years by Manetho, according to Josephus, and is divided into three stages. First, "they had our rulers in their hands . . . and inflicted every barbarity." Next, "At length they made one of themselves king," and the six reigns occupying 260 years are specified. Then "these six were the first rulers amongst them," and the "shepherd kings and their descendants retained possession of Egypt 511 years." Here there is first a period of harrying and plundering the native rulers; second, a fixed Hyksos rule, well organised and long-lived; third, the rule of their descendants, extending altogether to a dominion of 511 years. This total period is terminated by the expulsion of the Hyksos, and the establishment of the XVIIIth dynasty.

Now, the essential difference between the summaries of Africanus and Eusebius is, that the latter puts the Hyksos at the end of the dark period; while Africanus inserts them between the XIVth and XVIIth dynasties. As the account of Eusebius does not agree with Josephus, while that of Africanus agrees in the number of Hyksos kings and their reigns, it appears that Africanus is the better guide. His XVIth dynasty is, however, evidently the summary of the whole Hyksos period, 518 years, according with the 511 of Josephus; and therefore including the 284 years stated before it, and the 151 years stated after it. The XVIIth dynasty of Africanus seems to be corrupt as to the number of kings, stated as forty-three shepherd kings and forty-three Thebans, who reigned together 151 years. The equality of the numbers shows some corruption, and the reigns are very short.

Some clue in this confusion may be reached by seeing what dynasties will agree to the total Hyksos period. The last 151 years of the Hyksos appears to have been a joint rule of Hyksos suzerains and Egyptian vassals, as shown in the tale of Apepa and Seqenenra. There will therefore be 260 years of the great Hyksos kings, and 151 years of their descendants, making 411 years of their kings altogether. This would leave a round hundred years, out of the total of 511, for the confused period of their harrying of the Egyptians; as that was probably an indefinite period, of a gradual increase of power, it is very likely to have been put roundly at one century, which, added to the reigns of 411, made 511 years' total, or 518 years, according to Africanus.

How, then, does this stand in relation to Egyptian reigns? The 151 years at the end is a joint rule during the XVIIth dynasty. But what went on during the six great Hyksos kings and the confusion before them? Africanus gives no material here; but it seems not unlikely that the XVIth Theban dynasty of Eusebius refers to this age, five kings reigning 190 years, as we see that his XVth dynasty is apparently intended for the XVth dynasty of the six great Hyksos. This 190 years occurs in the old Egyptian chronicle in Syncellus as of eight kings, which is rather a more likely number. This, then, is the material which, on the Egyptian side, makes up the period of Hyksos rule.

About B.C.	EGYPTIANS.		HYKSOS.		About B.C.
2565					
2112	XIII. 60 kings, 453 years.				2098
1928	XIV. 76 kings, 184 ⎫		confusion 100 years. ⎫		1998
1738	XVI. 8 kings, 190 ⎬ 525		XV. 6 kings, 260 ⎬ 511		1738
1587	XVII. *x* kings, 151 ⎭		XVII. *x* kings, 151 ⎭		1587

Such seems, from this very confused material, to be the most likely original statement. If this be so, Africanus has formed his digest thus —

        His XIIIth is the Egyptian XIIIth.
        ,, XIV   ,,   Egyptian XIV.
        ,, XV   ,,   Hyksos XV.
        ,, XVI   ,,   Hyksos total.
        ,, XVII ,,   joint   XVII.

Eusebius, on the other hand, has compiled thus—

        His XIIIth is the Egyptian XIIIth.
        ,, XIV   ,,   Egyptian XIV.
        ,, XV   ,,   Hyksos XV. (called Theban, as they
                                    ruled over Thebes).
        ,, XVI   ,,   Egyptian XVI.
        ,, XVII ,,   joint   XVII.

Josephus has neglected the Egyptians altogether, and given only the Hyksos material, according to his object. The practical equivalence of the 511 years of the Hyksos, the 518 years in Africanus, and the 525 years of the three Egyptian dynasties, is our best clue through this tangle; and the small differences between these amounts may readily be accounted for by the count of 100 years in round numbers for the confusion beginning the Hyksos domination, and by some one king being reckoned as independent at the beginning of the XIVth or end of the XVIIth dynasty.

If we accept the above settlement, we may divide the periods thus in detail—

XIII.—60 kings, 453 years
XIV.—76 kings { 14 years before Hyksos
                100 years harried by the Hyksos
                70 years under the great Hyksos } 260 yrs. } 511 yrs.
XVI.— 8 kings, 190 years ,,   ,,   ,,
XVII.— x kings, 151 years' struggles with Hyksos

This arrangement is corroborated by a fragment of the Turin papyrus, which has been certainly misplaced hitherto; it is numbered 32, but cannot belong to the IVth dynasty (where it has been placed), both by the lengths of the reigns, and by the part of a name .....*zefa*. Nor can it be placed at any other part of the papyrus until we reach the end of the XIVth dynasty. Here are met a few other fragments which agree with it in the spacing, the writing, and the plain back (122, 133, 135). And in the XIVth dynasty before it are at least three kings ending in .....*zefa*, so that the type of name was not then uncommon. The lengths of reigns also accord better with this age of the XVIth dynasty than with any other unsettled period. The numbers are 6, 6, 24, 24, 21, 8 years. The 6 year reigns might be the end of the XIVth dynasty; and if four reigns occupy 77 years, that would leave 113 years for the remaining four reigns in the XVIth dynasty; not at all an unlikely number, when we have two of 24 years already here before us.

Until, then, some further material may come to light, it does not seem that we can do better than accept provisionally the arrangement which we have here outlined. And on this basis we shall now proceed to deal with the details of this period.

XIIIth dynasty, about 2565–2112 B.C.
According to the Turin papyrus.
"Mon." refers to account of monuments, following this.

		YEARS.
1	Ra·khu·taui	
2	Ra·sekhem·ka . Mon.	6
3	Ra·amen·em·hat	
4	Ra·s·hotep·ab	
5	Aufni	
6	⎧ Ra·s·ankh·ab . Mon. ⎨ (Ameny Antef Amenemhat)	
7	Ra·s·men·ka	
8	Ra·s·hotep·ab . Mon.	
9	........ka	
10	Ra·nezem·ab	
11	Ra·sebek(hote)p Mon.	
12	Ren·senb	
13	Ra·fu·ab . . Mon.	
14	Ra·sezef (a·ab)	
15	⎧ Ra·sekhem·khu·taui ⎨ Sebek·hotep (I.) Mon.	
16	Ra·user......ra	
17	⎧ Ra(smenkh)ka . Mon. ⎨ Mer·meshau	
18	⎧ ....ka ⎨ Anu	
19	..user·ur..	
20	⎧ Ra(sekhem·suaz·taui) ⎨ Sebek·hotep (II.) Mon.	3
21	⎧ Ra·kha·(seshes) . Mon. ⎨ Nefer·hotep	11
22	Ra·hat·heru·sa	
23	⎧ Ra·kha·nefer . Mon. ⎨ Sebek·hotep (III.) [Brugsch supposes two lost here, namely Ra·kha·ka	
24	⎧ Ra·kha·ankh ⎨ Sebek·hotep (IV. ?) ⎧ Ra·kha·hotep . Mon. ⎨ Sebekhotep (V. ?) 4y. 8m. 29d.	

		YEARS.
25	⎧ Ra·uah·ab . . Mon. ⎨ Aā·ab . 10y. 8m. 28d.	
26	⎧ Ra·mer·nefer . . Mon. ⎨ (Ay) . . 23y. 8m. 18d.	
27	Ra·mer·hotep Mon. 2y. 2m. 9d.	
28	⎧ Ra·sankh·n ⎨ Set hetu ? . 3y. 2m.	
29	⎧ Ra·mer·sekhem ? 3y. 1m. ⎨ An·ren	
30	⎧ Ra·suaz·ka . . 1+·y. ⎨ Hora	
31	.....m...... . . . 2+·y.	
32 to 35	lost.	
36	Ra·mer·kheper	
37	⎧ (Ra)·mer? ka . Mon. ⎨ (Sebek·hotep VI. ?)	
38	........ka	
39	Lost.	
40	......mes	
41	⎧ Ra...maāt . . Mon. ⎨ Aba .	
42	⎧ Ra...uben ⎨ Hora ?	
43	.....ka	
44	Ra...maā	
45	Ra	
46	....	
47	Ha..... ⎫
48	Sa ⎬ Fragments, 4 and 89
49	Hapu ⎬
50	Shemsu ⎬
51	Mena.... ⎬
52	Ur.... ⎭
53	Ra·nehesi . . Mon. ?	
54	Ra·kha·thi	
55	...neb·fu . . 1y. 5m. 15d.	

A fresh heading begins at the next entry; and as the above section contains nearly the number of kings (fifty-five or fifty-seven) in Manetho's XIIIth dynasty, it is probable that at this point is the end of this dynasty. The names that follow in the papyrus have a new type, three of them ending in ....zefa, which has not occurred in the foregoing part.

We shall now refer only to those kings of whom some remains are known; leaving, with the above mention, those who are only recorded in the Turin papyrus.

XIII. 2. SEKHEM·KA·RA   about 2560 B.C.

A stele naming this king was found, probably at Benha, and subsequently copied by Brugsch at Alexandria (B.T. 1455); its place is now unknown. It is a tablet of a noble, a king's son, named Mery·ra (perhaps the same of whom a scarab remains, P.I. viii. 40). On the upper part a Nile figure kneels, offering vases bearing *ankh·ded·uas* to the hawk on the *ka* name, *S·ankh· taui*: the cartouche of Sekhem·ka·ra comes next to this. His third year is named on a papyrus from Kahun (G.K. ix.).

XIII. 6. SANKH·AB·RA   about 2520 B.C.

AMENY·ANTEF·AMEN·EM·HAT

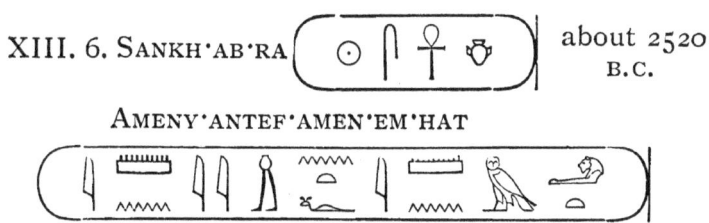

Of this king a noble table of offerings was found at Karnak. It consists of two square blocks of quartzite, carved with twenty small cup hollows in rows on the top, and bearing the various titles and names of the king around the sides (G. Mus.; M.K. ix.–x.).

XIII. 8. RA·SEHOTEP·AB 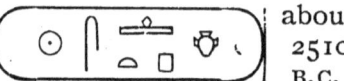 about 2510 B.C.

Some scarabs bearing this name (P. Mus.; F.P. Coll.) are so rude in workmanship that they cannot be assigned to the reign of Amenemhat I., in which fine work prevailed.

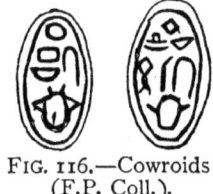

FIG. 116.—Cowroids (F.P. Coll.).

XIII. 11. RA SEBEK·HOTEP  about 2490 B.C.

Two scarabs of this king are known (F.P. and H. Colls.).

FIG. 117.—Scarabs (F.P. and H. Colls.).

XIII. 13. RA·FU·AB

The pyramid of this king has been identified this year with the south brick pyramid of Dahshur. In this was found the coffin and an ebony statue of this king. Near this pyramid was the tomb of a princess, Nub·hetep·ta·khrudet, found intact with all the furniture. Particulars have not yet been published.

XIII. 15. RA·SEKHEM·KHU·TAUI

SEBEK·HOTEP I.   about 2460 B.C.

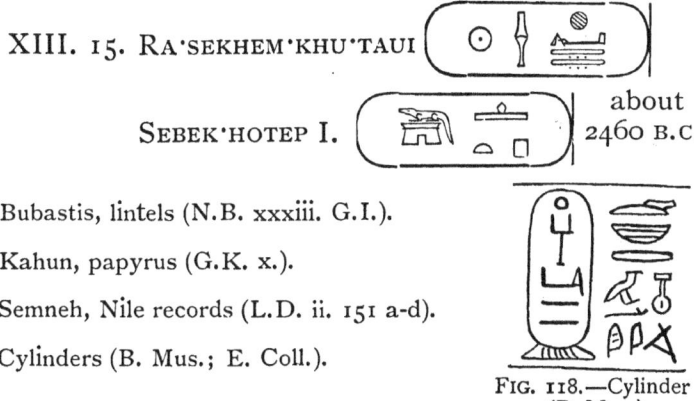

Bubastis, lintels (N.B. xxxiii. G.I.).

Kahun, papyrus (G.K. x.).

Semneh, Nile records (L.D. ii. 151 a-d).

Cylinders (B. Mus.; E. Coll.).

FIG. 118.—Cylinder (B. Mus.).

This king appears as a builder at Bubastis, two lintel blocks bearing his name. At Kahun a papyrus was found dated in his third year. The records of the high Nile at Semneh are of each year to the fourth. And some cylinders bear his throne name; while many scarabs inscribed only Sebekhotep are probably of his age.

XIII. 17. RA·SMENKH·KA

MER·MESHAU   about 2450 B.C.

Two large statues of grey syenite at Tanis bear these names (P.T. I. iii. 16). They are finely and massively executed, and differ much in style from the slender and shallow work in red granite of Sebekhotep III.; but this difference of style is easily due to the different local schools of art at different quarries. The statues were afterwards appropriated by Apepa, who carved his name on the arm (P.T. I. xiii. 6). There is some doubt as to the position of the king represented by these statues. In the Turin papyrus this No. 17 has only *ka* left at the end of the cartouche, and following it *mer-mesha*, as the personal name or title. As that, however, was a common military title, and also the title of the high priest of Mendes, there might be more than one king so called. On the other hand, a later king, No. 79, is named *Ra·smen* . . . .; but he is not so likely to have erected statues, as by that time the Hyksos were in the land, and it is rather in the first fifty-five names that this must be sought, though it might be any one of ten missing names in this period.

FIG. 119.—Grey syenite statue of Mermeshau, Tanis.

On the whole, it is probable that the seventeenth king is the one represented. Whether he were a general or the high priest has been debated; but as on the statues he is said to be loved of Ptah, and not of the Mendesian Ba·neb·dad, he is more likely to have been a general.

XIII. 20.
RA·SEKHEM·SUAZ·TAUI

SEBEK·HOTEP II.

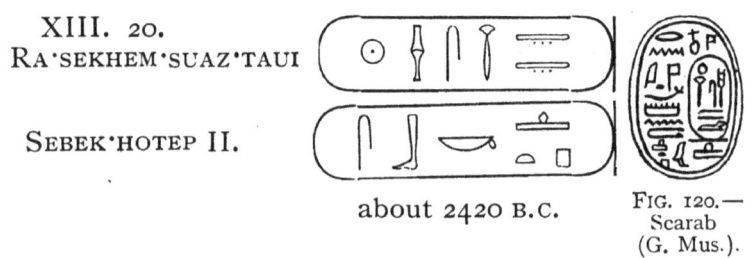

about 2420 B.C.

FIG. 120.—
Scarab
(G. Mus.).

This king is known on monuments with these two names; but of the first cartouche only the Ra is certain in the Turin papyrus, and the rest is blotted and broken. As, however, there is no other Sebekhotep without a fixed place in the papyrus, it is probable that this position No. 20 belongs to this king. His principal monument is a stele bearing his names in the Louvre (Pr. M. viii.) (Fig. 121); the scene represents two deceased daughters of a king adoring Min. They are Auhet·abu and Anqet·dudu, born of the queen Nen·na. What relation they were to the king Sebekhotep II. is not stated. They can hardly have been his sisters, as his mother is stated on the scarabs to have been Auhet·abu, and not Nen·na. But they might have been his daughters or aunts. It has been supposed that this deceased Auhet·abu is the same as his mother, but in that case she would certainly have been given the higher title of royal mother, and not only royal daughter.

More is recorded of the family on scarabs, and on a tablet at Vienna (Rec. vii. 188). From

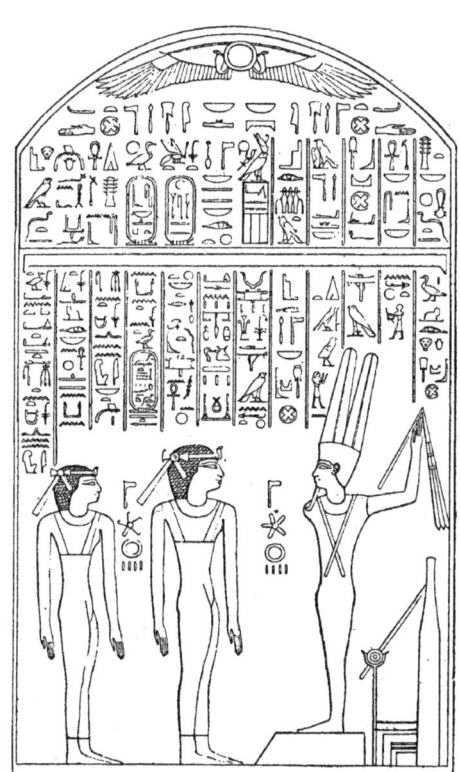

FIG. 121.—Stele of Sebekhotep II. Royal daughters adoring Min.

these we learn that the parents of Sebekhotep II. were the divine father Mentuhotep (P. Mus.; G. Mus.), and the royal mother Auhet·abu (G. Mus.; M. Coll.). The tablet is of a prince Senb, whose parents were likewise

Mentuhotep and the king's mother Auhet·abu, pretty certainly the same persons. Further, the children of Senb are stated as Sebekhotep, Auhet·abu, Hent, and Mentuhotep.

This king is mentioned in the tomb of Sebek·nekht at El Kab, as having given lands to the temple at that place (L.D. iii. 13 b).

XIII. 21. RA·KHA·SESHES

about 2410 B.C.

NEFER·HOTEP

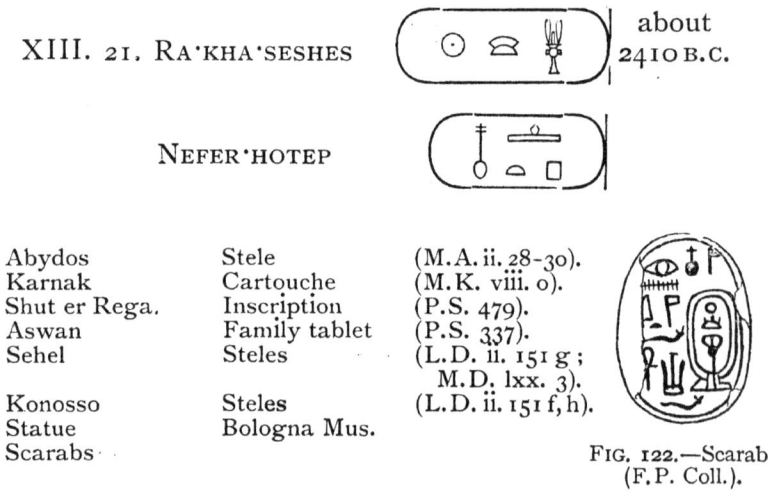

Abydos	Stele	(M.A. ii. 28-30).
Karnak	Cartouche	(M.K. viii. o).
Shut er Rega.	Inscription	(P.S. 479).
Aswan	Family tablet	(P.S. 337).
Sehel	Steles	(L.D. ii. 151 g ; M.D. lxx. 3).
Konosso	Steles	(L.D. ii. 151 f, h).
Statue	Bologna Mus.	
Scarabs		

FIG. 122.—Scarab (F.P. Coll.).

The large stele of this king found at Abydos records his sending to repair the temple there according to the directions of the sacred books, and to learn the will of the god ; for when he had unrolled and read the writings, he desired to honour the god according to all that he had seen in the books. There is some reason to suspect from the style of this stele that it may not be really of this age ; and the matter of it is so likely to have served to excite the liberality of some later king, that we may pause before fully accepting it. One small point is of value, that the king sends a messenger southward to Abydos, which suggests that the XIIIth dynasty did not live at Thebes. It is possible, as Sebek was constantly adored by them, and the statue of Neferhotep calls him beloved of Sebek in the midst of Shed (or Crocodilopolis), that the seat of government was really in the Fayum; having remained there since the close of the XIIth dynasty, the remains of which time are mainly in that province. A smaller stele found at Abydos shows Neferhotep before the god Min (M.A. 768).

A block at Karnak, which bears the cartouches of both Neferhotep and Sebekhotep III. (M.K. viii. n, o) shows that very probably they were coregents. We know from the scarabs that the father of each of these kings bore the same name, Ha·ankh·f, and the mother of a Sebekhotep was Kema, like the mother of Neferhotep. Hence we can hardly doubt that they were brothers. But two rock inscriptions at Aswan (P.S. 337) and Sehel (M.D. lxx. 3) record more of the family. From these we gather that Ha·ankh·f and Kema were the parents of Neferhotep; that Senbsen was his wife, and that there were four royal children, Hat·hor·sa, Sebekhotep, Ha·ankh·f, and Kema. The repetition of family names leaves the relationships dubious. We can only state them thus—

Fig. 123.—Statuette of Neferhotep.

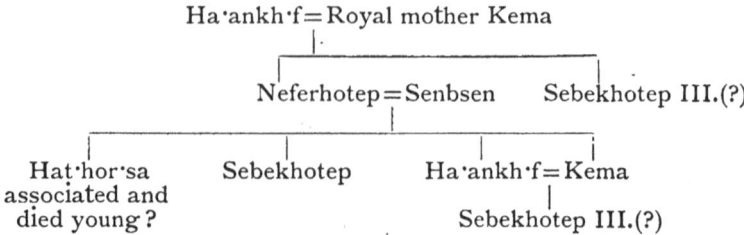

leaving yet unsettled the question of whether Sebekhotep III. was brother or grandson of Neferhotep.

At Shut er Regal, near Silsileh, is a cartouche of

Fig. 124.—Black basalt statuette of Neferhotep (Bologna Mus.).

Neferhotep; and at Sehel and Konosso, at the First Cataract, are other steles which only show Neferhotep with Anqet, Min, and Sati.

An excellent work of this reign is the seated statuette of black basalt in the Bologna Museum (Figs. 123, 124). It has the old traditions of Egyptian statuary, but with a certain weakness and youthfulness of expression which is different from any earlier works. In this it shows kinship to the large statues of the other brother, Sebekhotep III.

The scarabs of Neferhotep confirm the parentage reported by the tablet at Aswan, but are not of further interest.

XIII. 23. RA·KHA·NEFER about 2400 B.C.

SEBEKHOTEP (III.)

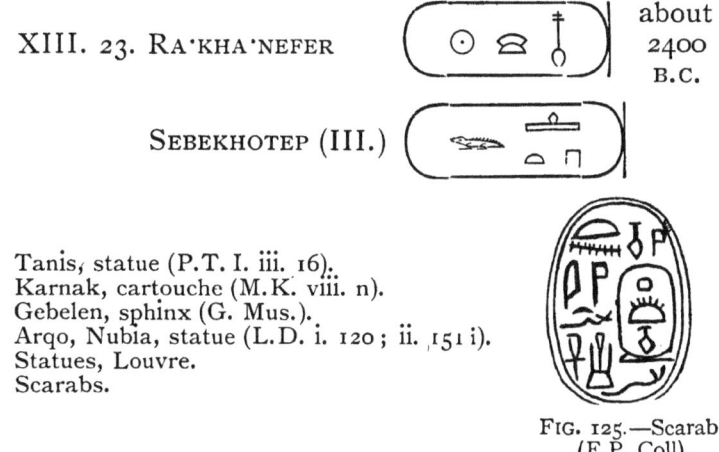

Tanis, statue (P.T. I. iii. 16).
Karnak, cartouche (M.K. viii. n).
Gebelen, sphinx (G. Mus.).
Arqo, Nubia, statue (L.D. i. 120; ii. 151 i).
Statues, Louvre.
Scarabs.

FIG. 125.—Scarab (F.P. Coll).

The remains of this king are more widespread than those of any other reign in this dynasty. A fine statue in brown-red granite lies at Tanis (Fig 126) (P.T. I. iii. 16); and a fellow-statue of double life size in the Louvre, of uncertain source, probably came from the same place. There is also a statue almost life size in black granite (P. Mus.). These statues are finely and gracefully wrought, but without the vigour of earlier work, or even of the Mer·meshau statue carved shortly before them; and as they have never been usurped by any king, they have not been brought at a later date from elsewhere. A small sphinx of black granite was found at Gebelen (G. Mus.).

The cartouche occurs at Karnak (M.K. viii. n) with that of Neferhotep, as we have noticed before. And there was found also an adoration to this king from a *mer·meshau* named Amenemhat (M.K. viii. p).

But the most astonishing remains of this dynasty are

FIG. 126.—Red granite statue of Sebekhotep III., Tanis.

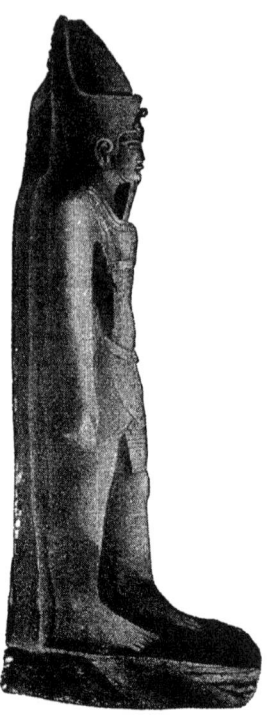

FIG. 127.— Grey granite colossus of Sebekhotep III., Island of Arqo.

the statues lying on the island of Arqo above the Third Cataract (see Hoskins' Ethiopia, p. 213). These are two colossi of grey granite, 23 feet high, lying upon their backs, one of them yet whole (Fig. 127). One is inscribed with the full names and titles of this king (L.D. i. 120; ii. 51 i). A remarkable point of decoration is a wreath around the top of the crown of Lower Egypt on one statue; such is unknown on any other Egyptian figure. These figures cannot have been brought up the cataracts, and must therefore have been cut in Upper Nubia, probably in a quarry at Tombos. They formed part of a temple there, of which some figures of baboons yet remain, together with a seated statue of Sebekhotep with inscriptions. There is then the proof that as late as the middle of the XIIIth dynasty the Egyptians held the country far above Semneh, which had been the frontier of the XIIth dynasty. With power thus widely extended, we see no sign of foreign invasion, nor of internal weakness. Why it is that there are so few remains of this dynasty must rather be attributed to the lack of taste for building than to the lack of power.

The scarabs of Sebekhotep III. are common, and usually combine both of his names.

RA·KHA·KA 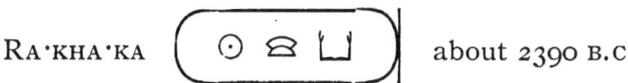 about 2390 B.C.

In the table of Karnak, amid the originally confused and now fragmentary sequences of that record, there occur in successive order Ra·sankh·ab, Ra·sekhem·khu·taui, Ra·sekhem·suaz·taui? ; Ra·kha·seshes, and Ra·kha·nefer, or the 6th, 15th, 20th, 21st, and 22nd kings of the Turin papyrus; then comes a lost piece which is restored by Lepsius as Ra·kha·ka, though as that part was missing even when Burton made his copy early in this century, it is difficult to know on what ground Lepsius—or L'Hote, from whom he copied—ventured on this restoration. Coming to the next line, we see Ra·kha·ankh, Ra·kha·(hotep?), and then three kings which cannot be identified in this part of the Turin list, before reaching Ra·mer·kau, the 37th king of Turin. This discrepancy shows that we cannot assign much weight, even in a favourable passage, to the sequence in the Karnak list. However, on the strength of that list, Brugsch has inserted two kings, Ra·kha·ka and Ra·kha·ankh (Sebekhotep) at the foot of the broken column of the Turin papyrus, ending now at No. 23, before the next column begins at No. 24.

The best ground for this is the difficulty of finding any other place for Ra·kha·ankh among the known names of the Turin papyrus; but as at least half a dozen names are wholly lost out of the XIIIth dynasty, that matter might easily have another resolution. All we can say is that this king belongs to some position before the decadence of the dynasty, and that the Karnak list suggests the place for him, and also for a king Ra·kha·ka, if the restoration of Lepsius has any authority.

Of Ra·kha·ka there is one scarab (F.P. Coll.), which can hardly be attributed to the other king of that name in the preceding dynasty, as it is coarsely made of pottery.

FIG. 128.—Scarab (F.P. Coll.).

RA·KHA·ANKH 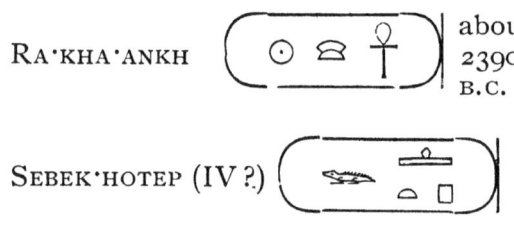 about 2390 B.C.

SEBEK·HOTEP (IV?)

FIG. 129.—Scarab (G. Coll.).

Koptos, part of stele.
Stele, Leyden.
Slabs from temple (P. Mus.; B 4, 5; C 9, 10).
Scarab (G. Coll.).
Queen? Nub·em·hat.
Daughter? Sebek·em·heb.

At Koptos a fragment of a private stele names the king's daughter Sebek·em·heb, whose mother (?) was the great royal wife Nub·em·hat, and mentions the *Hor sam taui*, apparently Sebekhotep IV. still living; the inscription is for Per·nub, who seems to have been the daughter of the son of a royal courtier Amena, who was son of a queen Ha·ankh·s. This would put Ha·ankh·s about two or three generations before

Sebekhotep IV., and thus she might be of the same age as Ha·ankh·f, the father of Sebekhotep III.

Four slabs sawn from the building of some temple are in the Louvre, on which the king is shown offering to Min and Ptah. A stele is also in Leyden, and one rude scarab is known (G. Coll.).

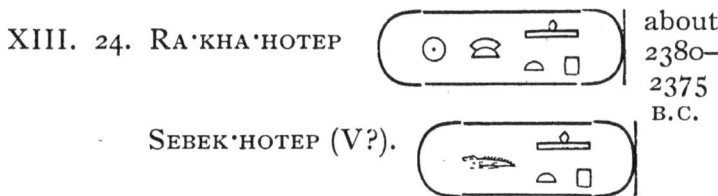

XIII. 24. RA·KHA·HOTEP   about 2380–2375 B.C.

SEBEK·HOTEP (V?).

Of this king only two scarabs are known; they are of the same type, with throne name and personal name, thus proving the cartouches to be of one king (P. Mus.; G. Mus.).

FIG. 130.—Scarab (G. Mus.).

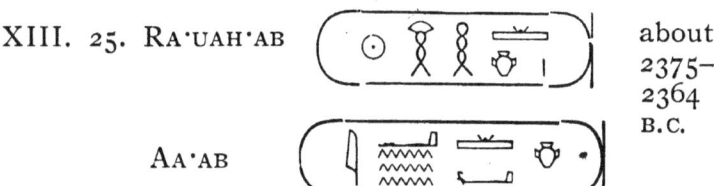

XIII. 25. RA·UAH·AB   about 2375–2364 B.C.

AA·AB

A cylinder of this king, naming him "beloved of Sebek, lord of Su·uaz" (G. Coll.), and a scarab (F.P. Coll.) are known. Also a piece of blue glazed cup from Kahun with the beginning of a royal name Ra·uah .... is probably of this reign (P.K. x. 72).

FIG. 131.—Scarab (F. P. Coll.).

XIII. 26.
RA·MER·NEFER

AY

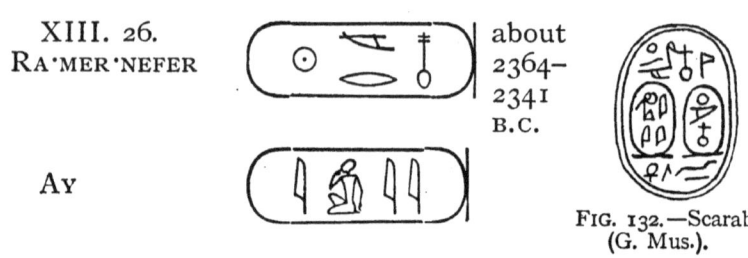

about
2364–
2341
B.C.

FIG. 132.—Scarab
(G. Mus.).

Here again scarabs are the only memorial. A few bear the throne name, and one (in G. Mus.) has both names.

XIII. 27.
RA·MER·HOTEP

ANA

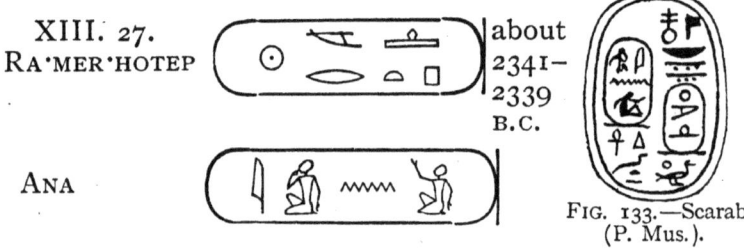

about
2341–
2339
B.C.

FIG. 133.—Scarab
(P. Mus.).

One scarab in the Louvre is the only contemporary object bearing the names of this king.

XIII. 37. RA·MER?KAU

SEBEKHOTEP (VI. ?).

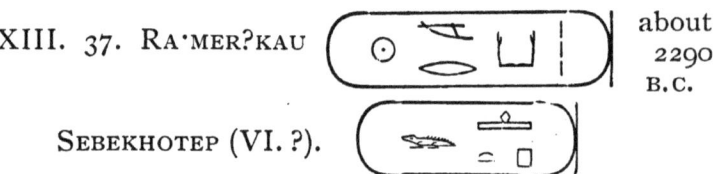

about
2290
B.C.

Of this king there is only a seated porphyry statue at Karnak, and no other remains (M.K. viii. 6).

XIII. 41.
RA·NEB·MAAT
about 2260 B.C.

ABA

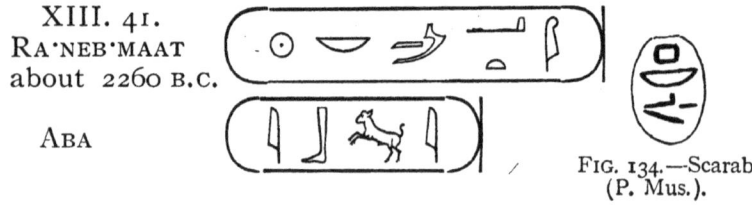

FIG. 134.—Scarab
(P. Mus.).

One scarab may be attributed to this period by the style of it, and there is no other name but the broken Ra . . . maāt in the Turin list to which it can be referred.

XIII. 47–52. This fragment (No. 41) of the Turin papyrus has hitherto been unplaced, or rather hopelessly misplaced in the VIth dynasty. There is no position possible for it until we reach this point, which the style of the writing on the back would indicate. A fragment placed in this column by the restorers (No. 89) would fit No. 41 well in the spacing of lines on both sides, and their relative positions. The names on this are of a peculiar type; they are simple personal names, but revert to the most high-flown origin, recalling the god Hapi, the Shemsu-hor, king Mena, and "the great" somebody. In the names shortly before this we see the same brief style, Aba and Hora: so that we might regard these as the last efforts to retain some dignity in an expiring dynasty, who had not even the heart to adopt the Ra names and full royal title; somewhat like the Roman Empire closing with a Julius and a Romulus before its extinction in the barbarian flood.

XIII. 53. Nehesi, the successor of these kings, appears to have been a negro; either a conqueror from the south, which is hardly likely, as his remains are in the extreme north; or more probably a Sudani slave or soldier raised into power, as the only hope of an expiring rule. In the list of Turin we read No. 53 as Ra·nehesi. On the statue from Tell Mokdam near Bubastis M. Naville has read the name of the king as Nehesi, or "the negro" (N.A. iv. 28). On a piece of an obelisk at Tanis (P.T. I. iii. 19) "the king's eldest son Nehesi" is twice named, as erecting monuments to Set. And a scarab remains of "the king's son Nehesi" (Brent Coll.) (Fig. 135).

FIG. 135.—Scarab (Brent Coll.).

Before entering on the XIVth dynasty, we must notice some kings whose names remain on monuments, but whose historical position is doubtful. Some of these kings were apparently powerful, and have left respectable remains; and the question is whether they belong to the gaps in the XIIIth dynasty, and are lost from the Turin papyrus, or whether they were among the long-reigned kings of the XVIth dynasty. The connection of name with that of Rahotep, who is again connected by his titles with the early XVIIIth dynasty, seems to point to all these belonging to the lost XVIth Egyptian dynasty under the great Hyksos kings.

In the XIIIth dynasty, however, there are seventeen kings out of forty-six known names to whom some remains can be assigned, or about one monumental king in three names; and about nine or ten names are almost entirely lost, which might therefore well include three or four monumental kings. Hence there is fairly room in the gaps of the Turin papyrus of the XIIIth dynasty for most of the following names, which are here ranked in order of their importance.

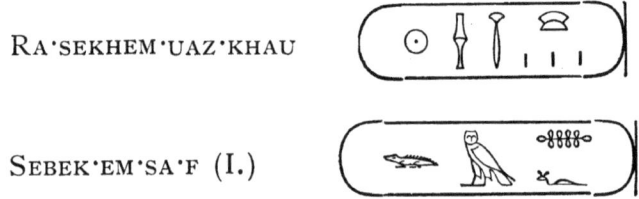

RA·SEKHEM·UAZ·KHAU

SEBEK·EM·SA·F (I.)

A standing statue of red granite three-quarters life size was found at Abydos (G. Mus.), with the names of this king (M.A. ii. 26); and a relief sculptured on the block by the legs, shows his son Sebekemsaf as deceased, which proves that this was not the son known as Sebekemsaf II. Another and smaller seated

SEBEK·EM·SA·F I

figure of the king in black basalt, was probably found at Thebes (Fig. 136); it is headless, but bears the king's names down the front of the throne. The work is cold and formal, and the signs rudely marked (F.P. Coll.; P.S. xxi. 2).

Two steles in the Wady Hammamat show the king adoring Min, and bear both of his cartouches (L.D. ii. 151, k, l). And at Shut er Regal the cartouche also occurs (P.S. 385). Some objects from the royal tomb have come to light, through Arab hands; a heart scarab (B. Mus.), a box (Leyden Mus.), and a gold plated scarab with the personal name, probably of this king (H. Coll.).

FIG. 136.—Basalt statuette of Sebekemsaf. Thebes (F.P. Coll.).

RA·SEKHEM·S·SHEDI·TAUI

SEBEK·EM·SAUF (II.)

This king is only known from the Abbott and Amherst papyri, which record the official inquiry concerning the royal tombs in the XXth dynasty. In the Abbott papyrus we read: "It was found that the thieves had violated the tomb by undermining the chamber of the ground level of the pyramid, from the great exterior chamber of the sepulchre of the overseer of the granaries, Neb-Amen, of the king Men·kheper·ra. The place of sepulture of the king was found to be void of its occupant; so was the place of sepulture of the principal royal spouse, Nub·kha·s, his royal wife; the thieves had laid hands on them" (R.P. xii. 106). The Amherst papyrus gives the confession which was afterwards extracted from one of the thieves. He states that they broke into the passage, and found the tomb "protected and surrounded by masonry and covered with roofing; we destroyed it completely, and found them (the king and queen) reposing. We opened their sarcophagi and their coffins in which they were. We found the august mummy of the king with his divine axe beside him, and many amulets and ornaments of gold about his neck. His head was overlaid above with gold, and the august body of the king was wholly covered with gold; his coffins were burnished with gold and silver, within and without, and inlaid with all kinds of stones. We took the gold which we found on the august mummy of the god, and the amulets and ornaments that were about his neck and the coffins in which he lay. Having also found the royal wife, we likewise took all that which we found with her; and we set fire to their coffins, and stole their furniture which we found with them, vases of gold, of silver, and of bronze, and divided them. We parted the gold which we found with the god, in their august mummies, the amulets, the ornaments, and the coffins, into eight lots" (C.E. ii. 9–12). We have here the example of what has gone on in all ages in the tombs of the kings and great men of Egypt. From the Abbott papyrus we learn that Nub·kha·s was the queen of Sebek·em·sauf, and can date a stele in the Louvre which is dedicated in the name of the "great heiress, the greatly favoured, the ruler of all women, the great royal wife, united to the crown, Nub·kha·s" (P.R.

SEBEK·EM·SAUF II

ii, 5). This stele gives an interesting family genealogy of the queen. She was daughter of the chief of the judges, Sebekdudu; and he appears to have had four wives. The more important part of the family stands thus—

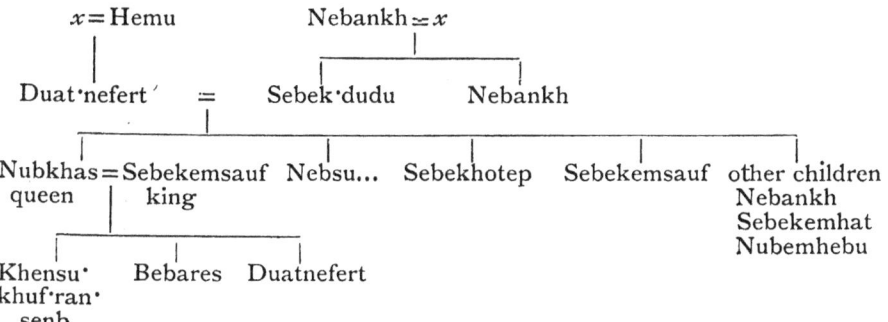

By a wife, Hemtsuten, Sebekdudu had Theti·antef.

By a wife, Dudut, Sebekdudu had Mentunesu and Hapiu.

By a wife, Senankh, Sebekdudu had Sebekhotep, who appears to have married his half-sister Hapiu, and had two children, Ada and Senankh, the latter of whom had a daughter Hapiu.

From the name of Sebek, and the use of *Shedi* by the second Sebekemsauf, it seems that these kings had their seat in the Fayum.

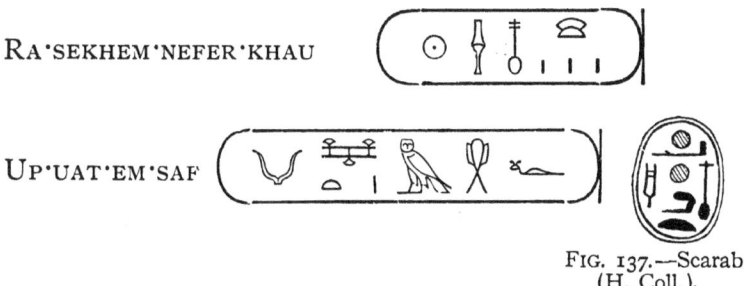

RA·SEKHEM·NEFER·KHAU

UP·UAT·EM·SAF

FIG. 137.—Scarab (H. Coll.).

This king is found on a stele formerly belonging to Harris (B. Mus.). And a scarab (H. Coll.) seems to bear the same name, with the addition of *Khe·ha*, which may be part of a *ka* name combined with it.

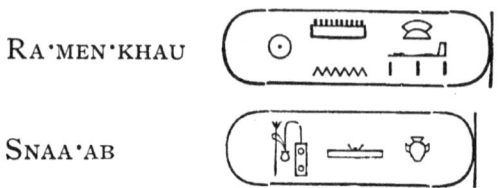

RA·MEN·KHAU

SNAA·AB

On a tablet found at Abydos (G. Mus.), this king is represented adoring Min (M.A. 771 ; ii. 27 b), but there is nothing to throw light on the age or connection of it. The style, however, is ruder than that of the other monuments of this dynasty.

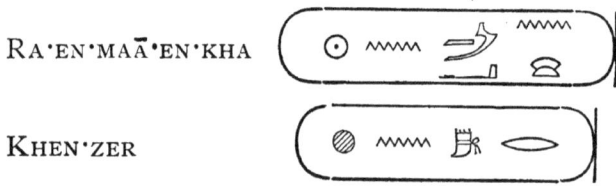

RA·EN·MAĀ·EN·KHA

KHEN·ZER

A stele bearing these two cartouches of one king is in the Louvre, recording the repairs of the temple of Usertesen I. at Abydos by Ameny-senb (C.E. iii. 2, 203 ; L.A. x.) (Fig. 138).

These five kings comprise all the unplaced ones that are likely to belong to the XIIIth dynasty.

The positions of these kings may well be either between Nos. 23 and 24, or in 31 to 35 of the Turin papyrus, but more cannot be said ; three of these ending in *Khau* suggests that they belong together, and links them with Rahotep.

FIG. 138.—Cartouches of Khen·zer (P. Mus.).

The name read Ra·sekhem·up·taui is probably

Sebekhotep I. misread ; Ra·nefer·kheper·ka is Tahutmes I. misread ; Ra·en·mut·er·ka is doubtful, and may be Ra·en·zer·ka.

XIVth Dynasty, about 2112–1928 B.C.

According to the Turin papyrus.

The numbering is consecutive with that of the XIIIth dynasty.

		YEARS.			YEARS.
56	Ra·seheb	3	82	to 86 (lost)	
57	Ra·mer·zefau	3+	87	Ra·snefer....	Mon.
58	Ra·senb·ka	1	88	Ra·men....	
59	Ra·ra·neb·zefau	1	89	...uah.....	
60	Ra·uben	4 ?	90	(lost)	
61	(lost)				
	(After this point the various fragments may be arranged in many ways, and have unknown spaces between them.)		91	(lost)	
			92	(lost)	
			93	?	
			94	A.....	
			95	A.....	
			96	...... ka	
62	.....zefa	4	97	(lost)	
63	.....uben		98	..... Hapu	
64	....ut·ab		99	..... ka Nenu	
65	Ra·her·ab		100	.....ka Bebnm....	
66	Ra·neb·sen		101	(lost)	
67	(lost)		102	Ra.......	
68	Ra...		103	Ra·ha.....	
69	Ra·skheper·en		104	Ra·ha.....	
70	Ra·dad·kheru		105	Ra·ses.....	
71	Ra·sankh....		106	Ra·neb·ati·au	
72	Ra·nefertum...		107	Ra·neb·ati·au	
73	Ra·sekhem.....		108	Ra·smen....	
74	Ra·ka.....ab ?		109	Ra·se·user	12
75	Ra·nefer·ab	Mon.	110	Ra·ha·shed.....	
76	Ra·a......				
77	Ra·kha.....		111	Ra·ha....	
78	Ra·ankh·ka.....	5	112	(lost)	
79	Ra·smen......				
80	(lost)		113	114 (lost)	

		YEARS.			YEARS.
115	R·a......		130	to 132 (lost)	
116	(lost)		133	(lost)	
	(Summation)		134	(lost) . . .	6
117	Ra·user.....		135	....zefa· . .	6
118	Ra·user.....		136	(lost) . . .	24
			137	(lost) . . .	24
119	120 (lost)		138	(lost) . . .	21
			139	(lost) . . .	8
121	A..f....		140	to 142 (lost)	
122	Set.....			(This last piece (frag. 32)	
123	Sunu....			has been formerly mis-	
124	Hor....			placed in the IVth	
				dynasty; but there is	
125	An·ab			no place possible for it	
126	Ra.....s			until we reach the long	
127	Penens..n sept			reigns of the XVIth	
128	Pedu nebti			dynasty; it appears to	
				join with fragments 122,	
129	.......heb·ra			133, and 135.)	
	(Summation ?)				

In these fragments is seen the same breakdown of the Ra names toward the close, and a reversion to private names alone, which we noticed before on a piece which is probably of the close of the previous dynasty. The fragments with names, 91 to 95 and 121–124, have been attributed to the Hyksos, apparently on the ground of the names beginning with Set.... and A.... (like Staan and Apepi); but as the other entries do not agree to the known Hyksos names, it seems probable that they may belong to the XIVth dynasty, when that was contemporary with Hyksos kings, and followed the style of their names.

We have already discussed the arrangement of the dynasties of this age, and will just recapitulate the order at which we arrived.

	EGYPTIANS.	HYKSOS.
XIV.	76 kings 14 years before Hyksos?	
	100 years harried by Hyksos	100 years' confusion
	70 years under great Hyksos ⎫	260 years. Great
XVI.	8 kings 190 years under great Hyksos ⎭	Hyksos kings.
XVII.	x kings 151 years struggles with Hyksos	151 years kings.

From this we gather that the average reigns of the XIVth dynasty were but two and a half years each; and the average of the thirteen reigns, assigned and unassigned, that remain in this latter part of the Turin papyrus is under three years, or, excepting one unusually long reign, it is two years. So the accordance of the average is very close, and gives us some confidence in Manetho's numbers of both years and kings. The total number of kings after the XIIIth is at least 85, and was probably about 110, in the Turin papyrus. This would accord to the $76 + 8 = 84$ kings of the XIVth and XVIth dynasties, with perhaps the other kings of the XVIIth dynasty.

Of only two kings of the XIVth dynasty can any remains be identified, namely, 75 Ra·nefer·ab. This cartouche is reported to have been copied on a stone in the mosque at Beni Ali (near Manfalut?) by Gliddon (MS. note by Dr. Birch); the *ka* name, though incompletely copied (..*u·taui*), is enough to show that this is not the name of Psamthek II. One scarab bears this name (T. Mus.) (Fig. 139).

FIG. 139.—Scarab (T. Mus.).

87 Ra·senefer. This may be the same king as on a scarab bearing Ra·senefer at Berlin.

Of other kings who belong to this period, some are known from the table of Karnak, which gives the kings of this age in the following order—

......ka	Turin list,	2 ?
Ra·suaz·en	,,	...
Ra·sankh·ab	,,	6
Ra·sekhem·khu·taui . .	,,	15
Ra·sekhem·suaz·taui ? . .	,,	20
Ra·kha·seshes . . .	,,	21
Ra·kha·nefer . . .	,,	23
Ra·kha·ka ? ? . . .	,,	23 a ?
Ra·kha·ankh	,,	23 b ?
Ra·kha (hotep ?) . . .	,,	24
Ra·snefer...	,,	87 ?
Ra...... . . .	,,	...
Ra·ses·user·taui . . .	,,	..
Ra·mer·kau . . .	,,	37

Ra·mer·sekhem		Turin list,	29
(Lost)		,,	...
Ra·sekhem·uaz·kau		,,	...
(Two lost) . . .		,,	...
Ra·khu·taui . . .		,,	1
Ra·mer·hotep . .		,,	27
Ra·suah·en . .		,,	...
Ra...uah·khau.	Sebekemsaf?	,,	...
(Three lost) . .		,,	...
Ra·za...... . .		,,	...
Ra·suaz·en . .		,,	...
Ra·snefer... . .		,,	87?
Ra..... . .		,,	...

We have here followed the lines of names in the reverse order to that in which they read, as this is evidently the sequence of the Sebekhotep family. The order seems, however, to be so wild in the later part that it is hopeless to trust to it for any historical ideas.

On scarabs we meet with one of these names, namely, Ra·suaz·en, on four scarabs of very rude work (B. Mus., P. Mus., Koptos, and Sayce). And some names are only known from scarabs, as—

Ra·nefer (common)
Ra·kheper
Ra·nefer·ankh
Ra·kha·neferui
Ra·neb·neferui
Ra·nub·neferui
{ Neferui·ka·dad·uah
{ Ka·ankh·et·nefer·kha
Uaz·neferui (vassal of the above)
Ra·nefer·nub
Ra·set·pehti
Ra·set·nub
Ra·peh·nub
Ra·nub·uaz
Ra·nub·hotep (common)

There are also many other groups of signs which may perhaps be personal names, or else merely ornaments or emblems. As these are already published (P. Sc.), it is not needful to go further into them.

An unanswered difficulty with regard to the XIVth dynasty is the position stated for its capital. Xois is

identified with Sakha, in the central Delta rather on the western side. How it came about that on the invasion of the country from the north-east, the native rulers should appear to have backed to the west, instead of retreating up the Nile valley,—how it was that they should have been known by the name of a Delta town in the region of the invaders, instead of a southern town such as Thebes or Aswan,—is a hard question. There are various solutions which should be kept in view, to see if any further light can be thrown on them.
(1) The dynasty may have originated at Xois, and have been dispossessed by the Hyksos southwards, holding yet a pre-eminence in the country above other native rulers as being the fighting frontier organisation to which others adhered. Thus it may not have ruled at Xois for any appreciable time, but have been a southern dynasty only starting from there. (2) Or the Hyksos may have overrun the country, and compelled the legitimate line to reside within their power in the Delta, so as to prevent revolt. (3) Or, as the Hyksos were a Syrian people not accustomed to wide rivers and marshes, it is possible that the lines of the Nile and canals were a better defence for the natives than any distance of retreat up the valley. At Sakha itself there are no signs of any important ancient town; and beyond one or two pieces of Roman work, it shows no antiquities; it might then be suspected that the real site of this dynasty was some southern city, the name of which was misread by Manetho, and converted into that of a town with which he must have been familiar, within a few hours' walk of his own home at Sebennytus. But no likely substitution can be suggested, such as that of Elephantine for Sakhebu in the Vth dynasty.

The nature of this dynasty, a long series of ephemeral rulers, reigning only two or three years on an average, is clearly artificial. They were, in fact, merely the puppets of the Hyksos power, the heads of the native administration which was maintained for taxing purposes; like the last Emperors of Rome, whose reigns also average two and a half years; or like the Coptic administration of Egypt, maintained during the supremacy of Islam as being the only practicable way of working the country. Later on, when the Hyksos had established a firm hold on all the land, and had a strong rule of their own, these native viceroys were permitted a longer tenure of power, and formed the XVIth dynasty contemporary with the great Hyksos kings.

CHAPTER X

FIFTEENTH TO SEVENTEENTH DYNASTIES. THE HYKSOS.
ABOUT 2098–1587 B.C.

THIS period of the foreign domination of Asiatic invaders is so strongly marked that we cannot but treat it as a whole. Unfortunately, there are very few materials for the study of it; almost all our information is in the extract which Josephus made from the history of Manetho, which shows also what a real history the account of Manetho was, and how the lists that we possess are the merest skeleton of his writings.

Apion has conferred a great benefit on history, by stinging Josephus into framing a splendidly mistaken theory of the glory of the Jewish race in Egypt, which he elaborated with nationalist fervour, calling in the Hyksos to figure as Hebrews domineering over Egyptians. It is through this valuable error that what was known of these invaders, by the later Egyptians, has been preserved. The account is so important that it should be read in full, so far as the Hyksos period is concerned. He quotes from Manetho :—

"We had formerly a king whose name was Timaios. In his time it came to pass, I know not how, that God was displeased with us; and there came up from the East in a strange manner men of an ignoble race, who had the confidence to invade our country, and easily subdued it by their power without a battle. And when they had our rulers in their hands, they burnt our cities, and demolished the temples of the gods, and inflicted every kind of barbarity upon the inhabitants, slaying some, and reducing the wives and children of others to a state of slavery.

"At length they made one of themselves king, whose name was Salatis : he lived at Memphis, and rendered both the upper and lower regions of Egypt tributary, and stationed garrisons in places which were best adapted for that purpose. But he directed his attention principally to the security of the eastern frontier; for he regarded with suspicion the increasing power of the Assyrians, who he foresaw would one day undertake an invasion of the kingdom. And observing in the Saite nome, upon the east of the Bubastite channel, a city which from some ancient theological reference was called Avaris; and finding it admirably adapted to his purpose, he rebuilt it, and strongly fortified it with walls, and garrisoned it with a force of 250,000 men completely armed. To this city Salatis repaired in summer, to collect his tribute and pay his troops, and to exercise his soldiers in order to strike terror into foreigners." (For Saite perhaps read Sethroite.)

"And Salatis died after a reign of nineteen years; after him reigned another king who was called Beon forty-four years; and he was succeeded by Apakhnas, who reigned thirty-six years and seven months; after him reigned Apophis sixty-one years, and Ianias fifty years and one month. After all these reigned Assis forty-nine years and two months. These six were the first rulers amongst them, and during the whole period of their dynasty they made war upon the Egyptians with the hope of exterminating the whole race.

"All this nation was styled Hyksōs, that is, Shepherd Kings; for the first syllable Hyk in the sacred dialect denotes a king, and sōs signifies a shepherd, but this only according to the vulgar tongue; and of these is compounded the term Hyksōs. Some say they were Arabians.. This people who were thus denominated

Shepherd Kings, and their descendants, retained possession of Egypt during the period of five hundred and eleven years.

"And after these things he relates that the kings of Thebais, and of the other provinces of Egypt, made an insurrection against the Shepherds, and that a long and mighty war was carried on between them, till the Shepherds were overcome by a king whose name was Misfragmouthōsis, and they were by him driven out of the other parts of Egypt, and hemmed up in a place containing about ten thousand acres which was called Avaris. All this tract (says Manetho) the Shepherds surrounded with a vast and strong wall, that they might retain all their property and their prey within hold of their strength.

"And Thummōsis, the son of Misfragmouthōsis, endeavoured to force them by a siege, and beleaguered the place with a body of four hundred and eighty thousand men; but at the moment when he despaired of reducing them by a siege, they agreed to a capitulation, that they would leave Egypt, and should be permitted to go out without molestation, wheresoever they pleased. And according to this stipulation, they departed from Egypt, with all their families and effects, in number not less than two hundred and forty thousand, and bent their way through the desert towards Syria. But as they stood in fear of the Assyrians, who then had dominion over Asia, they built a city in that country which is now called Judæa, of sufficient size to contain this multitude of men, and named it Hierosolyma."

Now, summarising this account, with the additional light of the other indications that we have, the following outline lies before us.

The country was disorganised, and incapable of resisting any active foe, when from the East there poured in a barbaric people, who settled, and seized on the government of the country, harrying and plundering, while the native rulers were at their mercy. After a century of this confusion they became more civilised, probably by the culture inherited from the Egyptian mothers of the second and third generation.

Then they established a monarchy of their own in the Egyptian fashion, adopting the usages of the country, and keeping native administrators in their power to claim the allegiance of the people. Six kings of this stable period are recorded; Salatis, the first, rebuilt Hauar—probably Tanis—as a stronghold, while Memphis was adopted by him as his capital. The succession of the great kings was as follows—

	XVTH DYNASTY.	B.C. about
Salatis	19 years	1998
Beon (Bnōn)	44	1979
Apakhnas (Pakhnan)	36 y. 7 mo.	1935
Apōfis	61	1898
Ianias (Sethōs)	50 y. 1 mo.	1837
Assis (Kērtōs + Asēth)	49 y. 2 mo.	1787
		1738

The variants are those of Syncellus and Africanus; but the latter alters the order, omitting the last two kings, and inserting after Pakhnan the names of Staan 50 years, and Arkhles 49 years—the same reigns as the last two here, but different names and successions. This is probably an error of Africanus, but may well embody two more of the Hyksos names, Staan and Arkhles, from a part of their list now lost to us.

The whole duration of the foreign dominion of this people and their descendants was 511 years. Then the Thebaid revolted, expelled them under Aahmes (Misfragmouthosis is quite a possible form from the known titles of the king, Aahmes·pa·her·nub·thes·taui), and restricted them to Tanis. Lastly, Tahutmes I. forced them to retreat into Syria, where they settled in the region of the hill country from which they had come (for the statement that Hebron was built seven years before Zoan, Num. xiii. 22, links the two cities together), or through which they had passed on their migration into Egypt.

As to the origin of the Hyksos race much has been written, though but little is certain. We cannot improve on the origin of the name given by Manetho: *hyk* or *heq*, a prince, and *sôs* or *shasu*, the generic name of the shepherds or pastoral races of the eastern deserts. On later monuments the Shasu are represented as typical Arabs. This usage of *heq* for the chief is like that of the *heq setu* or "chief of the deserts," the title of the Semitic Absha in the XIIth dynasty, and of Khyan before him.

One evidence regarding the race, which has been largely relied on, is the peculiar physiognomy of many statues and sphinxes which have been attributed to this period (Figs. 140–143). The so-called Hyksos sphinxes of Tanis, the statue from the Fayum, that of the Esquiline at Rome, the colossi of Bubastis, and some smaller pieces in museums, all show one type of face,—high cheek-bones, flat cheeks, both in one plane, a massive nose, firm projecting lips, and thick hair, with an austere and almost savage expression of power, characterise all these works. That they are as old as the Hyksos cannot be doubted, as they bear Hyksos names cut upon them; but lately it has been ques-

FIG. 140.—Black granite fish-offerers, Tanis.

tioned whether they are not much older than these invaders. Though the Hyksos names are the oldest now legible on the figures, they are merely inscribed lightly on the right shoulder, like the name of Apepa on the right shoulder of Mermeshau at Tanis; and no Hyksos name occurs on the breast or between the paws of the sphinxes. Meyer has concluded that they belong to the invaders of the VIIIth–Xth dynasty; and as now Khyan is probably fixed to that period, we know that fine work in black granite or syenite was being done then. Unfortunately, the head of the Khyan statue has not been found; no matter how battered, it would have sufficed to show whether the "Hyksos type" belonged to the earlier or later invaders.

FIG. 141.—Black granite sphinx, Tanis.

A new theory has just been proposed by Golenischeff (Rec. xv. 131), that the so-called Hyksos statues represent Amenemhat III. A statue of his, Fig. 108 (now at St. Petersburg) has some resemblance to the strange type; and a nameless statue belonging to Professor Golenischeff, which he illustrates along with the others, is undoubtedly of that type. But yet the Amenemhat is sufficiently distinct, in the lips, the chin, and the angle of the face,—even in its battered condition,—to make it difficult to accept it as a real origin of this strange type. If, however, that type belongs to Asiatic invaders during the IXth–Xth dynasty, it is obvious how the XIIth may have intermarried with their descendants, and have shown-some traits of their features. The admirable photographs which accompany the paper (in Rec. xv.) will enable a judgment to be formed on the question.

The only foreign parallel to this type of face is found among the foes of Ramessu II. in North Syria; but as the question whether this peculiar race and their works

Fig. 142.—Granite head, Bubastis.

are to be classed with the IXth or the XVth dynasty cannot yet be really determined, the subject of the physiognomy of the Hyksos and their origin must still await a decisive settlement.

The question of portraiture being thus in abeyance, there is but one clue left to the origin of the Hyksos, in the names of their kings. Now, doubtful as such a clue might be in one or two cases, yet when we find that the Greek forms would well represent such Semitic names as "the ruler," "the governor," "the oppressor," "the firm," and "the destroyer," it seems to give some weight to a Semitic origin for the people. Such names are more likely than a prominent

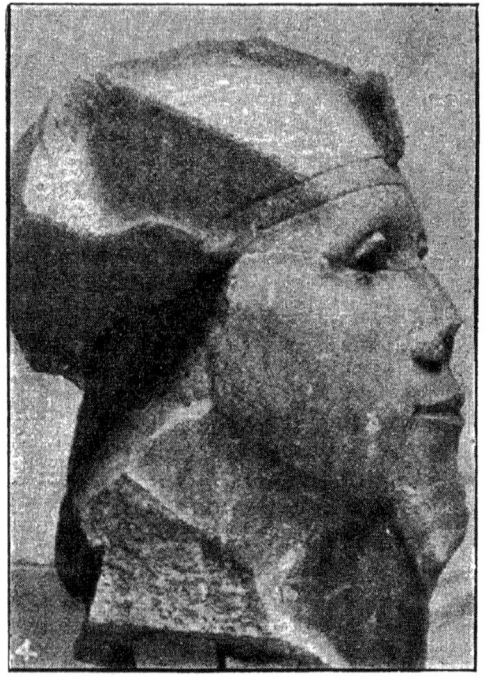

FIG. 143.—Granite head, Bubastis.

Semitic name of our own century, Jezzar Pasha, "the cutter" or "butcher"; and they are much in keeping with the character given to the Hyksos.

Of the actual remains there are but very few belonging to the Hyksos kings, and those only of Apepa I. and II.

XV. 4. RA·ĀA·USER — about 1898–1837 B.C.

APEPA I.

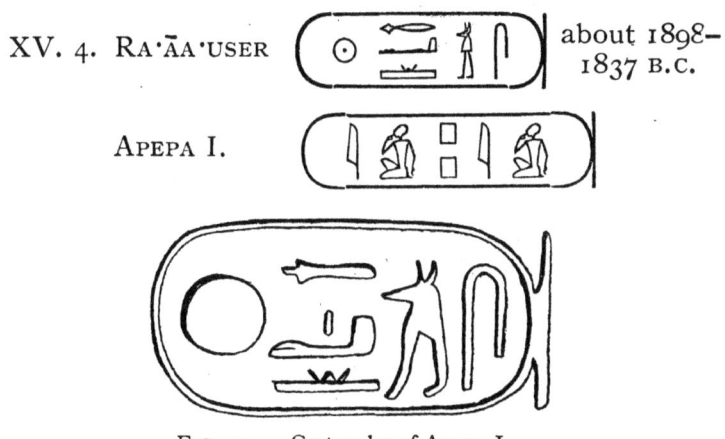

FIG. 144.—Cartouche of Apepa I., Gebelen (G. Mus.).

Bubastis,	Inscription	(N.B. xxxv., c).
Kahun,	Stamp	(P.K. xii. 16).
Gebelen,	Inscription	(Rec. xiv. 26).
Papyrus mathematical		(B. Mus.).
Palettes		(Berlin).
Scarabs.		

The inscription at Bubastis with the name Apepa is upon red granite, and therefore was probably due to the first Apepa, one of the six great kings, who ruled the whole of Egypt. It records how Apepa had erected "many columns and a gate of brass to this god" (N.B. xxii. A, xxxv. c).

A wooden stamp found at Kahun (P.K. xii. 16) may belong to the king, or to a private person (F.P. Coll.).

A lintel found at Gebelen (Fig. 144) bears the name of "the living good god, Ra·āa·user," twice repeated (Rec. xiv. 26; G. Mus.). This is of great value as showing, what Manetho states, that both Upper and Lower Egypt were reduced by the great Hyksos kings.

Of small objects, there is a mathematical papyrus (B. Mus.) written in the thirty-third year of the reign

APEPA I [DYN. XV.

of this king (A.Z. xiii. 40; S.B.A. xiv. 29). Also two palettes at Berlin, with both names of the king (S.B.A. iii. 97). Several scarabs (Fig. 145) with the throne

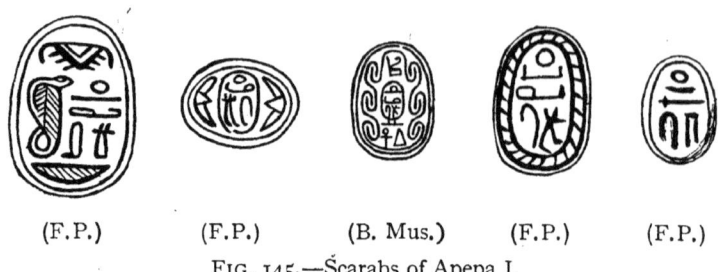

(F.P.)   (F.P.)   (B. Mus.)   (F.P.)   (F.P.)

FIG. 145.—Scarabs of Apepa I.

name are known, some of them very rude and blundered (B. Mus. 3; P. Mus. 2; Leyden; F.P. Coll. 4).

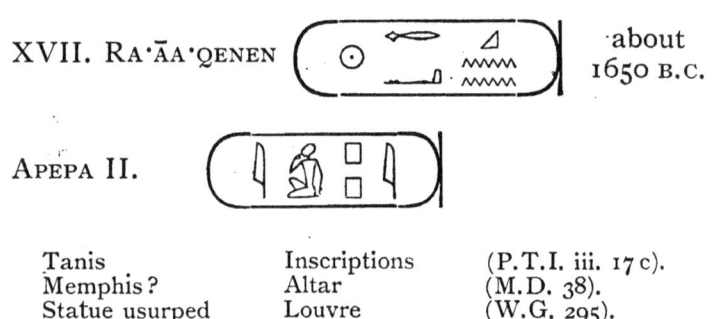

XVII. RA·ĀA·QENEN   about 1650 B.C.

APEPA II.

Tanis	Inscriptions	(P.T.I. iii. 17 c).
Memphis?	Altar	(M.D. 38).
Statue usurped	Louvre	(W.G. 295).

The statues of Mer·meshau, at Tanis, have down the right shoulder of each a line of added inscription, small, and not very disfiguring. It reads: "Good God, Ra·aa·qenen, son of the Sun, Apepa, giving life, beloved of Set." The figure of Set was, however, honourably placed first in the inscription, but was carefully hammered out in later times. Very probably the other lines of erased inscriptions on the right shoulders of the sphinxes at Tanis were also of this

[B.C. ABOUT 1650.] APEPA II. 243

king. And a sphinx at Ismailiyeh (from Tell Mas-khuta) has a line of similar erasure on the shoulder, and the whole head has been recut, and the mat of hair on the shoulders and chest removed, by Ramessu II.

In Cairo a fine and perfect altar of black granite (Fig. 146) was found, dedicated to Set of Hauar, or Avaris, by this king; it probably came from Memphis or Heliopolis (M.D. 38). Now in Ghizeh Museum.

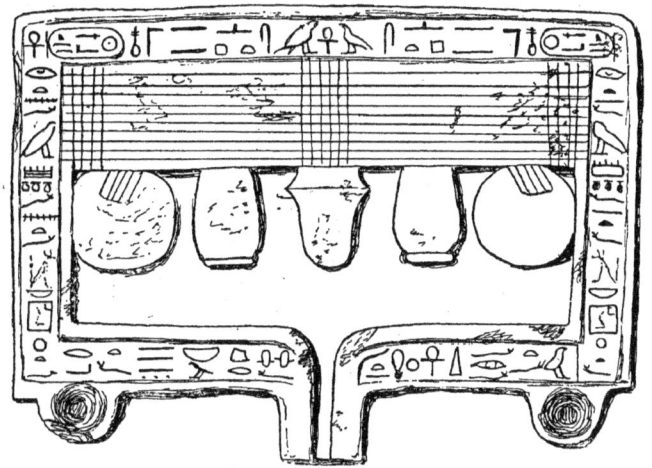

FIG. 146.—Black granite altar of Apepa II., Cairo (G. Mus.).

A statue in the Louvre has been read as of Apepa originally (W.G. 295), but usurped later by Amen-hotep III. It does not seem at all certain that the list of thirty-six conquered Nubian races belonged to the first owner, and it may be an addition put on by the usurper. That this king belongs to the XVIIth dynasty is indicated by his name, Aā·qenen·ra, being of the same type as that of Se·qenen·ra Ta·āā, with whom he is also associated in the tale of Apepa and Seqenenra (Sall. Pap. 1).

Perhaps of this same age is an obelisk at Tanis (Fig. 147), inscribed on all sides by a king RA·ĀA·SEH 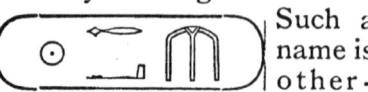 Such a name is otherwise unknown; but agrees in type to the throne names of the Apepas (P.T. I. ii. 20).

Lastly, there is the celebrated monument of Ramessu II., dated in the 400th year of "the king of Upper and Lower Egypt, Set·āa·pehti, son of the Sun,

FIG. 147.—Obelisk of Ra·āa·seh, Tanis.

Nubti·set, beloved of Horakhti" (A.Z. iii. 34). As this is the only monument dated with a fixed era in Egypt, it has naturally received much attention. The most reasonable view seems to be that this was a reckoning established by a Hyksos king, and used at Tanis continuously to the time of Ramessu II. It has also been shown that an entry in the lists of Africanus at the close of the XXIVth dynasty, of 990 years, is perhaps in accord with this era (A.Z. xvii. 138). As the last of the great Hyksos kings, Aseth (or Assis), is stated by Syncellus in his extracts to have revised the calendar, it is the more likely that some such era was established then. This statement is not, however, satisfactory, as he is said to have added the 5 days to the year of 360 days, which are known to have been in use long before his time; but it may well be that some other reformation has been thus misstated. The actual interval from Aseth to Ramessu I. is about 151 + 260 years or 411 years, thus leaving nothing for the reign of Sety I., and for the portions of the end of the reign of Aseth and beginning of that of Ramessu II.

The period of 990 years from the time of Beken·ran·f of the XXIVth dynasty, would yield about 720 + 990 = 1710 B.C. for the date of king Set·aa·pehti, within about

5 years of uncertainty; and similarly the date 720+590 = 1310 B.C. ought to fall within the reign of Ramessu II. But from the chronology, so far as we can now reckon it, this would be about 35 years too early for Ramessu II., though the Hyksos date would easily fall within the wide limits of their period. Hence this use of the 990 years does not seem very satisfactory.

A few names that are hitherto quite unfixed in position, but which probably precede the XVIIth and XVIIIth dynasties, require to be mentioned.

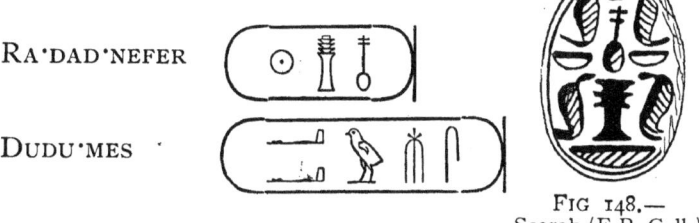

RA·DAD·NEFER

DUDU·MES

FIG 148.—Scarab (F.P. Coll.).

This king has been found on a scene at Gebelen, representing him being conducted by Khonsu to Anpu. He is referred to the XVIth dynasty by Daressy (Rec. xiv. 26); but from the occurrence of the name with graffiti of Pepy, he is placed in the VIIth–VIIIth dynasty by Sayce. From the style of a scarab of his (F.P. Coll.), it appears that the Xth dynasty would be about his period (Fig. 148).

RA·SE·BEQ·KA

This name occurs on a cylinder (Fig. 149) from Kahun (P.I. viii. 36) as the name of a king, "nefer neter... beloved of Sebek lord of Sunu." It belongs to the XIIIth or XIVth

FIG. 149.—Cylinders (F.P. Coll.).

dynasty apparently; and a similar cylinder was recently sold at Luxor (both F.P. Coll.).

RA SA?

HOTEP

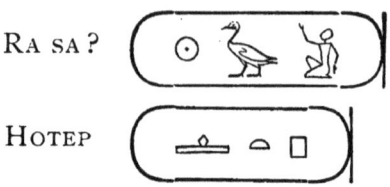

These names occur together on the rock (Fig. 150) of the Shut er Regal valley (P.S. 430). Possibly the bird reads *sa*, and this might thus be the same as No. 48 in the Turin list.

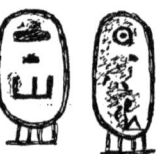

FIG. 150.—Rock marking, Silsileh.

SENB·MA·IU

This occurs on a stone at Gebelen (S.B.A. xv. 498).

RA·SEKHEM·UAH·KHA

RA·HOTEP

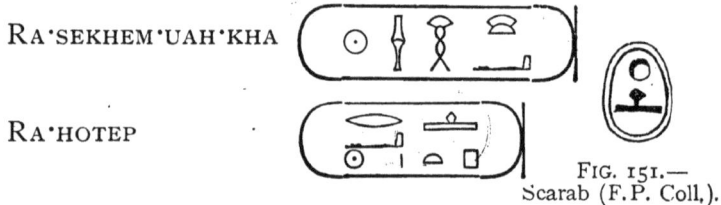

FIG. 151.— Scarab (F.P. Coll.).

Stele. Koptos.
Ostraka, subsequent tale (P. Mus.; F. Mus.).
Scarabs.

The only contemporary monument of this king is a much broken stele just found at Koptos. From that it appears that he had rearranged and endowed the temple there after a period of decay. His date and position are yet unfixed, but the titles, *Hor Uah·ankh*, lord of vulture and uraeus *User·ra·renpitu*, *Hor nub Uaz*...., are akin to those of the early XVIIIth dynasty, and indicate that he did not long precede that. On the other hand, the resemblance of the throne name to those of Sebekemsaf I. and Upuatemsaf would point to a close connection with the XIIIth dynasty. Possibly this group of kings may be those of the XVIth dynasty under the great Hyksos kings, midway between the XIIIth and the XVIIIth, to each of which the names bear a resemblance. The stele is of rather rough work, and unhappily the top scene has nearly all been lost.

The portions of a tale concerning Rahotep are on ostraka of a later age, about the XXth dynasty (P. Mus.; F. Mus.), in which mention is made of going to the tomb of king Rahotep, and at that place a mummy speaks, and states that "When I lived on earth I was treasurer of king Rahotep, and I died in the 14th year of king Ra·men·hotep" (Rec. iii. 3, xvi. 31; Contes Populaires, 291). Some few scarabs are known, all of small size, and not distinctive.

CHAPTER XI

Notes on Chronology

ALTHOUGH the questions of the Egyptian chronology are among the most difficult, they are also among the most essential to be considered. The various data that exist need that full discussion, in the light of modern knowledge of the subject, which they have never yet had. To treat them properly would entail a length of research, and an elaboration of treatment, which is quite beyond the scope of a history such as this. Yet, until such a work is undertaken, some provisional results are required for use; and I only propose here to go briefly over the outline of the materials which we have already noticed, and to connect that with the most prominent fixed data that we have. The results must, of course, be stated in years according with our era, but that will not therefore imply that we are certain of our results to within a year; only that, as we have often to consider short spaces of time during a dynasty, it is needlessly clumsy to deal with only round tens or hundreds of years. The figures in years, then, are only good for short differences of age, and we must always remember what our uncertainties are. The chronology rests on two modes of reckoning: (1) that by "dead reckoning," or adding the dynasties up one on another; (2) by certain fixed astronomical data, into the interpretation and calculation of which various uncertainties may enter. The more apart these modes can be kept the better, as then they serve to check each other.

The fundamental fact on which all of our astronomically fixed points depend is the imperfection of the Egyptian calendar. Using a year of 365 days, it followed that the nominal beginning of each year was a quarter of a day too soon: just as if we were to neglect the 29th of February in leap years, and go on always from 28th February direct to 1st March. Thus every four years a day was slipped, and the nominal months of the year were begun a day too soon. In $4 \times 7 = 28$ years they began, then, a week too soon. In $4 \times 30 = 120$ years they began a month too soon; and after twelve months and five days thus slipped, or in 1460 years, they began a year too soon, and so had rotated the nominal months through all the seasons. This would not cause any trouble to any one generation of men, as the change in one man's life would not be more than two or three weeks; hence this slow shift would be unperceived in the affairs of daily life; and as the Egyptians were not addicted much to historical researches, they would not be thrown out by finding that the harvest or inundation could occur in any month of the year, according to the date of their research.

This loss of the day in four years was, however, soon known to the Egyptians, and used by them as a mode of constructing a great cycle, which in Ptolemaic times became very prominent, and entered into all their fanciful adjustments of history and myths.

Some mode of noting the absolute months, as related to the seasonal periods, became a necessity; and, of course, the place of the sun among the stars most truly shows the exact length of the year. But how to observe both sun and stars, when without any mode of time-dividing,—such as clepsydra or clock,—was an essential difficulty. This was got over by noting on what day a particular star could be first seen, at its emerging from the glow of the sunlight. In actual practice they observed Sirius (or Sothis), the dog-star; and as the stars all rise and set earlier and earlier every night, they observed what was the first night in the year on which Sirius could just be seen emerging from the glow of sunlight at dawn, and this was entitled the heliacal rising. Hence, from using Sothis for this observation, the whole period during which the months rotated in the seasons was called the Sothic period of 1460 years. We have some definite statements as to this in Roman times. Censorinus, writing in 239 A.D., states that the Egyptian New Year's day, 1st of Thoth, fell on the 25th of June ; and a hundred years before, in 139 A.D., it fell on the 21st July, " on which day Sirius regularly rises in Egypt." Hence the beginning of a Sothic period of 1460 years, or the New Year's day falling on the 21st of July at the heliacal rising of Sirius, took place in 139 A.D. ; likewise in 1322 B.C., in 2784 B.C., and in 4242 B.C., or thereabouts.

From this it is plain, that, as the nominal months rotated round all the seasons once in each of these cycles, therefore, if we only know the day of the nominal month in which any seasonal event happened,—such as the rising of Sirius, or the inundation,—we can find on what part of the cycle of 1460 years such a coincidence can have fallen.

It is from data such as this that Mahler has lately calculated, by the rising of Sirius, and also the new moons, that Tahutmes III. reigned from 20th March 1503 B.C., to 14th February 1449. And though it would be very desirable to use all the data of the kind together in one general discussion, yet until this is done we may provisionally accept Mahler's calculation as a basis.

This, fortunately, has two checks, one on either side of it ; and, for the sake of clearness, we will use Mahler's datum provisionally. First, we must outline the dates of the XVIIIth–XIXth dynasty, as reckoned out by the best information we have, on the reigns and the relationships ; and though we may be doubtful within ten years about it, yet it will suffice to show if the other astronomical dates are near the mark.

The reasons for this arrangement of the XVIIIth dynasty cannot be entered on here, but will be dis-

NOTES ON CHRONOLOGY 251

cussed in the next volume. Provisionally, I arrange it thus—

	B.C.		B.C.
Aahmes I.	1587	Amenhotep IV.	1383
Amenhotep I.	1562	Rasmenkhka.	1365
Tahutmes I.	1541	Tutankhamen.	1353
Tahutmes II.	1516	Ay.	1344
Hatshepsut.	1503	Horemheb.	1332
Tahutmes III.	1481	Ramessu I.	1328
Amenhotep II.	1449	Sety I.	1327
Tahutmes IV.	1423	Ramessu II.	1275
Amenhotep III.	1414	Merenptah.	1208
	1383		

But many small questions, of coregencies, etc., are necessarily uncertain. The total for the XVIIIth dynasty comes out as 260 years against Manetho's 263.

Now, one good datum is, that Merenptah celebrated in the second year of his reign a festival of the rising of Sirius on the 29th of the month Thoth. Mahler has fixed the rising of Sirius, recorded on 28th Epiphi under Tahutmes III., as in 1470 B.C. From 28th Epiphi to 29th Thoth is 66 days, which the heliacal rising would change to in the course of 4 × 66 years, or 264 years. This, from 1470, gives 1206 B.C. for the second year of Merenptah, or 1208 B.C. for his accession, which is just the date we have reached by the approximate summing of the reigns.

Another datum on the other side is the calendar of the Ebers papyrus, which records the rising of Sirius on the 9th of Epiphi in the ninth year of Amenhotep I. The reading of the king's name has been much debated; but this is the last, and probable, conclusion. Now, from the 28th to the 9th of Epiphi is 19 days, which Sirius would change through in 76 years; so that the rising on the 9th of Epiphi took place in 1470 + 76 =

1546 B.C.; and the first year of Amenhotep I. would be thus fixed in 1555 B.C. The date before reached is 1562 B.C., equal to a difference of less than 2 days in the time of Sirius' rising. This, at least, shows that there is no great discrepancy. Thus there are three data for the rising of Sirius, which agree within a few years, though at considerably different epochs. The whole question of the exact epoch depends on the observations and calculations as to the rising of Sirius; those, however, cannot be very far in doubt, and these three data leave no doubt of the general interpretation of the materials, and assure us of the general position of our results.

We therefore have as a starting-point for our backward reckoning the accession of the XVIIIth dynasty about 1587 B.C. From this we can reckon in the dynastic data given by Manetho; following this account rather than the totals of reigns, as he appears to have omitted periods when dynasties were contemporary, as in the 43 years for the XIth after the close of the Xth. Thus, from the above starting-point of 1587 B.C., we reach the following results, solely by using material which has been discussed and settled in this history on its own merits alone, and without any ulterior reckoning in total periods.

	YEARS.	B.C.		YEARS.	B.C.
		4777			3006
Dynasty I.	263		Dynasty X.	185	
		4514			2821
,, II.	302		,, XI.	43	
		4212			2778
,, III.	214		,, XII.	213 (T.P.)	
		3998			2565
,, IV.	277		,, XIII.	453	
		3721			2112
V.	218		,, XIV.	184	
		3503			1928
.. VI.	181 (T.P.)		,, XVI.	190	
		3322			1738
,, VII.	70		,, XVII.	151	
		3252			1587
,, VIII.	146		,, XVIII.	260	
		3106			1327
,, IX.	100		,, XIX.		
		3006			

NOTES ON CHRONOLOGY

For all the earlier periods we have but one check, and that a vague one. We know that when Una quarried alabaster at Hat-nub—or Tell el Amarna—he did it in 17 days of the month Epiphi; and that yet he could not get it down to the pyramid before the Nile began to subside. There are some rather vague points about this, as the part of the month of 30 days in which the 17 fell, the time required to get down, which would perhaps be only 6 or 8 days (as Hat-nub is not so far up the Nile as was supposed when this was considered before, P.S. 20), and the time of the Nile falling. Putting the fall at about November 5, the boat would have left Hat-nub about October 28; and the 17 days would be to October 11. Hence Epiphi would fall within 6 days of October 5 to November 5. This date would be that of Epiphi at about 3350 B.C., if we reckon the 1460 year periods back from 139 A.D. What small differences might be made by a fuller consideration of the details of the 1460 period we cannot at present say. At least, the result would not be widely different from this, probably within a century of it. Having, then, 3350 B.C. for the reign of Merenra, and adding about 60 years, we reach about 3410 B.C. for the beginning of the VIth dynasty, with an uncertainty (to put it liberally) of 50 or 100 years.

This 3410 B.C., then, should be equal to the date that we find by the dead reckoning of dynasties back from the XVIIIth to the VIth, which is given in that way as 3503 B.C. And this shows that we have to deal with errors which are probably within a century, and that we are not left with several centuries of uncertainty.

In the present rough state of the astronomical data, and the doubts as to the MS. authorities, we have reached quite as close an equivalence as we may hope for; and at least there is enough to show us that we may trust to the nearest century with fair grounds of belief.

These dates, then, are what I have provisionally adopted in this history; and though they are stated to the nearest year, for the sake of intercomparison, it must always be remembered that they only profess to go to within a century in the earlier parts of the scale. I only wish it were possible to repeat this on every occasion of stating a date ; it cannot be too well remembered.

INDEX

All Ra names of kings are placed together under Ra. K, King, Q, Queen, pr., Priest.

Āa, K., 109, 117.
Aa·ab, K., 206, 219.
Aa·hotep·ra, K., 109, 117.
Aam, Q., 132.
Aam (Lower W. Nubia), 94, 99.
Aasen, pr., 23.
Aba, pr., 102.
Absha, 172.
Abydos, table of kings, 17.
Ada, 151.
Adu, pr., 91, 98, 102.
Affa, pr., 71.
Ahy, pr., 98.
Aimery, pr., 42, 72, 73, 74.
Aimhetep, K., 30, 31, 66.
Aken, 181.
Akherkin, 163.
Akhet·hotep, tomb of, 26.
Akhet·hotep, pr., 76, 78, 79, 84.
Akhet·hotep·her, pr., 73.
Alabaster quarry, 45, 95, 253.
,,   vases, 76, 88, 104.
Amenemhat I., K., 145, 148.
,,   II., K., 145, 164.
,,   III., K., 145, 184.
,,   IV., K., 145, 196.
Ameny (short for Amenemhat), 165.
Ameny Antef Amenemhat, K., 206, 207.
Ameny·senb, 103.

Amtes, Q., 94.
Amu (Eastern Semites), 94, 120, 155, 172, 193.
An, K., 75.
Ana, K., 206, 220.
Ana·ankh, 76.
An·ab (see Snaa·ab), K., 226.
An·ab, K., 228.
Anket·dudu, 211.
Ankh·ef, pr., 23.
Ankh·em·aka, pr., 72, 76.
Ankh·hapi, pr., 34.
Annu, K., 109.
An·ren, K., 206.
Antef (official), 151.
Antef·a (prince), 126.
Antef I., K., 109, 124, 127.
,,   II., K., 109, 124, 128.
,,   III., K., 109, 124, 129.
,,   IV., K., 109, 124, 133.
,,   V., K., 109, 124, 135.
,,   VI., K., 124, 141.
Anu, K., 206.
Anu (Nubians), 183.
Apa·ankh, 88.
Apakhnas, K., 234, 236.
Apepa I., K., 234, 236, 241.
,,   II., K., 242.
Apis, titles of, 26.
Apophis, K., 234, 236.
Aquiline race, 10.

Arqo, 216.
Art, teaching of, 140.
Arthet (Upper W. Nubia), 94, 99.
Asa, pr., 87.
Assa, K., 79, 100.
Assa·kha, pr., 91.
Assis, K., 234, 236.
Asyut tombs, 115.
Ata, K., 20.
Ata, pr., 72, 73, 76, 91.
Ateth, K., 20.
Ati, pr., 78.
Atmu·neferu, 171, 175.
Atush, pr., 79.
Aty, K., 86, 88.
Aufni, K., 206.
Auhet·abu, Q., 211.
Ay, K., 206, 220.

BA·NETERU, K., 21, 23.
Basalt of Khankah, 3, 22.
Ba·ur·dedu, 100.
Bebn·m......, K., 227.
Beni Hasan tombs, 149, 159, 165, 172.
Beon, K., 234, 236.
Bezau, K., 21, 22.
Birket Qurun, 190.
Brickwork, panelling of, 51.
Bubastis, chasm at, 22.
Bulls, worship of, 22.
Burial customs, 11, 28, 37.

CANAL of the cataract, 179.
Caverns collapsed, 4.
Chronology, vi, 95, 110, 146, 198, 201, 244, 248–254.
Chronology, absence of early, 9.
Chronology, compilation of, 17.
Copper tools, 7.
Cylinders, earliest, 55.

DAD·KA·SHEMA·RA, K., 108.
Dates of dynasties, 252. (See Chronology.)
Dating on monuments, 157.
Debehen, 55.
Delta, structure of, 7.

Deng, dancer, 100.
Dep·em·ankh, pr., 34, 42, 53, 55, 71, 72, 84.
Deposition decree, 136.
Divine dynasties, 9.
Dogs on Antef stele, 134.
Dudu, pr., 34.
Dudumes, K., 245.
Dynastic lists, authority of, 16–20.
Dynasties, divine, 9.
,, Thinite kings, 9.
,, Ist–IIIrd, 16.
,, ,, remains of, 26.
,, Ist, 20.
,, IInd, 21.
,, IIIrd, 21.
,, IVth, 30.
,, Vth, 68.
,, VIth, 86.
,, VIIth–Xth, 108.
,, XIth, 124.
,, growth of, 143.
,, XIIth, 145.
,, character of, 199.
,, XIIIth, 201, 206.
,, XIVth, 201, 227.
,, XVth, 201, 236, 241.
,, XVIth, 201.
,, XVIIth, 201.
,, XVIIIth, reigns of, 251.
,, dates of, 252.

EDOM, 154.
Egyptians, origin of, 13, 28, 29. (See Races.)
Elephantine, 70.

FAULT in Nile valley, 2.
Fayum, 2, 151, 159, 168, 193, 213.
Fayum, development of, 190.
Female succession, 23.
Fetish pole of Min, 14.
Flints, worked, 5–8.
Foreign invaders, 118, 172.
Four hundred year stele, 244.
Funeral customs, 11, 28, 37, 155.

INDEX

GEOLOGY of Egypt, 1.
Gods, dynasties of, 9.
Granite temple, 48.
Gravels of Nile, 2.
Griffith, Mr. F. Ll., vii.

HA·ANKH·F, 213.
Ha·ankh·s, Q., 218.
Hapa, pr., 87.
Hapi·dua, pr., 76.
Hapu, K., 206, 221, 227.
Hatnub quarry, 46, 253.
Hatshepsut, Q., 62.
Hawara, 184-189.
Heliopolis, temple of, 157.
Heliopolitan gods, 10.
    ,,   Vth dynasty, 69, 85.
Heni, K., 21, 24.
Hent·sen, 38.
Hent·taui, Q., 176, 183.
Herodotos, 40, 191, 193.
Hesat, pr., 79.
Hesepti, K., 20, 24.
Hesy, panels of, 26-28.
Hetep·hers, pr., 42.
Hewn stone first used, 23.
Hezefa...p, K., 21.
History, early, compilation of, 19.
Hor... (or Har, or Heru), K., 228.
Hor, pr., 153.
Hora, K., 206.
Hor·akau, K., 75.
Hor·dad·f, 63.
Hor·kau·ra, K., 109.
Hor·meren, K., 108.
Hor·nefer, 144.
Hor·nefer·hen, K., 106.
Hor·nefer·ka, K., 108.
Hor·shesu (see Shemsu·har), 10.
Hor·uah·ankh, K., 133.
Hotep, K., 246.
Hotep·ankh·menkh (*ka*), K., 26.
Hull, Professor, 3.
Hyksos, 201-205, 228, 231, 233-247.

Hyksos statues, so-called, 237-240.
Hymn to Usertesen III., 182.

IANIAS, 234, 236.
Im·hotep (see Aim·hetep), 30, 31, 66.

JEBEL AHMAR, 3, 154.
Jewellery of Sat·hathor, 177.

KA names, 26, 148.
Ka·ankh·et·nefer·ka, 230.
Kaau, 94.
Ka·em·nefert, pr., 42, 53, 72, 76.
Ka·em·retu, pr., 76.
Kahun flints, 7, 8.
    ,,   town, 171.
Kaka, pr., 92.
Ka·ka·a, K., 74.
Ka·ka·hekenu, Q., 74.
Ka·kau, K., 21, 22.
Karnak, list of, 17, 229.
Kas, 163.
Kay, pr., 42.
Kebh, K., 20.
Ked·khenes, pr., 78.
Kema, 213.
Kertos, K., 236.
Khafra, K., 30.
Khemten, pr., 42.
Khen·zer, K., 226.
Khesaa, 163.
Khety, K., 108, 109, 114, 115.
Khety (vizier), 139.
Khnum·ab·ra, 23.
Khnum·hotep, pr., 71.
    ,,   ,,   tomb, 149, 165.
Khnum Khuf, K., 43.
Khua, 95.
Khufu, K., 30, 38.
Khufu·ka·aru, pr., 42, 47.
Khyan, K., 109, 118.
Kings, 17. (See Lists and Ra.)
Kokhome, 22.
Koptos, clay modelling, 23.
    ,,   earliest settlement, 13, 14.
Koptos, statues at, 13, 14.
Kush, 160.

LABYRINTH, 187.
Large-eyed race, 11.
Lisht, fragments at, 53.
Lists of kings, 17. (See Dynasties.)
Lists of kings, compilation of, 19.

MAA·AB·RA, K., 109, 116.
Maat·kha, 64.
Manefer, pr., 79.
Manetho, 16, 19.
„ on dynasties, Ist–IIIrd, 22, 23.
Mastaba form, 32, 33.
Mastabat el Faraun, 83.
Medum pyramid, 32.
„ tombs, 36.
Mehti·em·saf, 86, 97, 104.
Mena, K., 16, 22, 23, 24.
„ K. (XIIIth dyn.), 206, 221.
Mendes, 22.
Men·ka·ra, Q. (VIth dyn.), 86, 104.
Men·kau·hor, K., 61, 68, 78.
Men·kau·ra, K. (IVth dyn.), 30, 55.
Mentu·hotep I., K., 109, 124, 127.
Mentu·hotep II., K., 109, 124, 131.
Mentu·hotep III., K., 109, 124, 138.
Mentu·hotep, Q., 144.
„ divine father, 211.
Mera, pr., 87, 91.
Mer·ab, pr., 42.
Mer·ba·pen, K., 20.
Mer·en·ra, K., 86, 97, 104.
Mer·meshau, K., 206, 209, 242.
Mer·seker, Q., 183.
Mer·tisen, artist, 140.
Mertit·tefs, Q., 10, 31, 35.
Mery, tomb of, 26.
Merysankh, Q., 31, 35.
Mesniu, 10.
Methen, pr., 34.
Mezau (S. Nubians), 94, 152.
Min, prehistoric statues, 14.

Min·hon, pr., 71.
Moeris, lake, 190.
Mud, rate of deposit, 6.
Mythical period of gods, 9.

NEB·HOTEP, K., 127.
Neb·ka, K., 21, 23, 24, 25.
Neb·ka·ra, K., 21.
Neb·ka·n·ra, K., 24.
Nebt, 95.
Neby, K., 108, 113.
Nefer·ab·ra, pr., 42.
Nefer·ar·ka·ra, K. (Vth dyn.), 68, 73.
Nefer·ar·ka·ra, K. (VIIIth dyn.), 109.
Nefer·art·nef, pr., 72.
Nefer·f·ra, K., 68, 75.
Nefer·hotep, K., 206, 212.
Nefer·ka, K., 108.
Nefer·ka·ra, K. (IInd dyn.), 21, 23.
Nefer·ka·ra (IIIrd dyn.), 21.
Nefer·ka·ra (VIth dyn.), 86, 101.
Nefer·ka·ra (VIIIth dyn.), 108, 113.
Nefer·maāt, tomb, 36.
„ pr., 53.
Nefer·s, K., 108.
Nefert, Q., 174.
Nefert·kau, 31, 35.
Neferui·ka·dad·uah, K., 230.
Nehesi, K., 221.
Ne·ka·ankh, pr., 71.
Nekht·abs, pr., 76.
Nen·khetef·ka, pr., 71, 72.
Nenna, Q., 211.
Nenu, K., 227.
Net·aqerti, Q., 86, 104.
Neter·ka·ra, K., 86, 104.
Neteru (*ka*), 26.
Nile deposit, rate of, 6.
„ levels of, 3, 5, 193, 209.
„ regulation of, 192.
Nile valley, fault, 2.
„ submergence, 5, 6.
Nitokris, Q., 105.
Nub·em·hat, Q., 218.
Nub·hotep·ta·khredet, 208.

INDEX

Nubian affairs (Vth dyn.), 94, 99.
Nubian affairs (XIIth dyn.), 152, 160, 163, 178-181.
Nub·kha·s, Q., 224.

OBELISK of Begig, 150.
Obelisks, caps of, 157.
Obelisks of Ra, 65, 71.
Organisation of government, 149.

PAKHNAN, K., 236.
Palæolithic flint, 5.
Palermo stone, 72.
Papyri, early kings in, 24.
Papyrus, oldest dated, 81.
Pa·seb·khanu, K., 44.
Pedunebti, K., 228.
Pehenuka, pr., 71, 73.
Penens...n·sept, K., 228.
Pepy I., K., 86, 89.
Pepy II., K., 86, 101.
Pepy·na, pr., 91, 98.
Pepy·senb, K., 109.
Per·ab·sen, K., 23.
Persen, 63.
Philistines, 15.
Phœnician race, 15.
Poem of praise, 182.
Pre-historic age, 1-15.
Psemtek, pr., 63.
Psemtek·menkh, pr., 42, 53, 63.
Ptah·bau·nefer, pr., 42, 72, 73, 76.
Ptah·du·aau, pr., 63.
Ptah·en·kau, 89.
Ptah·en·maāt, pr., 73.
Ptah·hotep, pr., 71, 74, 75, 78.
,, proverbs of, 81.
Ptah·kha·bau, pr., 72, 73, 75, 76.
Ptah·nefer·art, pr., 78.
Ptah·neferu, 187, 188, 195.
Ptah·ru·en, pr., 73.
Ptah·se·ankh, pr., 91.
Ptah·shepses, 64.
,, pr., 84, 87.
Ptolemy Soter, K., 192.
Punt, 12, 14, 100, 141, 167.

Pyramids, design of, 39, 57, 90, 169, 176, 184.
Pyramids, development of, 32, 33.
,, sections of, 32, 57, 83.
,, theory of restoration, 58.
,, two of one king, 34, 55, 84.
Pyramids of Abu Roash, 56.
,, of Abu Sir, 71, 76.
,, of Dahshur, 176.
,, of Gizeh, 38, 47, 56.
,, of Hawara, 184.
,, of Illahun, 168.
,, of Medum, 32, 39.
,, of Riqqeh, 77.
,, of Sakkara, 82, 87, 90, 97.
,, of Thebes, 133.

KINGS' NAMES.
RA·AA·HOTEP, 109, 117.
Ra·aa·qenen, 242.
Ra·aa·seh, 244.
Ra·aa·user, 241.
Ra·ab·mery, 109, 114.
Ra·amen·em·hat, 206.
Ra·ankh·ka......, 227.
Ra·dad·ef, 63.
Ra·dad·ka, 79.
Ra·dad·kheru, 227.
Ra·dad·nefer, 245.
Ra·en·ka, 108, 113.
Ra·en·maa·en·kha, 226.
Ra·en·maat, 184.
Ra·en·user, 75.
Ra·fu·ab, 206, 208.
Ra·ha·shed......, 227.
Ra·hathor·sa, 206.
Ra·her·ab, 227.
Ra·hotep, 246.
Ra·ka......ab, 227.
Ra·ka·mery, 109, 115.
Ra·kha......, 227.
Ra·kha·ankh, 206, 218, 229.
Ra·khaf, 47.
Ra·kha·hotep, 206, 219, 229.
Ra·kha·ka, 206, 217, 229.
Ra·kha·kau, 176.

Ra·kha·kheper, 168.
Ra·kha·nefer, 206, 215, 229.
Ra·kha·neferui, 230.
Ra·kha·seshes, 206, 212, 22(.
Ra·kha·thi, 206.
Ra·kha·user, 109, 117.
Ra·kheper, 230.
Ra·kheper·ka, 156.
Ra·kheper·kha, 168.
Ra·khu·taui, 206, 230.
Ra·maa·ab, 109, 116.
Ra·men·hotep, 247.
Ra·men·ka, 104.
Ra·men·kau, 55.
Ra·men·khau, 226.
Ra·mer·en, 97, 104.
Ra·mer·hotep, 206, 220, 230.
Ra·mer·kau, 206, 220, 229.
Ra·mer·kheper, 206.
Ra·mer·nefer, 206, 220.
Ra·mer·sekhem, 206, 230.
Ra·mery, 89.
Ra·mer·zefau, 227.
Ra·messu II., 171.
Ra·neb, 26.
Ra·neb·ati·au, 227.
Ra·neb·ka, 21, 26.
Ra·neb·kha, 106.
Ra·neb·kher, 138.
Ra·neb·maat, 206, 220.
Ra·neb·neferui, 230.
Ra·neb·sen, 227.
Ra·nefer, 230.
Ra·nefer·ab, 227, 229.
Ra·nefer·ankh, 230.
Ra·nefer·ar·ka, 73, 109.
Ra·nefer·f, 75.
Ra·nefer·ka (IInd dyn.), 21.
   ,,   (IIIrd dyn.), 21, 26.
Ra·nefer·ka (VIth dyn.), 101.
   ,,   (VIIIth dyn.), 108, 113.
Ra·nefer·kau, 109.
Ra·nefer·nub, 230.
Ra·nefer·tum......, 227.
Ra·nehesi, 206, 221.
Ra·neter·ka, 104.
Ra·nezem·ab, 206.
Ra·nub·hotep, 230.

Ra·nub·kau, 164.
Ra·nub·kheperu, 134.
Ra·nub·neferui, 230.
Ra·nub·uaz, 230.
Ra·peh·nub,. 230.
Ra·ra·neb·zefau, 227.
Ra·sa, 246.
Ra·sahu, 71.
Ra·se·ankh......, 227.
Ra·se·ankh·ab, 206, 207, 229.
Ra·se·ankh·ka, 141.
Ra·se·ankh·n, 206.
Ra·sebek·hotep, 206, 208.
Ra·sebek·ka, 65.
Ra·sebek·neferu, 197.
Ra·se·beq·ka, 245.
Ra·se·heb, 227.
Ra·se·hotep·ab, 148, 206, 208.
Ra·se·kha·n, 109, 116.
Ra·sekhem......, 227.
Ra·sekhem·ka, 206, 207.
Ra·sekhem·khu·taui, 206, 209, 229.
Ra·sekhem·nefer·khau, 225.
Ra·sekhem·s·shedti·taui, 223.
Ra·sekhem·se·uaz·taui, 206, 210, 229.
Ra·sekhem·uah·ka, 246.
Ra·sekhem·uaz·khau, 222, 230.
Ra·se·kheper·en, 227.
Ra·se·men·ka, 206, 227.
Ra·se·menkh·ka, 206, 209.
Ra·se·men......, 227.
Ra·senb·ka, 227.
Ra·se·nefer·ka, 227, 229, 230.
Ra·seshes·her·her·maat, 127.
Ra·seshes·up·maat, 129.
Ra·ses·user·taui, 229.
Ra·set·nub, 230.
Ra·set·pehti, 230.
Ra·se·uah·en, 230.
Ra·se·uaz·en, 229, 230.
Ra·se·uaz·ka, 206.
Ra·se·user......, 227.
Ra·se·user·en, 118.
Ra·se·zefa·ab, 206.
Ra·shepses·ka, 74.
Ra·uah·ab, 206, 219.
Ra·uben, 206, 227.
Ra·user......, 228.

INDEX

Ra·user......ra, 206.
Ra·user·ka, 88.

Ra, descent from, 69.
Ra, obelisks of, 65, 71.
Ra·ankh·ema, pr., 75, 78.
Ra·en·kau, pr., 71, 75.
Ra·hent, pr., 84, 88.
Ra·hotep (IVth dyn.), 36.
Ra·ka·pu, pr., 79.
Ra·nefer·ab, pr., 42.
Ra·se·ankh, statue, 26.
Races, aquiline, 10.
„ large-eyed, 11.
„ snouty, 11.
Rainfall, ancient, 4.
References, v.
Restoration of pyramids, theory, 58.
Restoration of scarabs, 69.
Riqqeh, 77.

SABU, pr., 84, 87.
Sahura, K., 68, 71.
Sakha, 231.
Sakhebu, 70.
Sakkara, list of, 17. (See Pyramids.)
Salatis, K., 234, 236.
Sanehat, adventures of, 153.
Sankh·ka·ra, K., 124, 141.
Sat·hathor, 177.
Sati (Asiatics), 152.
Scarabs, restored, 62.
Search for stone, 151.
Sebek·em·heb, 218.
Sebek·em·saf I., K., 222.
Sebek·em·sauf II., K., 223.
Sebek·hotep I., K., 206, 209.
„ II., K., 206, 210.
„ III., K., 206, 215.
„ IV., K., 206, 218.
„ V., K., 206, 219.
„ VI., K., 206, 220.
Sebek·ka·ra, K., 30, 31, 65.
Sebek·neferu, Q., 145, 187, 195, 197.
Sed festivals, 93, 131, 251.
Seden·maat, pr., 73, 75, 76.
Se·hotep·ab·ra, K., 148.

Seker·ka·bau, tomb, 26.
Seker·nefer·ka, K., 21, 23.
Sem·en·ptah, K., 20, 22, 24.
Sem·nefer, 74, 75 ; pr., 78, 79.
Semneh and Kummeh, 181, 193.
Sen·amen, 75.
Senb, 211.
Senb·f, pr., 23.
Senb·maiu, K., 246.
Send, K., 21, 23, 24.
Sennu·ankh, pr., 71, 72.
Sent, Q., 144.
Sent·s·senb, 176.
Sepa, statue of, 26.
Sesa, pr., 91, 102.
Set ...., K., 228.
Set·hetu, K., 206.
Sethos, K., 236.
Sethu (Upper E. Nubia), 99.
Sety I., compiled history, 19.
Se·user·en·ra, K., 118.
Sezes, K., 21.
Shat, 163.
Shemsu, K., 206, 221.
Shemsu·har, 10.
Shemyk, 163.
Shepses·kaf, K., 30, 64.
Shepses·kaf·ankh, pr., 42, 72, 73.
Shepses·ka·ra, K., 68, 74.
Shera, pr., 23, 24.
Shert·sat, Q., 144.
Shesha, pr., 91.
Shut er regal, tablets, 139, 142.
Sickles of flint, 8.
Sinai tablets, 35, 43, 71, 78, 80, 92, 102, 158, 165, 189, 196.
Sirius cycle, 249.
„ festivals, 251.
S·kha·n·ra, K., 109, 116.
Snaa·ab, K., 226.
S·nefer·ka, K., 108, 109.
S·neferu, K., 30, 31.
S·neferu·nefer, pr., 78, 79.
S·nezem·ab, pr., 71, 73, 74, 75, 76, 84.
S·nezem·ab·antha, pr., 42.
Snouty race, 11.
Sothis cycle, 249.
„ „ in mythology, 10.

INDEX

Sothis festivals, 251.
Sphinx of Gizeh, 51.
,, in Louvre, 92.
Stele of 400 years, 244.
Suhtes, K., 74.
Sunu........, K., 228.

TABLET of 400 years, 244.
Tablet of Sphinx, so-called, 44.
Tahutmes III., list of, 17.
,, ,, date of, 250.
,, IV., 52.
Tefaba, 115.
Temehu (Oasis), 94, 99, 153.
Temple of Gizeh, 48.
,, of Illahun, 171.
,, of Medum, 34.
Tererel or Tereru, K., 108.
Teta, K. (Athothis), 20, 21, 22, 23, 24.
Teta, K. (VIth dyn.), 86, 87.
Tetu, pr., 138.
Thentha, pr., 34, 42.
Theta, 92.
Theta, pr., 53.
This, kings of, 9, 10, 13.
Thunury, list of, 17.
Thuthu, 79.
Thy, pr., 73, 76.
Tombs, plundering of, 224.
Tosorthos, K., 23.
Town of Kahun, 171.
Transliteration, xv.
Tumem, Q., 141.
Turin papyrus, 17, 18, 31, 84, 108, 110, 201-205, 221.

UASH, pr., 53.
Uazed, K., 109, 121.

Uaz·neferui, K., 230.
Uaz·nes, K., 21.
Uenefes, K., 22.
Uha, pr., 92.
Una, pr., 91, 98.
,, inscription of, 94.
Unas, K., 68, 82.
Un·nefer, pr., 23.
Up·uat·em·saf, K., 225.
Ur........, K., 206.
Urarna, pr., 71.
Ur·khuu, pr., 55, 73.
User·en·ra, K., 68, 75.
User·ka·f, K., 68, 70.
User·ka·ra, K., 86, 88.
User·tesen I., K., 145, 156.
,, II., K., 145, 168.
,, III., K., 145, 176.
Uta, pr., 55.

WAWAT (Lower E. Nubia), 94, 152.
Weight, earliest, 46.
,, of Hormera, 164.
Westcar papyrus, 20, 21, 29, 69.
Women, succession of, 23.

XOIS, 230.

YA·PEQ·HER, K., 109, 122.

ZAU, pr., 95, 102.
Zauta, pr., 91, 98, 102.
Zautaker, 151.
Zazai, K., 21.
Zeser, K., 23, 24, 26.
Zeser·sa, K., 21.
Zeserti, K., 21.

www.ingramcontent.com/pod-product-compliance
Lightning Source LLC
Chambersburg PA
CBHW061247230426
43663CB00021B/2936